THE DIVINE CAMPAIGNS

TimeFrame AD 1100-1200

WESTERN EUROPE

THE MIDDLE EAST

TimeFrame AD 1100-1200

THE DIVINE CAMPAIGNS

TimeFrame AD 1100-1200

BY THE EDITORS OF TIME-LIFE BOOKS

TIME-LIFE BOOKS, ALEXANDRIA, VIRGINIA

Time-Life Books Inc.
is a wholly owned subsidiary of
TIME INCORPORATED

FOUNDER: Henry R. Luce 1898-1967

Editor-in-Chief: Jason McManus
Chairman and Chief Executive Officer:
J. Richard Munro
President and Chief Operating Officer:
N. J. Nicholas, Jr.
Editorial Director: Ray Cave
Executive Vice President, Books:
Kelso F. Sutton
Vice President, Books: George Artandi

TIME-LIFE BOOKS INC.

EDITOR: George Constable
Executive Editor: Ellen Phillips
Director of Design: Louis Klein
Director of Editorial Resources:
Phyllis K. Wise
Editorial Board: Russell B. Adams, Jr.,
Dale M. Brown, Roberta Conlan,
Thomas H. Flaherty, Lee Hassig, Donia
Ann Steele, Rosalind Stubenberg
Director of Photography and Research:
John Conrad Weiser
Assistant Director of Editorial Resources:
Elise Ritter Gibson

EUROPEAN EDITOR: Kit van Tulleken
Assistant European Editor: Gillian Moore
Design Director: Ed Skyner
Assistant Design Director: Mary Staples
Chief of Research: Vanessa Kramer
Chief Sub-Editor: Ilse Gray

PRESIDENT: Christopher T. Linen
Chief Operating Officer: John M. Fahey, Jr.
Senior Vice Presidents: Robert M.
DeSena, James L. Mercer, Paul R.
Stewart
Vice Presidents: Stephen L. Bair, Ralph J.
Cuomo, Neal Goff, Stephen L. Goldstein,
Juanita T. James, Hallett Johnson III,
Carol Kaplan, Susan J. Maruyama,
Robert H. Smith, Joseph J. Ward
Director of Production Services:
Robert J. Passantino

Correspondents: Elisabeth Kraemer-Singh
(Bonn); Maria Vincenza Aloisi (Paris);
Ann Natanson (Rome). Valuable assis-
tance was also provided by Jane Walker
(Madrid); Deepak Puri (New Delhi);
Dick Berry (Tokyo).

TIME FRAME
(published in Britain as
TIME-LIFE HISTORY OF THE WORLD)

SERIES EDITOR: Tony Allan

Editorial Staff for *The Divine Campaigns:*
Designer: Lynne Brown
Writer: Fergus Fleming
Researchers: Louise Tucker (principal),
Caroline Alcock
Sub-Editor: Diana Hill
Design Assistant: Rachel Gibson
Editorial Assistant: Molly Sutherland
Picture Department: Patricia Murray
(administrator), Amanda Hindley (picture
coordinator)

Editorial Production
Chief: Maureen Kelly
Production Assistant: Samantha Hill
Editorial Department: Theresa John,
Debra Lelliott

U.S. EDITION

Assistant Editor: Barbara Fairchild
Quarmby
Copy Coordinator: Jarelle S. Stein
Picture Coordinator: Robert H.
Wooldridge, Jr.

Editorial Operations
Copy Chief: Diane Ullius
Production: Celia Beattie
Library: Louise D. Forstall

Special Contributors: Douglas Botting,
Windsor Chorlton, John Cottrell, Stephen
Downes, Ellen Galford (text); Timothy
Fraser, Barbara Hicks, David Nicolle,
Linda Proud (research); Roy Nanovic
(index)

CONSULTANTS

General:
GEOFFREY PARKER, Professor of Histo-
ry, University of Illinois, Urbana-
Champaign, Illinois

General and India:
C. A. BAYLY, Reader in Modern Indian
History, St. Catharine's College, Cam-
bridge University, Cambridge, England

Middle East:
JONATHAN RILEY-SMITH, Professor of
History, Royal Holloway and Bedford
New College, University of London, Lon-
don, England

Southeast Asia:
JAN WISSEMAN CHRISTIE, Honorary
Fellow, Centre for South-East Asian Stud-
ies, University of Hull, Hull, England

Western Europe:
CHRISTOPHER GIVEN-WILSON, Lectur-
er in Medieval History, University of St.
Andrews, Fife, Scotland

**Library of Congress Cataloging in
Publication Data**

The Divine campaigns.
 (Time frame)
 Bibiography: p.
 Includes index.
  1. Twelfth century.   I. Time-Life Books.
II. Series.
D201.8.D58   1988   909'.1   88-29542
ISBN 0-8094-6433-0
ISBN 0-8094-6434-9 (lib. bdg.)

Time-Life Books Inc. offers a wide range of fine
recordings, including a *Rock 'n' Roll Era* series.
For subscription information, call 1-800-621-
7026 or write Time-Life Music, P.O. Box C-
32068, Richmond, Virginia 23261-2068.

CONTENTS

EUROPE'S FEUDAL ORDER

1

On an April day in the year 1127, a glittering company assembled on the broad open ground called the Sands, just west of the town of Bruges near the North Sea coast. From manor houses on the surrounding plain, from fortresses lowering over the gray estuaries, from the rich abbeys of Saint Bertin and Saint Omer, nobles and churchmen had gathered to do homage to William, the new count of Flanders.

A notary named Galbert of Bruges stood by to record the words and deeds of this solemn ceremony. One after another, in a sequence prescribed by rank and dignity, the men laid aside their swords, uncovered their heads, and knelt before the count, who asked each one the same question:

"Do you wish, without reservation, to become my man?"

"I wish it."

The count enclosed the hands of the petitioner between his own and sealed the compact with a kiss on the lips. Then he motioned for an attendant to bring forward a jeweled casket holding relics of the saints—fragments of bone, nail parings, ringlets of hair—sacred objects on which each nobleman swore his oath:

"I promise by my faith that from this time forward I will be faithful to Count William and will maintain toward him my homage entirely against every man, in good faith and without any deception."

Next the count of Flanders reached out and touched each man with a wand, investing each as his vassal. Thus the bond between them was forged. By doing homage, the men had placed themselves at William's disposal, and William in exchange pledged that he would protect his vassals.

Count William's position was more precarious than it looked on that festive day. He had acquired his title only because his predecessor, Charles the Good, had been murdered by enemies while attending mass. Nor would William enjoy his rank for long: In a matter of months, he too would be dead, overthrown by Flemish rebels. Peace was uncertain, harmony—where it existed at all—hard won. The solemn oaths and bonds of fealty had grown out of the desperate need to impose some order on western Europe.

From the fifth century to almost within living memory stretched a bleak and bloody era of chaos. Invaders from east and north and south had swept across Europe, gutting cities and effacing any semblance of government. For those on western Europe's fringes, the torment peaked in the tenth century, as seaborne Northmen from Scandinavia descended upon the settlements of France and Britain, North African Muslims menaced France from the Mediterranean, and wild Magyar horsemen from central Asia thundered into Germany.

By the tenth century, however, recovery had already begun in the less ravaged heartlands. Progress was painfully slow, measured not in years or decades but in

In an illustration from a German manuscript history of the Welfs—one of the great medieval German families—King Frederick Barbarossa ("Red Beard") of Germany sits enthroned, holding the orb and scepter that signify his sovereign power, flanked by his son Henry. (Although not himself a Welf, Barbarossa had Welf blood.) One of the most dynamic rulers of his age, Barbarossa attempted to exert his authority over his ambitious nobles but was diverted by campaigns in northern Italy too frequently to retain thorough control of his own territory. Henry, who as Henry VI succeeded his father, found the German nobles equally as troublesome but through marriage gained a new realm in Sicily and southern Italy.

generations. Gradually, power came to reside in the hands of the local lords, barricaded in their fortresses, warring with their neighbors and dominating the lesser folk who lived in their shadow. Some lords ruled justly, others held sway through tyranny and terror, but their unwritten contracts with their dependents were based on a mutually satisfactory bargain: protection and maintenance in return for allegiance and service. The social system that grew out of these relationships came later to be known as feudalism. First formulated in eighth-century France, feudalism was firmly established throughout most of France, England, Germany, and northern Italy by the beginning of the twelfth century.

In the course of the century, each of these countries developed along its own route. In France, power gradually shifted away from the petty lords and toward the monarch, who stood at the pinnacle of the feudal system. In England, where feudalism had been imposed from above, an already-strong monarchy tightened its grip. In

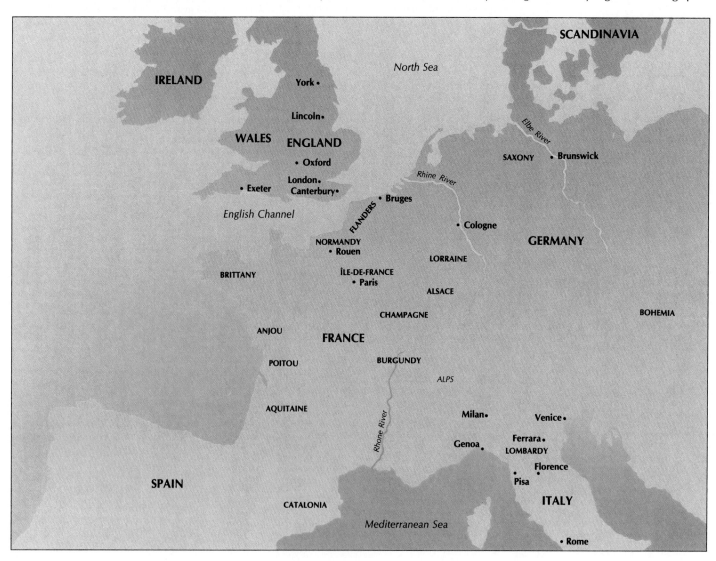

Germany, by contrast, the independent-minded nobles proved more than a match for the kings. Meanwhile, in northern Italy, there flourished cities larger and more prosperous than any others in Europe, and a middle class growing in influence; the developments in Italy hinted at the rise of towns throughout Europe and the eventual rotting of the constricting bonds of feudalism.

Against the flux of earthly affairs the Europeans of the twelfth century set the certainties of heaven. Nobles and kings saw themselves as God's men, bound to fight God's wars as any man was bound to fight for his earthly master. The faith of Europe found its most dramatic expression in the Crusades against the Muslims who occupied Jerusalem and the Holy Land.

Throughout the century, great armies from northern Europe made the hazardous journey to the east to do battle in the name of Christ. The Muslim Middle East began the twelfth century rent by conflicts and unable to offer a concerted defense. The Crusaders established an outpost of Catholic Christendom in the Levant and held Jerusalem for eighty-eight years. They lost the city only after the Islamic rulers in their turn invoked the concept of holy war to unite their own subjects.

In the meantime, Muslims themselves were expanding eastward, beckoned by the rich land of India. The decadent and inward-looking Rajput rulers of the subcontinent's northern fringe were no match for the Muslim warriors: The last decade of the twelfth century saw the Muslim conquest of northern India—a conquest spurred both by lust for empire and by the desire to spread the worship of Allah. The conquerors established the Delhi sultanate, a Muslim dynasty that was to rule northern India for three centuries.

Ambitious ventures inspired by matters of faith were not confined to the Christian and Muslim worlds. Far to the east, in the hinterland of Southeast Asia, the rulers of two expansionary kingdoms were embarking on gigantic temple-building projects that reflected the newfound wealth of empire. In Cambodia, temple construction glorified the kings as much as the gods, for the great temples of Angkor Wat and Angkor Thom also served as royal mausoleums; in the Buddhist state of Pagan, in Burma, the architectural achievements of the kings were believed to result in the reincarnation into a better life not only of the rulers themselves but of all their subjects. For a while, both the Angkor state and Pagan flourished exceedingly, then both faded, to be long outlasted by the monuments they erected. Neither kingdom created as robust a society as the one that emerged in western Europe after the barbarian depredations came to an end.

The unwritten contracts of feudal Europe imposed obligations on the members of every level of the rural community. The weakest and poorest owed their lord labor in the fields. Over these peasants the lord held virtually absolute power: He could flog them into obedience, hang them when they committed crimes, or withhold their right to marry. Men who had the strength and skill to fight, and the financial wherewithal to arm themselves, were treated with more respect. These warriors became the vassals of the lord.

The bond between lord and vassal offered both parties loyalty and support, backed by tangible benefits. A strong lord would come to a vassal's assistance if land or person were threatened by enemies. He would also guide the vassal in the management of personal affairs. To cement the ties between them, the lord would grant his man a fief—usually a gift of land, but occasionally a retaining fee in cash.

The vassal had obligations in return. By swearing an oath of fealty, as Count William's vassals did at Bruges, the vassal promised to safeguard his lord's life, property, and honor. He was expected to provide military assistance to his superior—fighting in battles, bringing such men as he himself could command, or making a financial contribution to the war chest. The vassal also promised to attend his master's court and give counsel when required. To display his fealty to the world, he might also be expected to perform certain services of honor, such as waiting at his lord's table or holding the stirrup when his lord mounted a horse.

A lord himself could serve as vassal to a greater lord, and the latter might be a vassal of a mightier magnate still. A vassal could hold land from more than one lord at a time, although in most cases there would be one superior—known as the liege lord—whose claims on his loyalties took priority.

The Church was an integral part of the system: Abbots and bishops possessed more land than many secular nobles and were often direct vassals of the king. But ecclesiastics owed a greater allegiance to the pope in Rome, and their dual loyalties made for conflict. More than one monarch of the twelfth century met his deepest humiliation at the hands of the Church.

The king himself possessed many priestly attributes. According to the teachings of the Church, the king was God's representative on earth, set apart from lesser mortals not simply by his royal birth, but by the religious rites of his coronation. When the time came to crown a king, the deed was done in church, in a solemn ceremony performed by a bishop. The new monarch was placed on the throne, anointed with the same holy oil used to consecrate priests, and invested with the royal regalia—the ring, the sword, the scepter—that conferred upon him the obligation to dispense justice and defend the Christian faith. From that moment, a king stood above the law: Indeed, he was the law's living embodiment. He alone among mortals was deemed by clergy to shed blood without sin, and his own flesh was sacrosanct. The king's very touch, many believed, could cure disease.

With the Church in control of the rites of kingmaking, a monarch could claim with conviction that God's grace had made him ruler. But earthly politics also counted. The firstborn son of a reigning king did not necessarily stand to inherit his father's crown. In Germany, kingship was subject to election: A royal family collectively inherited the right to rule, but it was up to the realm's mightiest nobles to decide which member of that house was worthy of the throne. In France and England, by the twelfth century, the eldest son was the usual choice. In these lands, it was the custom for the reigning king to name his eldest son as heir, summon the high nobles to assent to the choice, and see his successor crowned in his own lifetime.

The king stood at the apex of the feudal pyramid: Only he could truly own land. Lesser men held land purely as tenants, in exchange for the services and loyalty they owed their overlord. But, throughout the twelfth century, a king was, in reality, only as powerful as the noble lords of his realm would allow him to be. For, although they might do him formal homage, some of these nobles possessed wealth and influence beyond anything their sovereign could command.

The sovereigns of France were members of the Capetian dynasty, descendants of Hugh Capet—the name means "Cap Wearer"—who had been elected king of the Franks in 987. During the eleventh century, weak Capetian kings had barely managed to control their personal domain, the territory of about 15,500 square miles

The image and legend on this silver seal-die identify its owner as Isabella of Hainault, queen of France, who died in 1190; she would have worn it as a pendant ornament. Stamping such a seal in wax created an impression that guaranteed a document's authenticity; this type of mark was also used on personal gifts and items of trade, and to fasten letters. As badges of status and safeguards against dishonesty, seals became increasingly popular during the twelfth century with merchants and clergy as well as aristocracy and royalty.

surrounding Paris known as the Île-de-France. The kings were entitled to homage from a handful of dukes and counts whose lands added up to what is approximately the area of present-day France, although they included slivers of present-day Belgium and Spain, and excluded much of what is now Alsace and Burgundy. Among the vassals of the French kings were the English kings, in their role of dukes of Normandy. At the beginning of the twelfth century, however, neither the kings nor the great landholders counted for very much in France. The country was a patchwork made up of small, virtually independent lordships. The landscape was dotted with castles— situated every twelve miles or so—and presiding over each of these strongholds and

An early thirteenth-century manuscript drawing depicts Roland, the legendary eighth-century champion of Christendom, being invested by the emperor Charlemagne with the sword and apparel that were the insignia of knighthood. The concept of a feudal contract binding a vassal to his lord developed between Charlemagne's age and that of the artist's, but the scene is drawn as if feudalism were already an institution. The submissive gesture of the young warrior's outstretched hands symbolizes his oath of fealty, by which he promises to fight for the honor of his lord in return for protection if his own life or territory are threatened.

its surrounding territory was a minor lord known as a castellan. Technically, the castellans were vassals of the great dukes and counts or, in the royal domain, of the king himself; in reality, these lordlings exercised control over their localities with almost a free hand.

The balance began to shift at the start of the twelfth century, when the great territorial princes of France began to assert their feudal rights. Among the newly forceful lords were the Capetian kings themselves, the dukes of Burgundy, the counts of Champagne and Flanders, and the English kings—who, in the middle of the century, acquired through inheritance or marriage the county of Anjou and the enormous region of Aquitaine in the south, thus becoming the most powerful princes in France.

The first task of the great lords was to tame the castellans. Some of these minor lords were decidedly unsavory characters, enthusiastic abusers of power who were unlikely to relinquish it without a fight. Louis VI, who ruled from 1108 to 1137, found himself up against petty tyrants such as Thomas of Marle, who controlled a territory northeast of Paris and whose cruelty was a byword among his contemporaries. One of them wrote of the pleasure Thomas took in punishing those who crossed him: "For he did not merely kill them outright with the sword and for definite offenses, as is usual, but by butchering them after horrible tortures. No one can tell how many people expired in his dungeons and chains from starvation, disease, and torture."

Thomas of Marle's hands were drenched in blood. He went to war against his own father, cut the throat of an ecclesiastical kinsman who had displeased him, took under his protection a band of rebels who had murdered the bishop of Laon, summarily appropriated properties belonging to the Church, and violated his feudal oath by taking up arms against his overlord, King Louis. In order to raise an army, the king—whose treasury was limited—had to call upon the Church for assistance. Desperate to be rid of this priest murderer and plunderer, one parish after another gathered funds. Yet when Louis was successful in destroying his enemy's formidable fortresses, he chose, for his own mysterious reasons, to grant Thomas a pardon. Only after the baron committed fresh atrocities did Louis take him prisoner and hold him in captivity until he died.

Through such victories as these, the twelfth-century princes gained confidence. But for Louis VI and his son Louis VII, who succeeded him in 1137, the strengthening of their hold was far more than a simple matter of dispatching punitive expeditions against unruly vassals. In order to govern the royal domain effectively, they established a new class of administrators, directly answerable to the king, to look after the Crown's interests, gather revenues and ensure their prudent use, protect the populace, and keep the peace. Outside the royal domain, the kings began, very gradually, to exercise their power as monarchs and as feudal overlords. They defended the Church against attack—as in the matter of Thomas of Marle—and called their vassals to attend court, in fulfillment of the feudal obligation to offer advice and counsel to their lord. And, when appeals were made to the kings by beleaguered vassals, they would intervene in disputes even outside the Île-de-France. It was a mark of the growing prestige of the Crown that in 1124 Louis VI was able to summon most of his vassals to fight off a German invasion of Lorraine, a duchy on the eastern frontier that owed allegiance to him.

Good order brought prosperity to the royal domain. The population flourished and the wealth of the land increased, enriching its royal landlords. For reasons of both perspicacity and piety, the Capetian kings transferred considerable amounts of this wealth to the coffers of the Church. Louis VII founded religious houses, constructed new churches or rebuilt old ones,

and conferred fiefs or other financial privileges on high ecclesiastics in exchange for their invaluable support.

Among these religious personages, none was more powerful than Suger, abbot of the ancient royal abbey of Saint Denis, situated a few miles from Paris. An intimate friend of both Louis VI and Louis VII, Suger wrote the life history of the former king after his death and served under the latter as a loyal regent of France, virtually ruling the country while Louis VII was absent on a crusade to liberate the Holy Land.

Suger professed two all-consuming ambitions: He desired to strengthen and glorify the Crown of France, and he wished to rebuild and embellish his abbey. For Suger, the two aspirations were intertwined. Saint Denis was the patron saint of all France, its chief protector after God Himself, and the abbey dedicated to him should, the abbot thought, be a symbol of the French nation. Generations of young French princes had been schooled at the abbey; most of the kings of France were entombed within its precincts; the oriflamme, by legend the standard of the eighth-century emperor Charlemagne, hung above its altar.

To achieve his dream of making Saint Denis worthy of its status as a national shrine, Suger summoned artists and artisans from all over France and persuaded king and high nobles alike to dig deep into their coffers to support the enterprise. These efforts yielded the first flowering of the Gothic style—a glorious synthesis of soaring pointed arches that drew the eye toward heaven, luminous stained-glass windows, and intricate carvings of mortals and angels, saints and monsters, brought to vibrant life in wood and stone.

At every stage of the work on the abbey, Suger saw himself as impresario. In his own account of the project, he describes how he lay awake at night pondering the right source of wood for the roof beams and leaped out of bed in the morning to hustle his carpenters out to the forest to consider his choice. He composed verses to be inscribed on Saint Denis's main doors and did not hesitate to engrave on the doors that it was Suger who had caused these things to be made.

As Suger had planned, the new Saint Denis became a shrine not only to God but to the Crown of France. In the course of rearranging the libraries of the abbey, monks found—or possibly forged—old charters and documents that linked the Capetian dynasty with Charlemagne. And thenceforth the kings of France would pay an annual ceremonial visit to the abbey church to place coins upon its altar, reminding the world that they were heaven's vassals and that France was the fief they held by the grace of God. Church and Crown worked hand in hand, each benefiting from the support of the other.

On these sturdy foundations, the century's last and greatest French king, Philip II, would elevate the monarchy to heights undreamed of by his predecessors. He was to regain many of the lands held by the English kings and exert real power over the

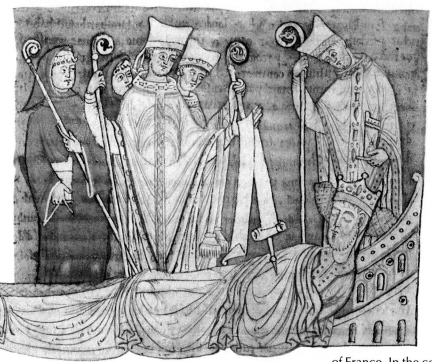

Lying helpless in his bed, Henry I of England is shown surrounded by a swarm of angry bishops and abbots *(below)*, by knights in armor who have unsheathed their swords *(far left)*, and by peasants wielding scythes and pitchforks *(left)*. These nightmare visions of rebellion by the three social orders of his realm were reminders of the fragility of power: The king remained king only for so long as his subjects chose to obey him. Based on dreams that Henry confided to his physician, the illustrations formed part of an early twelfth-century chronicle compiled by two monks of Worcester.

The high ceiling vaults of the abbey church of Saint Denis are supported by a skeleton of stone ribs and pointed arches. The open structure of the ambulatory—a semicircular aisle running behind the altar—allows sunlight to suffuse the choir.

A porphyry vase transformed by goldsmiths into the shape of an eagle and a jewel-encrusted chalice of sardonyx, a type of quartz, adorned the high altar with majesty.

A Royal Sanctum Renewed

In the mid-twelfth century, the crumbling abbey of Saint Denis, a few miles north of Paris, was magnificently rebuilt to express the glory not only of God but of the French monarchy. Saint Denis was the patron saint of France, and in the abbey dedicated to him, the kings of France had been buried since the sixth century. The abbey's altar was adorned with the oriflamme, a scarlet flag believed to have been the standard of Charlemagne. By emphasizing the role of the king as vassal of France's spiritual protector, the refurbished abbey both enhanced the prestige of the monarchy and helped unite the king and his nobles in their common allegiance to God.

The genius behind the building was a churchman and politician of peasant origins named Suger. Appointed abbot of Saint Denis in 1122, Suger also served as chief adviser to Louis VI and Louis VII. Between 1137 and 1144, Suger supervised the building of a new porch and facade for his abbey and, at the east end, the focal point of the liturgical rites, a choir and an ambulatory from which side chapels radiated.

On the portal of the church, Suger inscribed a quotation from an early medieval mystical text that encapsulated his own fervent beliefs: "The dull mind of man rises to truth through that which is material. And, seeing the light, is resurrected from its former submersion." Suger's guiding principles were light and splendor. He erected a great cross of gold over the tomb of Saint Denis and assembled a treasury of precious vessels and sacred relics adorned with jewels. For the choir and ambulatory, Suger made use of tall columns linked by pointed arches instead of solid walls, thus flooding the east end of the church with light, which poured through translucent stained-glass windows. The result—an engineering feat achieved with the structural support of flying buttresses and ribbed ceiling vaults—was the first example of a style of architecture that later became known as Gothic.

great princes. By the time of his death in 1223, France would possess Europe's first—and for a long time only—true royal capital, a center not only of government and commerce but of scholarship, with a university that would make Paris the center of Europe's intellectual life for centuries to come.

While the Capetians were strengthening their monarchy, a similar process was taking place on the opposite side of the English Channel. At the start of the twelfth century, England's feudal system was more orderly than that of France. When William, duke of Normandy, conquered the Anglo-Saxon kingdom in 1066 and became William I of England, he had placed his own loyal followers in charge of all the great estates. These vassals did not have to be wooed or worried into loyalty: Their castles were the strongholds of the occupying forces rather than centers of resistance to royal control. Henry I of England, who mounted the throne in 1100, continued William's work of establishing an efficient, centralized monarchy. Most notably, he began the practice of sending out itinerant justices to hear cases on his behalf—cases that would otherwise have been judged by local lords.

But after Henry's death, the country deteriorated into a state of near anarchy during a succession quarrel. Stephen of Blois, a grandchild of William the Conqueror, seized the English throne. But for nearly twenty years, another grandchild of William's—Matilda, widow of the German emperor and wife to Geoffrey Plantagenet, count of Anjou—contested the crown. Meanwhile, the nobles of England warred among themselves. Henry's administrative and judicial systems virtually disintegrated, causing one contemporary observer to lament that England, formerly the home of peace, piety, and justice, had become "a place of perversity, a house of strife, a school of disorder, and the teacher of every kind of rebellion."

With the death of Stephen in 1154, the conflict resolved itself. Stephen's named heir was Matilda's son, Henry Plantagenet. As Henry II, he set to work rebuilding the shattered kingdom. Most of the war-weary English nobility welcomed his efforts. With their assistance, he destroyed or confiscated the fortresses of local despots who had taken advantage of the power vacuum to harry the populace. He rounded up and expelled the bands of foreign mercenaries that Stephen had imported in his vain attempts to quell rebellion.

The country breathed a collective sigh of relief as Henry organized his administration. He sought out able people to help him rule. Some of his appointees were experienced officials from the first Henry's reign. But he also recruited talented newcomers, not necessarily of exalted birth, such as Thomas Becket, son of a London merchant, who became his chancellor.

The first task was to put the royal treasury in order. Henry's treasurer, Richard Fitznigel, observed: "We are, of course, aware that kingdoms are governed, and laws maintained, primarily by prudence, fortitude, temperance, justice, and the other virtues, for which reason the rulers of the world must practice them with all their might. But there are occasions on which sound and wise policies take effect rather quicker through the agency of money."

Henry agreed. He restored and extended his grandfather Henry I's system for assessing and collecting revenues from the royal domain and from feudal vassals, relying on a countrywide network of sheriffs. Twice a year, these local administrators were summoned to present their accounts at the Royal Exchequer. The king's department of accounts took its name from a long table covered with a checkered cloth.

At one end presided the chief justiciar—the head, under the king, of the royal administration. At the other end, no doubt sweating under his tunic, sat the sheriff whose accounts were under scrutiny. In between these parties, lesser functionaries moved counters representing sums of money from one square to another to represent incomes and expenditures in a manner that even an innumerate sheriff could follow. Scribes stood by, recording the results.

With the funds received, Henry was able to initiate reforms in other areas. A prime ambition was to make the attainment of justice quicker and more uniform, thereby reducing the possibility that litigants would resort to violence to resolve their differences. Henry had no desire to take over the entire burden of judging cases from his feudal vassals: The resources of the Crown could not have coped. His aim was to provide an effective appeal procedure. To accelerate the appeal process, Henry revived his grandfather's innovation of sending judges across the land to hear cases in the name of the king. He provided for special assizes to deal with cases of eviction, which in the past had frequently been handled dishonestly by feudal lords feathering their own nests. Under Henry, the jury system, initiated by Northmen who had settled in England in the tenth century, was institutionalized and extended to cover civil, as well as criminal, trials.

Henry's dream of subjecting all in his realm to the law of the land met with fierce resistance from one important group, whose members reserved the right to judge themselves. The clergy had their own ecclesiastical courts for settling disputes over church property and judging those men of the cloth who so forgot themselves as to commit crimes. Perhaps one in six of England's adult male population were qualified to be judged in ecclesiastical courts. Most of them were not priests but were in the so-called minor orders. They had taken the initial vows that admitted them into the ranks of deacons or stipendiary vicars; in theory, they were looking forward to ordination. But for many, the special status that even minor orders brought was an end in itself, and ordination was put off indefinitely.

Henry accepted the role of the Church courts in civil cases, but he found it intolerable that a sizable segment of the population should remain exempt from the criminal law of the realm. In 1163, his advisers reported that, in the nine years since his coronation, at least one hundred murders, and innumerable lesser crimes of theft and violence, had been perpetrated by "criminous clerks" beyond the reach of royal justice. The worst sentence that a Church court could impose on such wrongdoers was defrocking. Henry wanted clergy defrocked by Church courts to come next before lay courts and submit to far more severe verdicts.

As part of his long struggle to bring the Church to heel, Henry appointed his trusted chancellor, Thomas Becket, to fill the vacant archbishopric of Canterbury. The king was untroubled by the fact that Becket was not even a priest; it was a simple matter to have him ordained in time for the enthronement. But Henry faced a rude awakening. Becket flung himself with passion into his new role and transformed himself overnight from a loyal servant of the king to the staunch defender of the Church. He refused to countenance a second trial for defrocked clergy; he argued, quoting from the Bible, that no one should be judged twice for the same crime.

The quarrel raged for years. Not all clergy supported Becket's militant resistance to royal power. Even the pope sent messages from Rome urging his archbishop to compromise with the king.

In 1164, Henry called together the great barons and ecclesiastics of the realm and

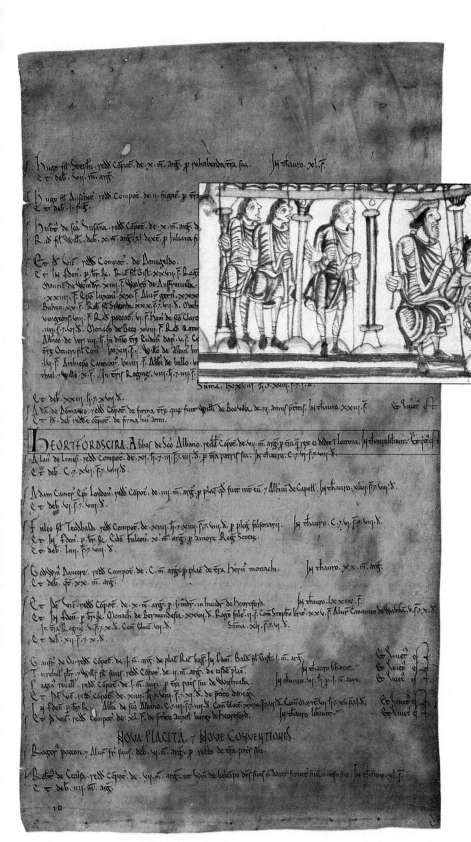

Using scales to check that the correct amount is received, a royal officer collects taxes from the subjects in his division of the country. Twice a year, a sheriff—the king's representative in each of England's thirty-seven shires—submitted his accounts to the Royal Exchequer in the form of a written parchment scroll; the outlined area on the scroll shown on the left records that, in Hertfordshire, the abbot of Saint Albans had owed seven marks of silver for land that the king had granted him but had paid his debt in full. The regular scrutiny of sheriffs' accounts was established by Henry I, who also took stern measures to protect the currency; the silver penny opposite, minted at Chichester, dates from the period following Henry's inquiry into forgery and the minting of substandard coins in 1125.

promulgated a document known as the Constitutions of Clarendon, which he presented as an effort to codify the time-honored legal customs of the kingdom in matters where Church and State were in dispute. The Constitutions removed or restricted many of the privileges claimed on behalf of the Church by canonical lawyers. Thomas promptly defied the Constitutions by trying a case in his own ecclesiastical court in a way that violated the new restrictions. He was summoned to appear before the king to explain his conduct.

Becket's fellow clergy found themselves in an awkward position: The bishops, in their capacity as royal vassals, were expected to sit in judgment upon him. But Thomas, as their ecclesiastical superior, forbade his bishops to attend the court. While the bishops negotiated with the king over a course of action that would salve their consciences, Becket fled to the Continent.

For six years, he remained in exile, exchanging attacks and threats with Henry. In 1170, an uneasy peace was achieved, and Becket was prevailed upon to return. The day before he embarked, Becket provocatively excommunicated three bishops for taking part in the coronation of the king's son—a role that he claimed as the archbishop of Canterbury's alone. When the monarch heard the news, he cried aloud that he wished someone would rid him of "this turbulent priest."

Four knights of the royal household took their sovereign at his word, hastened to Canterbury, and murdered the archbishop in his own cathedral. All of Europe recoiled in horror at the crime. Henry protested his own innocence, but he was well aware that, as far as Christendom was concerned, Thomas Becket's blood was on his hands. On the 12th of July, 1174, he came to Canterbury and submitted himself to be flogged by priests in the place where his old friend and enemy had died. He had to endure not only the public humiliation but the knowledge that the Church had beaten him. The Constitutions of Clarendon were revised to accommodate Becket's position, and the clergy were to remain beyond the reach of England's criminal law until, four centuries later, an English king was ready to deny Rome any say in the affairs of his country.

Despite his failure to bring the Church into line, Henry succeeded in bringing a degree of justice and order to a chaotic realm. An equally daunting task faced his royal counterpart in Germany, Frederick Barbarossa.

Germany—the eastern half of the great empire won in the eighth century by Charlemagne—consisted of present-day West Germany, Austria, and the Netherlands, most of Belgium and Alsace, some of Switzerland, and a fraction of East Germany. Like France, it was a collection of territories ruled by virtually autonomous princes. Officially, these magnates were the vassals of the German monarch, who following Charlemagne's precedent was styled Holy Roman Emperor and was regarded as the secular protector of the Church. Again harking back to Charlemagne, the German kings claimed dominion over northern Italy almost as far south as Rome. But they were masters of Italy in name only and presided with little real power over a Germany riven by warfare between two noble clans.

When the princes of the realm elected

Thomas Becket is cut down before the altar of Saint Benedict in Canterbury Cathedral by four impetuous knights. The assassination, on December 29, 1170, was the final act in a bitter dispute between Archbishop Becket and Henry II of England, whose determination to restrict ecclesiastical courts was opposed by Becket. The knights' belief that their act would aid the king proved mistaken: Public outrage forced Henry to withdraw his demands, and Becket—depicted here in an English manuscript illustration from the 1190s—was canonized by the pope only three years after his death.

Frederick I as their king in 1152, he was welcomed by all parties as an enlightened choice: He was kin to both opposing factions, the Welfs and the Hohenstaufens, yet was not seen as the ally of either side. By all accounts, Frederick was a charismatic figure: He was broad shouldered and amiable of countenance, and he sported fair, almost reddish, whiskers that earned him the sobriquet Barbarossa—meaning "Red Beard" in Italian.

Within a few years, Barbarossa brought a semblance of order to his battle-scarred, famine-ravaged realm. Charm alone was not enough; he had to shed a considerable amount of blood to whip unruly nobles into line. Chroniclers spoke of many people hanged, castles destroyed, towns and even churches put to the torch. But Frederick succeeded in imposing a set of legal codes and agreements, known as the Land Peaces, that touched the lives of all his subjects. He compelled all males, from the age of eighteen to seventy years, to swear an oath, renewable at regular intervals, to keep the peace. The Crown undertook to help the hungry by fixing an official price for grain after every harvest.

While Frederick remained in Germany, the peace endured. But Barbarossa's imperial ambitions drew him away from home: He wished to stake his claim to the growing wealth of Italy. Whenever he made one of his numerous and lengthy sorties across the Alps, the German nobles fell again to fighting among themselves.

To ensure that during his absences his nobles remained loyal to the Crown, Frederick allowed them a virtually free hand in the control of their own territories and granted many of them a higher feudal status: The margrave of Austria became a duke, the duke of Bohemia a king. The noble who took the most advantage of Frederick's liberality was Henry the Lion, duke of Saxony.

By the standards of any age, Henry was a flamboyant figure. His residence at Brunswick was like a royal court in miniature, outshining any of Barbarossa's palaces in grandeur. Within its handsome walls, artists and master artisans labored to glorify their patron, and foreign envoys came to pay their respects. The king of England, Henry II, sent his daughter Matilda to be the Lion's bride. The duke was a patron of commerce as well as art, founding towns and supporting merchant ventures. Above all, he was a formidable warlord and a brilliant military strategist.

The Lion's land lust knew no limits. He made forays into territories claimed by other nobles, thereby making a great number of powerful enemies. Arbitrating among his vassals, Frederick summoned Henry to trial. Henry ignored the imperial order. Then Frederick went on the offensive: In 1180, he broke up Henry's ducal holdings and distributed them to other lords. The Saxon became an outlaw but still possessed enough loyal allies to raise a powerful army.

Frederick hounded Henry stubbornly. Gradually, Barbarossa wore the Lion down, defeating some of the duke's supporters in battle, persuading others to desert the cause. One by one, the rebel fortresses fell. By 1182, Henry was forced to surrender. The emperor displayed a restraint that undoubtedly infuriated the duke's old enemies: Instead of drawing and quartering his victim—the usual fate of traitors—Frederick officially forgave him, then banished Henry to the court of his father-in-law, Henry II of England, for personal safety. After Barbarossa's death, Henry the Lion returned to Germany and revived his old quarrels. Only shortly before his death in 1195 was he reconciled with the new emperor.

Since Barbarossa, with all his energy and military skill, could barely manage to control an upstart vassal such as Henry, it is not surprising that his successors failed completely. While France and England grew steadily more centralized, Germany fragmented. The German nobles consolidated the powerful position they had gained under Frederick, and after his reign, no ruler was to impose unity on Germany for hundreds of years.

Throughout Europe, the nobility encompassed not only wealthy potentates like Henry the Lion, capable of challenging the sovereignty of kings, but also many minor figures, almost as poor as peasants. Yet a powerful bond united the greatest magnate and the landless knight: Both were enrolled in the international fraternity of warriors. Encased in iron shells of armor, mounted on chargers, thrusting cruelly pointed lances, they hurled themselves across the battlegrounds of Europe.

The training for knighthood began early. Boys from noble families were usually sent away from home around the age of six to be fostered in other knightly households. There, usually with others of their own age, they were taught horsemanship and the arts of fighting with lance and sword. Nor were the less martial aspects of their education neglected: They were instructed in etiquette, taught to dance, and possibly helped to an appreciation of music and poetry by the ladies of the house. When a youth had absorbed these lessons to his guardians' satisfaction, he was ritually dubbed a knight.

In 1128, young Geoffrey the Fair of Anjou celebrated his initiation into knighthood in the Norman city of Rouen. As the scion of a princely family, he enjoyed a coming-of-age of considerable splendor, but the ritual was, in essence, that which any noble fledgling would expect to undergo. It is not recorded if Geoffrey spent the night before the ceremony on his knees in church, mounting a vigil over his weapons; not all families viewed this spiritual act as an essential step. Geoffrey did, however, begin the great day itself with a ritual bath, to purify himself at the beginning of his new life. Duly cleansed, he donned a tunic made of gold cloth and a purple cloak, and slipped his feet into silken shoes.

At the proper moment, he was led before Henry I, duke of Normandy and king of England. In the presence of the cream of the Norman nobility, Geoffrey was given his knightly accouterments: golden spurs, a breastplate of superior craft, equipped with a double layer of mail, and a spear of ash and iron. A shield, adorned with painted lions, was hung about his neck. The king himself reached out to gird Geoffrey with a sword of ancient provenance, then touched the young man with his own sword to dub him a knight. Thirty noble youths, friends and companions of Geoffrey's, were knighted at the same ceremony and presented with gifts of weapons and horses from the king. Once these solemnities were over, the whole company launched into a solid week of feasts and festivity. Prominent on the agenda were the war games known as tournaments, where two teams of knights fought each other on horseback, wielding lances and swords.

For later generations, the tournament would become a stylized performance, when knights met in carefully regulated contests on a small and circumscribed ground. But in the twelfth century, it was often difficult to distinguish between a tournament and real warfare. The combat raged over the countryside: Fields, farms, and even hapless villages became part of the battleground, and fatalities were common. Prisoners were

This gilded bronze bust was commissioned by Frederick Barbarossa shortly after he became Holy Roman Emperor in 1155. Intended as a personal gift for his godfather, the bust conforms with contemporary written descriptions of Barbarossa and is probably a fairly realistic likeness of the youthful and energetic emperor. Breaking with the stylized conventions of official portraiture, many artists and sculptors of the twelfth century demonstrated an increasing concern with the actual physical appearance of their subjects.

Hunting, besides being a diversion and a source of meat, tested courage and displayed physical prowess. It also honed riding and weapons skills, and developed field craft.

Sword practice when wearing armor strengthened the wrist and arm. Knights delivered a series of furious blows at a wooden stump.

Domestic duties for a squire included looking after his knight's weapons and spare horse. As servant, the squire also helped the knight don his armor and his sword.

A squire attended his knight at table, learning the manners and concept of service essential to knighthood. He also learned by overhearing the warriors' conversations.

Youths in western Europe were trained to maneuver and fight as a unit. These close-packed and disciplined horsemen were central to the devastating Crusader cavalry charges.

Wrestling toughened a youngster and prepared him for infantry combat—a form of fighting that twelfth-century aristocrats did not shun as their successors would do.

Social training for a squire involved playing a musical instrument, dancing, and composing verses in praise of the lady he had chosen as the unattainable object of his devotion.

TRAINING A KNIGHT

By the twelfth century, western Europe's military elite was becoming a social and political aristocracy, yet knights remained fighting men, and their education emphasized martial qualities above all else. Their ideals, like those of the Dark Ages warriors who were their forebears, were physical strength, skill at arms, courage, and loyalty to their leaders.

During the twelfth century, such military virtues were joined by Christian ideas of service, humility, and mercy to form a chivalric code that spread throughout Europe. From his apprenticeship as a squire to his elevation to knighthood, a trainee warrior would learn not only the arts of combat but the ethics of gentlemanly conduct. Tournaments gave a knight the chance to impress with both his martial ability and his courtly behavior. Many knights were now literate, and in addition to extolling the glory of battle in verse, these aristocratic troubadours delighted in recounting the pain and the platonic pleasures of courtly love.

captured and held to ransom. The victors stripped the vanquished of their armor and kept it, along with their horses, as spoils of war.

Such encounters kept fighting skills from growing rusty and provided young knights a foretaste of what they would have to face on a wartime battlefield. The English chronicler Roger of Howden echoed the views of many of his contemporaries when he declared that "he is not fit for battle who has never seen his own blood flow, who has not heard his teeth crunch under the blow of an opponent, or felt the full weight of his adversary upon him."

For a knight of modest means, the tournament could provide a way of earning a living in peacetime. Good armor and well-trained horses were valuable prizes, and ransoms, if collected in sufficient number, were a healthy source of income. One soldier of fortune who supported himself in this way was William, later called the Marshal. He was the fourth son of a minor baron, with little wealth to help him make his way in the world. The day after William was dubbed a knight, he took part in a battle between two rival counts and acquitted himself so well that he became something of a celebrity. Reports of his bravery both in warfare and in tournaments soon reached Eleanor of Aquitaine, queen to Henry II of England, who hired him to teach her princely sons the arts of war.

As a knight in the royal court, William gained even greater fame and fortune. In 1177, he went into partnership with another warrior, attending tournaments throughout northern France with the intention of making money: Within ten months, he and his associate were reputed to have captured and raised ransoms on more than 100 knights. When William quarreled with his king, both the count of Flanders and the duke of Burgundy leaped into the breach and tried to tempt him into their service with the promise of lands and pensions, but in the end, William remained loyal to the Plantagenet princes he had tutored.

This early thirteenth-century ivory casket is decorated with scenes illustrating the love of the dying Tristan for Iseult, wife of the king of Cornwall. The legend of the ill-fated couple was one of many romances created at this time by French and German poets. Out of the reciting of such epics in the courts of Europe, there grew a set of chivalric conventions governing the conduct of a knight in thrall to a highborn lady. At the same time as this secular idealization of women came about, womanhood also gained a new significance through the growing cult of the Virgin Mary, who was coming to be revered as the foremost saint of Christendom. In a twelfth-century, silver-gilt French statue *(opposite)*, Mary is portrayed with the child Jesus.

William reached his position at the royal court through valor, but he could not have risen so high had he not been born into a knightly family. In the more fluid societies of the ninth and tenth centuries, knighthood had often been won by prowess in arms. By the twelfth century, the nobility was coalescing into a hereditary caste. Patents of arms were sometimes granted to eminent members of the bourgeoisie, but a gulf had opened between the honorable knight and the mercenary soldier who served for pay. In time, in England and France, another social division would become manifest: The highest nobles would draw apart from the lesser knights, who would gradually metamorphose into the English gentry and the French *petite noblesse*.

In Germany, the *ministeriales,* the equivalent of the gentry, emerged from quite different roots. The original ministeriales resembled serfs: They were bound to the services of a particular lord and were counted as his property. Yet in prestige and power, the ministeriales became far superior to peasants. They were members of the lord's household and served him as soldiers and administrators, defending his castles and managing his estates. Their lack of autonomy did not prevent these knights from amassing wealth: By the twelfth century, ministeriales were able to hold and inherit property of their own.

Whatever the differences in their status, the knights of Europe shared the same values. They saw themselves as the embodiments of chivalry, the exalted code of knightly conduct that was first nurtured in the great houses of France and spread rapidly through Europe. Chivalry embraced, but transcended, military heroism: It was based on courtesy, fairness, fidelity, and honor. Literature—more accessible as the nobility learned to read in increasing numbers—spelled out its ideals.

"Lords, look at the best knight you have ever seen," enjoined the author of one chivalric epic. "He is brave and courtly and skillful, noble and of good lineage, and eloquent; expert in hunting and falconry; he knows how to play chess and back-gammon, gaming and dicing." This pattern of perfection, the writer continued, "has honored the poor and lowly, and judges each according to his worth."

Such paragons did not often exist in fact, as the authors well knew. Much of the courtly literature may have been written tongue in cheek, making satirical capital on the gulf between ideal and reality. To point up the imperfect present, poets retold the legends of the distant past. The great deeds of Charlemagne's paladins and King Arthur's knights, the struggles of ancient Greek and Trojan heroes, were all recalled by the troubadours—the poets of love, lust, and valor who sang in the noble house-holds and princely courts of southern France.

The first troubadour to gain fame for his rhyming stanzas was himself a prince—Guilhelm, ninth count of Poitou and seventh duke of Aquitaine, who lived from 1071 to 1127. But lesser folk, both men and women, brought their verbal and musical talents to the art. One celebrated troubadour, named Marcabru, was said to have been a foundling, left in a bundle at a rich man's door. He wandered through southern France and Catalonia between 1130 and 1148, entertaining nobles in their courts and soldiers around their camp-fires, singing love lyrics, war songs, and ribald satires. Another, known as the Monk of Montaudon, left his monastery at the behest of the king of Aragon and migrated from one noble house to another, regaling his audiences with such unclerical sentiments as: "I like enjoyment and gaiety, / Good food and gifts and jousts for me! / I like a lady of courtesy, / Who is unembarrassed, ready, and free, / A rich man spending generously, / Sharp only to his enemy."

In their songs and stories, the troubadours opened a window on a glorious world where a knight not only did homage to his lord but dedicated himself, with passionate if chaste devotion, to the service of a highborn lady. Even love, so conceived, mirrored feudalism: The lover offered himself as the lady's vassal. He worshiped her from afar, revered her as a goddess, and reveled in the exquisite agonies of unrequited love: "Though such great torments I have known / through you alone, / I'd rather die for your harsh sake / than from another the least pleasure take."

If chivalric literature idealized the knight, it created an equally far-fetched image of his romances. In reality, the daughters of the nobility served as dynastic pawns.

A marriage could bring new territories to a lord as part of his wife's dowry, or—if she boasted higher birth than he—it could be a means to enhance his own prestige. Despite the Church's official views on the permanence of marriage, it was relatively easy for a prince or a king to put aside a wife, particularly if she failed to produce an heir. Among the much intermarried families of the nobility, it was always possible to discover—years after the wedding—that the rejected bride was too close a cousin, and the inconvenient marriage could be annulled.

But a few highborn women managed to wield power, and none more so than Eleanor, heiress to the rich French duchy of Aquitaine. She was first the queen of France, wife of Louis VII; she was divorced by him—probably because she failed to provide him with a male heir—and six weeks later married the English king Henry II. She extended Henry's domain by bringing her vast French landholdings as a dowry and engaged actively in politics, governing England as regent when her husband was absent from the kingdom. But this marriage, too, turned sour, and when it did Eleanor became a formidable foe. In 1173, she encouraged her sons to rebel against their father and so threatened the king that he took her prisoner and kept her in captivity until his death sixteen years later.

In spite of her fluctuating political fortunes, Eleanor exercised a profound influence on the aristocratic culture of western Europe. She loved literature and music, and created a court of troubadours and cultivated noblewomen who traveled with her, celebrating and refining the lore of chivalry and the mystique of courtly love. She was an enthusiastic patron of architecture. By her own example, she widened the intellectual horizons of many royal courts and noble households.

This intricate, ambitious world of knights and ladies, poets and prelates, troubadours and kings depended for its survival on one single, unlovely reality: the sweat of the peasants who worked the land. From the yields of his holdings, the noble vassal fed and clothed his household, and acquired the arms and horses he needed to meet his military obligations to his feudal lord. To ensure their continued control over the vital resource of peasant labor, the nobility had devised the notion of serfdom.

Serfdom, a status as old as the feudal system, tied a human being and his descendants to a landholding. Since the bond was to a landscape rather than to a particular owner, serfdom was not quite equivalent to slavery—but its restrictions were almost as great. Peasants had never accepted serf status joyfully, but if they were landless and starving, or if their lives were threatened by marauders, they had no alternative but to hand over their freedom. The serf gained protection and a patch of ground for his own use, and in return he owed his master certain services.

From one estate to another, the nature and number of these obligations varied. The serfs of a manor belonging to the bishop of Mâcon in Burgundy, for instance, were expected to plow, supplying their own draft animals for the purpose; to work in the vineyards; to cut and bring in the hay; to harvest the crops; to thresh the grain; and to tend the woodland that was used both as a fuel source and as a grazing place for swine. Peasant women had services of their own to perform: attendance in the lord's kitchen, spinning his wool, brewing his beer, and churning butter in his dairy.

In any time left over from these tasks, serfs were free to work the ground the lord had granted them. But if a serf sold vegetables from his own plot at market, the lord claimed a share of the profits. He expected his people to use his bakehouse and his mill, and to pay him handsomely for the privilege.

LIFE ON THE MANOR

The manor—a lord's house and surrounding land—was the basic unit of western European medieval society. Little changed from one generation to the next, and each inhabitant's role was prescribed by custom. The lord owed his protection to the peasants, and they in turn owed him service.

Bound to the land, peasants could leave only with the lord's permission and usually lived out their lives on the manor. Part of their time was spent in unpaid labor: Some owned no fields, and those who had land could cultivate it only after filling the master's work quota. On some manors, this amounted to three days a week, as well as extra work at harvesttime. If weather threatened the harvest, the peasants had to get their lord's crops in before their own.

In this illustration from "A Mirror for Maidens," a twelfth-century manuscript written to enlighten novice nuns, peasants of a feudal manor toil over the harvest. Workers hoe *(center)*, scatter seed *(center and bottom)*, reap and bind grain *(top and bottom)*, and carry it into a barn *(center)*.

For their services, the peasants received a small portion of the harvest, in addition to minor privileges—such as the right to graze their livestock on their lord's freshly harvested fields and to take anything from his woods that could be cut with their sickles.

In the untamed forest, the manor was an island of order. Manors such as this, in the English Cotswolds, were almost self-sufficient.

In the comfort of his stone hall, the lord of the manor ruled virtually as a king, controlling almost every aspect of life. Close by lived his officials: the bailiff, who ran the estate, and the reeve, who supervised the peasants' work. The church was built on land given by the lord, who often appointed and supported its rector.

The peasants—a dozen or as many as 1,000—usually included a miller, a smith, a weaver, and a cobbler. These were freemen, who could take their trade elsewhere but seldom did. Their houses were generally larger and better than those of the serfs, who lived with their livestock in smoky huts of timber, thatch, and mud. The countryside yielded wood for cups and bowls, straw to sleep on, and the occasional dish of birds or berries. Their only imported commodities were salt for preserving meat and iron for tools.

Around the village spread two or three large fields divided into strips known as furlongs. Some land was kept for the lord, but within the furlongs, plots were randomly allotted to the peasants, so that good and bad land was shared out fairly. Each field under cultivation was planted with a single crop, which often meant that a peasant daily trudged miles to tend his scattered plots of oats or barley or wheat. To allow the soil to recover, one field was left fallow every year.

Much of this manor's income came from wool; the lord's sheep grazed on the fallow field, and the villagers' animals fed in the common. Some wool was kept for the peasants' clothes. The rest was taken to market, where it commanded a high price from weavers all over Europe.

The serf population of western Europe was to reach its peak in the thirteenth century, but the twelfth century witnessed a temporary move away from the system. Sometimes serfs were able to purchase their freedom outright; more often, they were permitted to provide their lord with goods or money in place of services. One landlord, an abbot from Alsace, expostulated against "the negligence, the uselessness, the slackness, and the idleness" of serfs who grudgingly contributed their compulsory labor; he would far rather collect his rents in cash and use these funds to pay more willing workers.

The annual dues paid by a French peasant named Guichard—who lived in Burgundy not far from the estate of the bishop of Mâcon—were typical of these arrangements. Every Easter he gave his landlord, Canon Étienne, a lamb; in the haymaking season, he owed the landlord six pieces of money. When the grain harvest came around, Guichard was obliged to give Étienne a generous measure of oats, as well as clubbing together with some other peasants to entertain the canon to a feast. At the grape harvest, Guichard paid over another sum of money, three loaves of bread, and some wine. He was relieved of any obligation during the lean months of winter, until

A series of illustrations from a twelfth-century English calendar of religious feast days show the occupations traditionally associated with different months of the year. Feasting *(above)* celebrates the new year in January; the reveler here is the two-headed Roman god Janus, who gazes simultaneously back into the old year and forward into the new one. In April, trees are pruned and new ones planted; sheep are sheared in June or July; and in November, pigs are slaughtered to provide meat for the winter. In the twelfth century, the sequence of seasonal labors seemed inextricably linked with that of holy days and festivals, for each followed a fixed annual cycle in a little-changing world.

the beginning of Lent, when the canon expected a capon. In the middle of that penitential period, another six pieces of money were due, and soon thereafter it was time once more to sacrifice the Easter lamb.

The typical rural manor—the home and lands of a lord—was a largely self-contained world. It had its own church, its mill, a central brewhouse and bakehouse, possibly a tavern. The fields were divided between the peasants' smallholdings and those making up the lord's personal domain. The peasants' cottages were commonly grouped into a hamlet near a source of water; a great manor might contain several such villages. The lord had his own barns and cowsheds, usually in proximity to his substantial dwelling house or castle; his tenants often shared their cottages with a family cow or goat, and all but the poorest households kept a pig.

From one generation to the next, the rural scene hardly altered. The eighth century had brought western Europe watermills, deep, efficient plows, and the three-year cycle of crops—wheat, then oats or barley, then fallow—which fed both people and beasts and allowed the land to recover its fertility. By the twelfth century, these improvements were widespread, but the only recent innovations were windmills—becoming a familiar sight on the landscapes of East Anglia and northern France—and the greater use of draft horses. Sturdy workhorses, bred for the farm instead of the battlefield, could cover more ground, and work for longer, than the oxen that had pulled the plows since Roman times. But horses remained far more expensive than oxen and out of many peasants' reach.

While agricultural techniques remained all but unchanged, the number of mouths to feed was growing at an alarming rate. Thanks to the extended period of relative peace and stability, the population of Europe swelled from an estimated 48 million at the beginning of the century to 61 million at its end. Nowhere was the crisis more acute than in Germany. There the population surged from about 4 million in 1100 to 7 million only ten decades later. Not even five devastating famines, caused by widespread crop failure, stemmed the tide. In times of such extreme want, starving hordes rampaged through the countryside. Travelers trembled at the account of an archbishop and his entourage waylaid on their way to mass; a band of starving men forced them to dismount and stand aside while their horses were hacked to pieces and devoured on the spot.

With no means in sight of boosting yields from existing farmland, the one answer to the food crisis was to put virgin land under cultivation. Throughout western Europe, enlightened lords and monarchs encouraged new settlements, freeing serfs from their bonds and offering exemption from various taxes. Forests were felled, marshland drained, and land, especially in the Low Countries, was reclaimed from the sea itself. From the Elbe River in Germany to the Welsh Marches of England, the wilderness was tamed and colonized. But for Germans, colonizing virgin land within their country's borders was, at best, only a partial solution. Desperate for new territory to support its population, Germany looked to the east.

For centuries, the Germans had been enmeshed in a more or less permanent state of war with their eastern neighbors, the Slavs. Between the ninth century and the twelfth, chronicles recorded over 175 battles, as well as innumerable minor skirmishes. In 1157, Barbarossa invaded Poland and forced or persuaded many powerful Polish nobles to accept him as their feudal overlord; some, indeed, enthusiastically supported Barbarossa's cause against their own, much weaker, native monarchy. Meanwhile, the emperor's powerful vassal, Henry the Lion, conquered great tracts of hitherto undeveloped Slav borderlands beyond the Elbe River. As fast as German conquests pushed the border eastward, the German population filled up the land that is present-day East Germany—and beyond, into the fringes of Czechoslovakia and Poland. Princes transplanted peasants to raze forests. New towns were founded at a prodigious rate.

Throughout the century, the great part of Europe's wealth still came, as it had since time immemorial, from agriculture. But now that more and more land was becoming productive, surpluses began to appear. As strife diminished, traveling became safer. And thus commerce, in abeyance during Europe's centuries of turmoil, began to flourish once more.

The nobles, ever more prosperous as their lands expanded, took to conspicuous consumption. They demanded bright hangings to warm the stone walls of their castles, richly spiced delicacies to grace their tables, ornately carved coffers to store an ever increasing number of personal possessions. And even those whose work was warfare sought weapons and armor of the finest quality. The nobles' aspirations provided business for artisans of all sorts—jewelers and tailors, goldsmiths and furriers, master builders ready to turn a patron's charitable impulses into the soaring vaults of a new church.

Nor was affluence the sole preserve of the aristocracy. The social order was shifting. Formerly, the world seemed easily divisible into those who waged war, those who tilled the soil, and those in holy orders who prayed for the souls of the other two groups. Now there were new ways to earn a living: Professional administrators managed the increasingly complex government of the realm; lawyers profited as their sovereigns developed judicial systems; scholars resurrected the half-forgotten wisdom of the ancients and gathered students from all over Europe. And merchants, riding out along the roads or taking ship from the bustling sea and river ports, made comfortable livings by supplying the needs of these new customers.

Of all the goods that moved across the ever expanding commercial networks, none was more significant than Flanders cloth. As the population of Europe grew, so too did its demand for woolen clothing; as the sheep of England flourished, they produced far more wool than native weavers could handle.

Into this breach stepped the merchants of Flanders. Their homeland across the English Channel had a surplus of willing workers and a dearth of land. Flemish buyers became familiar visitors to the markets of Exeter, Winchester, Oxford, Lincoln, York, and other centers of English wool production. At home, Flemish weavers unceasingly worked the pedals of their looms, turning England's surplus wool into cloth.

Now the West had something to sell that the whole world wanted. Italian merchants carried shiploads to the Muslim East. Textiles became western Europe's most important export, outstripping more traditional wares, such as timber, salt, oil, and wine. In exchange, the wool traders were particularly eager to buy from the Italians Egyptian alum, a caustic used in cloth processing, and a range of eastern dyestuffs. They would also, if their own profits warranted, procure culinary spices such as pepper, cloves, and cinnamon, which had traveled from as far afield as India and Java, along with drugs highly prized for their curative powers—licorice, aloes, and galingale, a root resembling ginger. Europe also developed an appetite for North African leather and slaves and for gold and silks from India.

As far as possible, the goods were shifted by water, for boats provided easier, cheaper, and safer transit than rutted earth roads. The greatest trade axes, both east-west, were the Mediterranean and the North Sea. To transport goods between northern and southern Europe, most merchants used barges that were towed up the Rhine and the Rhone, and traveled overland between the two great rivers.

Traders met at fairs and markets strategically situated along the trade routes. No commercial rendezvous were more important than the great fairs held six times a year in the vine-clad French county of Champagne, between the Rhine and the Rhone. The exact site of the fair depended on the calendar: Troyes for the summer Warm Fair and the Cold Fair of All Souls' Day, Lagny for the New Year's Morrow Fair, Bar for mid-Lent, Provins for the Feast of the Ascension in May.

Whichever the destination, the travelers knew the routine that awaited them: an initial week when all merchandise was exempt from taxes, followed by a specialist cloth fair, a leather fair, and a fair for the exchange of wax, cotton, spices, and other merchandise sold by weight instead of measure. The round of fairs-within-the-fair would culminate in a period designated for the payment of bills and the settlement of debts. Notaries stood ready with ink and sealing wax to draw up contracts; officials patrolled the booths to see that all rules and regulations were scrupulously observed; a Court of Fairs sat in regular session to settle disputes and investigate complaints.

A rudimentary banking system, run by Italians and Jews, simplified the transactions

THE CITIES ON THE RISE

The twelfth century saw a spectacular rise of western Europe's cities. European cities had far to go to match the sophistication of such centers as Constantinople, Cairo, or Baghdad, which had populations of about 500,000, long-established trade links, and flourishing artistic traditions. But as relative peace allowed trade to expand, Florence, Milan, Venice, and Paris achieved populations close to 100,000, and another dozen cities boasted populations of 40,000 or more. It was no accident that Italian cities were in the vanguard: Italy had suffered less than lands farther north from barbarian depredations in the previous centuries and had never entirely lost the urban traditions inherited from the Roman Empire.

During the twelfth century, a new urban middle class emerged as the engineers of the cities' success. The merchants of Genoa and Pisa sent fleets to exploit the trading opportunities that had been opened up in the eastern Mediterranean by the Crusades. Venetian traders conducted a lucrative business with Byzantium, while Florentine magnates enriched themselves from the profits of the city's woolen-cloth industry.

Along with their wealth, the merchants achieved political prominence, as the guilds established to set standards of work and to protect members' interests gradually assumed responsibility for the organization of civic life. The eagle clutching a bale of wool that appears above was adopted as the badge of Florence's guild of merchants, which, together with its sister organizations, the guild of wool traders and the guild of moneychangers, controlled the city. The nobles of Florence were forced to renounce their feudal titles and take up commercial activities before they were eligible to join the ruling council.

Under the new leadership, towns in many parts of twelfth-century Europe enjoyed a degree of social freedom and prosperity unknown to the rural laborers who toiled in the service of a feudal overlord. The cities' wealth and freedom lured thousands of peasants from the soil.

The wealth also made the city-states a target for the expansionist ambitions of both the pope and the Holy Roman Emperor. Rivalries within and among the Italian cities threatened to undermine their resistance, but in the 1160s, some northern Italian cities formed the Lombard League and fought jointly to preserve their independence. Ultimately, the Lombard League succeeded in denying the authority of both pope and emperor.

Founded by the Romans on the north bank of the Arno River, Florence had expanded south of the river by the 1170s, when a new circle of walls was built to protect the inhabitants. Within the walls, tenements of brick, timber, and rubble were home to a teeming population of immigrants from the countryside, eager to share in the city's prosperity. Only the wealthiest families lived in relative privacy, their houses adorned with lofty towers that offered a retreat whenever the city's fragile political stability was rent by violence.

Established in the streets around the newly completed cathedral baptistry, the stalls and workshops of the cloth workers were the hub of the city's economy. By the twelfth century, Florence had established trading links throughout the Mediterranean and northern Europe, importing wool from as far away as England, Portugal, and North Africa. Brought to Italy as raw fleeces, the wool was spun by Florentine workers into thread for dyeing and weaving. The city's artisans were particularly renowned for their vivid scarlet dyes, while the quality of Florentine cloth was bettered only by that of the finest silks and velvets imported from Byzantium.

All textiles were sold by a standard measure, the braccio, which was equivalent to an arm's length. Although a few traders dealt in finished items—cloaks, breeches, and hats—most relied on the sale of unworked cloth, paid for in silver florins. So prosperous were the merchants of Florence that they established banking houses throughout northern Europe, and it was their loans—to figures such as the kings of England and the papacy—that financed many of the wars and political struggles of the Middle Ages.

at the fairs. Moneylenders, commanding a far-flung network of agents, would facilitate the transfer of money from one country to another, relieving merchants of the dangerous necessity of transporting chests of coins along the roads. And if a merchant ran short of cash or needed backing for a new venture, it was possible to arrange for credit. All these deals were conducted with the utmost confidence. It was recognized that every agreement made in Champagne was legally binding, wherever European merchants came together.

The natural habitats of these prospering merchants were the towns. The twelfth century saw many new towns created—often by royal charter—and old ones transformed beyond all recognition. Some of them became famous the world over for their wares: Milan was a byword for armor, Florence for cloth, London and Cologne for goldsmith's work. As the towns expanded and grew wealthy, they also grew in influence. Economically, politically, and culturally, the town dweller was now a force to be reckoned with.

Towns were magnets for countryfolk. For runaway serfs, the towns provided sanctuary. The Germans had a saying that "town air makes you free," since according to custom, a serf who dwelled within the walls for a year and a day was automatically liberated from his bonds. But even peasants who already had their freedom were attracted by the opportunities. New quarters of artisans' workshops and merchants' counting houses were under construction, and those able to learn a trade could be assured of gainful employment.

The urban ruling class was composed of burgesses—the merchants and master artisans who provided jobs and amassed an increasing share of society's wealth. In the early Middle Ages, the towns had fitted into the feudal system. Justice and administration fell under the control of the local lord, whether a prince or a count or a bishop. But sooner or later, almost every town began to chafe under the feudal system and to seek self-government. One way to obtain freedom was to pay the lord for a charter. The alternative was to go above the lord's head to the king—who looked to the towns as natural allies against too powerful magnates. Once liberty had been granted, the townspeople quickly became accustomed to managing their town's concerns as they pleased. The burgesses were a new breed, operating outside the old system of land-based feudal relationships. They were no one's vassals, and no landlord stood between them and the king.

Nowhere was urban autonomy more highly developed than in the city-states of northern Italy. Foreign visitors, such as the Jewish traveler Benjamin of Tudela, visiting Genoa, Pisa, and other towns in the 1160s, marveled at the freedom these communities enjoyed: "They possess neither kings nor princes to govern them, but only judges appointed by themselves."

City life in Italy had not suffered such grave damage at the hands of barbarian invaders as elsewhere in Europe. The urban tradition had carried on unchecked from Roman times. With this head start, the Italian towns were bigger than most others in Europe. Of the four western European cities with populations approaching 100,000 in the twelfth century, three—Venice, Milan, and Florence—were Italian. (Paris was the fourth.) Moreover, the gulf between town and countryside, the schisms between rural nobles and urban burgesses, did not exist here. Although the greatest part of their wealth came from trade, Italian cities were intimately meshed with their rural hinterlands. Noble, land-holding families moved into town and involved themselves in trade. Town-dwelling peasants daily walked out of the gates to tend their fields.

ARTISTRY IN ENAMEL

Polished to a jewel-like shine, the twin beauties of glass and metal combined in dazzling proliferation at the hands of twelfth-century enamelers. The most important enameling traditions in the twelfth century were the Limoges and the Mosan schools—named, respectively, after a city in central France and the Meuse River in northern France, although artisans in both schools were far-flung. Limoges enamels included both secular and religious items, whereas Mosan enamels—such as the plaque on the right showing Naaman being cured of leprosy in the Jordan River—were almost exclusively liturgical.

There were two chief ways of forming enameled ornaments. In the increasingly popular champlevé, or "raised-field," method, depressions were gouged out of a box, a cross, or other artifact of copper or bronze. Enamel—the constituent elements of glass mixed with a metallic coloring agent—was poured into the pits. The ridges between the pools of enamel were then gilded before the object was fired in a kiln. By this method, artisans were able to produce pieces that were, at the same time, larger and less costly than the cloisonné, or "cell-work" items, in which the enamel was inlaid between thin bands of intricately bent, but expensive, gold—the most malleable metal.

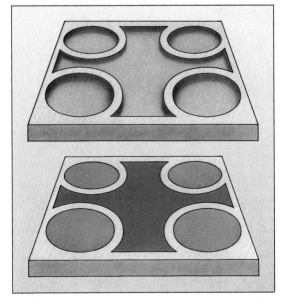

In the champlevé technique, hollows are gouged out of a metal base, leaving the intended design defined by narrow ridges.

Enamel of different colors is placed in the hollows of the base, which is then fired in a kiln.

Merchants, artisans, lawyers, and notaries used their mounting wealth to acquire land and sometimes knighthoods.

The knighthoods were not merely honorifics. The towns had need of their own armies, because city-states were all too willing to war among themselves, and mercenaries were expensive. "Our city," explained the Genoese chronicler Caffaro, writing in 1173, "thanks be to God, outshines others in strength, wealth, and agreeable qualities. If, therefore, we wish to preserve praise, nobility, and quiet, and to destroy utterly our hostile neighbors, it would be wise and most useful to create native-born knights in our city."

Some enemies came from within. The richest families of a town, who dominated its political and economic life, did not always share power amicably. Ancient blood feuds and vendettas, as well as new conflicts of interest, fueled violent rivalries. Slow to forget affronts but quick to avenge them, these clans built town houses that were virtual fortresses. Many mansions had a high tower, used not only for keeping lookout but for pelting opponents with stones and arrows. The towns made many efforts to curb this internal warfare. Pisan authorities, for instance, passed laws limiting the heights of the towers and imposed fines on anyone who used them to attack their neighbors. The ultimate sanction for a troublesome household was the demolition of its tower. (The rubble was carted away to provide ballast for the city's cargo fleet.)

The greatest threats to the peace of these Italian communities, however, came neither from their own citizens' feuds nor from the hostility of rival towns. Frederick Barbarossa was eying Italy, intent on asserting his imperial rights.

Barbarossa's predecessors had been far too preoccupied with their troubled German dominions to concern themselves with affairs in the southern parts of their empire. They were willing to tolerate—or were too weak to deny—virtual self-government by the Italian towns. Once Barbarossa had imposed peace, however

The enamelwork scenes of hunting and courtly love on this ornate twelfth-century casket reflect the contemporary subject matter of the troubadour poets of Provence. The bright colors of the enamels are indicative of the work of the Limoges school.

precarious, on Germany, the rich city-republics beckoned him, golden and tantalizing in the southern sun. He first crossed the Alps at the head of an army of German warriors in 1154. Over the next thirty years, Barbarossa launched six long and hard-fought Italian campaigns.

Not all the Italian towns resisted his domination. Barbarossa was shrewd enough to exploit the rifts between them. He tempted those who supported his imperial claims with promises of rich rewards. Others were totally opposed to German rule; the Holy Roman Empire, they believed, should be a loose confederation comprising independent city-states, duchies, and principalities, all enjoying clearly defined and inviolable rights.

Barbarossa used military might in his attempt to subdue those cities whose loyalty could not be purchased. He besieged rebel towns and, when necessary, flattened them with his superior forces. Where he took control, he sent in an administrator—a German knight or an Italian loyal to his cause. In theory, this official was supposed to be a civil servant, a manager rather than a politician, who would impose order and carry out the business of local government. Some of Frederick's representatives did, indeed, govern fairly; however, many others were petty dictators, who turned their cities into virtual police states, imposing crippling new taxes, confiscating property, and taking hostages to serve as sureties for the citizens' obedience.

A Mosan reliquary commissioned to house a splinter of wood believed to be from the True Cross of Christ, this crucifix is decorated with five Old Testament scenes considered to be prophetic of the Crucifixion.

In 1162, Barbarossa marched against his most implacable enemy, the city-republic of Milan—which, three times in the past four years, had pledged good faith and then risen up in armed rebellion against him. Barbarossa's army was augmented by forces from Pavia, Como, and Lodi, rival towns that had long resented Milanese domination of the region. With the help of his allies, Barbarossa besieged the Milanese for a year, threatening dire consequences if they failed to surrender. When at last he broke through Milan's defenses, Barbarossa was as ruthless as his word. He destroyed fortifications dating back to Roman times and razed the city. Its cathedral, its lesser churches, and most of its houses were smashed, reduced to rubble; witnesses reported that not one building in fifty was left standing. Those inhabitants who survived were driven out into the fields and forced to live in squalid encampments outside the city, exposed to all kinds of weather.

Armed terror was not Barbarossa's only tactic. He knew he would never control Italy unless he had the support of the pope in Rome. When he was not laying siege to a rebellious city, he was playing politics with the Vatican. After the death of Pope Adrian IV left the papal throne unoccupied, a minority of cardinals favorable to Barbarossa sought to ensure that his candidate was elected. When the majority of the cardinals opted for someone else, Barbarossa's man tried—

literally—to snatch the papal mantle from the victor's shoulders and threw open the doors of Saint Peter's Basilica to admit a horde of his own armed supporters. With one voice, they acclaimed him as the pope. The official incumbent managed to flee and went into hiding until he could be consecrated elsewhere.

The Church now had two pontiffs—the officially elected Alexander III and Barbarossa's antipope, Victor IV. The popes promptly excommunicated each other, and Alexander excoriated the German emperor as "the chief persecutor of God."

The wrath of Alexander and his supporters was echoed by the towns of Lombardy, furious at Barbarossa's attacks on their independence. Sixteen cities formed themselves into the Lombard League. They swore to support each other, vowed that none of them would make any separate peace or individual treaty with the emperor, and dedicated themselves to defending the claims of Alexander III as the one true pope. Throughout the 1160s, they enjoyed a succession of military victories.

Thanks to the fierce resistance of the Italian cities, Barbarossa was never able to consolidate his power in the south. He knew that his homeland suffered in his absence, but he was a man with an obsession: Italian resistance signified far more than an affront to his royal pride. By their defiance against their lord, the city-states challenged the entire structure of feudal society.

The words of a citizen of Ferrara, spoken in 1177, when the struggles with Barbarossa must have seemed as if they would go on forever, were enough to fill the heart of any king with fury—or with fear. For the orator vowed on behalf of his city "never to relinquish that liberty that we inherited from our fathers, grandfathers, and great-grandfathers. . . . We would rather meet a glorious death with liberty than live a wretched life in servitude."

Soon after these words were spoken, Barbarossa abandoned his quarrel with the pope, and in 1183, he made a formal peace, the Treaty of Constance, with the Lombard League. But the treaty with the Italian cities was not couched in the words of a king forgiving his rebellious vassals: It was a contract, on almost equal terms, between two former adversaries.

The proud cities of Italy faced further storms. The threats to peace and freedom would continue. But within a century they would win their struggle: The German emperors would count for virtually nothing in northern Italy. By their wealth, their creative energy, and their bid for autonomy, Italian cities intimated that something new was at work in the body politic. Life, they proved, could flourish outside the web of feudal bonds and vows. The seeds of change had been planted. They might take centuries to germinate and spread, but nothing now could stop their growth.

THE ROAD TO COMPOSTELA

Throughout the twelfth century, the pilgrim roads of Europe were thronged each spring and summer by travelers bound for shrines housing the bones, hair, clothes, and other relics of the saints. By going on pilgrimage, the faithful hoped to win remission of sins or be cured of disease; at the very least, the journey made an adventurous change from routine.

Three destinations were thought to confer special blessing on the pilgrim: Jerusalem, where it was possible to visit the True Cross and the sites of Christ's passion; Rome, with its relic-filled churches built to serve the papal court; and Compostela in the northwest of Spain—the land that Christian knights, to the jubilation of all Catholic Christendom, were reconquering from its Muslim occupiers.

Since the ninth century, Compostela had claimed possession of the tomb of Saint James the Apostle—"Santiago" in the Spanish language. Popular legend had it that after the death of Christ the saint had traveled from Jerusalem to Spain to preach the gospel. According to one of several versions of the story, he had returned to his own land to die a martyr, but his body had been miraculously transported to northern Spain in a ship built of stone. The remains of the saint were said not only to possess the power to slay Muslims but to work wondrous cures for many diseases.

The reputation of Compostela drew pilgrims from as far afield as Scotland and Greece. Once they reached France, they traveled along one of four southwesterly routes that met across the Pyrenees in northern Spain. The undertaking was described in a number of medieval guides, the fullest of which was written in 1139 by Aimery Picaud, a devout monk from the region of Poitiers in France, who had himself made the journey. Picaud offered practical advice on the marvelous, desolate, and dangerous spots the faithful would pass through on the pilgrimage.

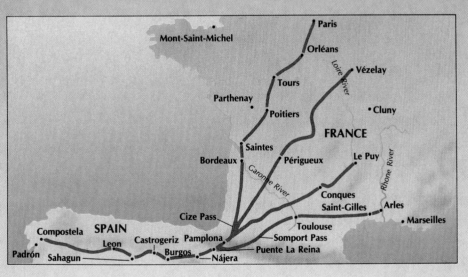

> *"There are four routes that go to Santiago de Compostela that all join together at Puente La Reina."*

Picaud began his guidebook by tracing each of the four routes to Compostela as it progressed toward the barrier of the Pyrenees. He also described various shrines en route that deserved a visit. He recommended, for example, a stop in Orléans, where the church of Saint Samson displayed a dish used at the Last Supper.

To complete one of the four routes took at least a month. Most pilgrims timed their departure for spring, hoping for good weather and passable roads. They displayed their holy endeavor by wearing long coarse tunics similar to monks' habits, and they carried wooden staffs, cut in their homelands and blessed by a local priest. The rich rode horseback and the very sick were carried on litters, but the majority walked. The pilgrimage was a rare opportunity for people of all nations and classes to share in a common enterprise, and along the way, the wealthy lent assistance to their poorer companions, providing them with food or the occasional use of a horse.

The pious provided a livelihood for many: peddlers, entertainers, moneychangers, and confidence tricksters abounded. Picaud warned his readers to beware of unscrupulous tradespeople who sold the unwary stale bread and rotten meat.

> *"Hospices give rest to the poor, help to the ill, salvation to the dead, and cheer to the living."*

Picaud assumed that most pilgrims, having finished their day's journey, would seek lodging in a hospice. Founded and endowed with land or money by noble patrons, these resting places were maintained partly by the donations of pilgrims. They were staffed by monks and laity able to deal with most of their visitors' needs—from the lancing of blisters to the burial of the dead. Typically, a hospice offered a dole of bread and meat and a ration of rough red wine.

Hospices were strung out along the routes to Compostela and often built on either side of the road, with an entrance porch spanning the way. Since most towns were walled and were locked at night for safety, many hospices were established outside towns so that the guests might still be received after dusk.

Besides providing sustenance, the hospices were much-needed places of refuge for weary travelers. By day some stretches of road were patrolled by knights of the military orders—the Templars and Hospitalers originally established in the Holy Land. Nevertheless, cutthroats and wolves remained an ever-present danger. Small wonder that, according to Picaud, "those entering hospices will think themselves in the Kingdom of Heaven."

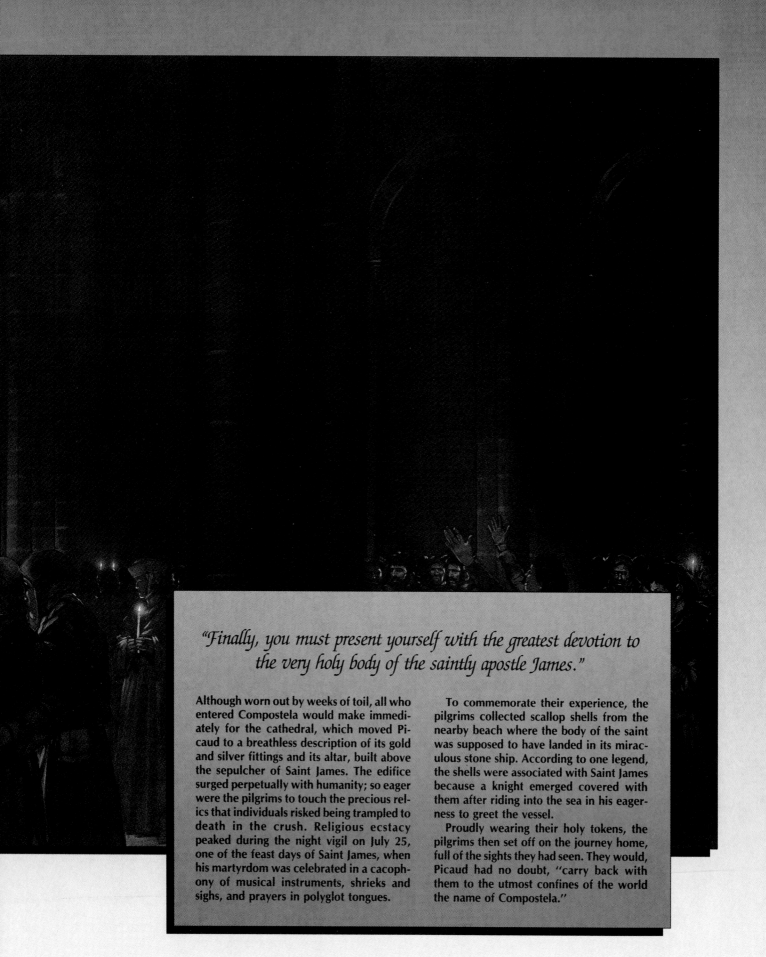

"Finally, you must present yourself with the greatest devotion to the very holy body of the saintly apostle James."

Although worn out by weeks of toil, all who entered Compostela would make immediately for the cathedral, which moved Picaud to a breathless description of its gold and silver fittings and its altar, built above the sepulcher of Saint James. The edifice surged perpetually with humanity; so eager were the pilgrims to touch the precious relics that individuals risked being trampled to death in the crush. Religious ecstacy peaked during the night vigil on July 25, one of the feast days of Saint James, when his martyrdom was celebrated in a cacophony of musical instruments, shrieks and sighs, and prayers in polyglot tongues.

To commemorate their experience, the pilgrims collected scallop shells from the nearby beach where the body of the saint was supposed to have landed in its miraculous stone ship. According to one legend, the shells were associated with Saint James because a knight emerged covered with them after riding into the sea in his eagerness to greet the vessel.

Proudly wearing their holy tokens, the pilgrims then set off on the journey home, full of the sights they had seen. They would, Picaud had no doubt, "carry back with them to the utmost confines of the world the name of Compostela."

THE POWER OF THE POPES

Clad in the coarse woolen tunics of penitents, Philip, king of France, and Bertrade, countess of Anjou, stood barefoot before a solemn conclave of prelates gathered in Paris. For nearly a decade, the two had lived together in sin. But now, in the year 1104, the couple promised to part forever. Reluctantly, they were bowing to the will of an ecclesiastic from another country, a man without royal blood, yet one to whom even kings and emperors bent the knee: the pope, head of the Catholic church and bishop of Rome.

As the earthly ambassador of the Kingdom of Heaven, the pope wielded weapons more terrible than those of any terrestrial army. To goad these two sinners back to the path of righteousness, Pope Pascal II had used the ultimate sanction: excommunication. They were barred from receiving the sacraments and denied all hope of heaven. But now, thanks to their long-awaited compliance, the ban was lifted.

Pascal's display of authority over a crowned head typified the confidence of the popes in their age of greatness. In the course of the twelfth century, the popes came to exert their will not only on spiritual but also on temporal matters until, by the close of the century, they were acting remarkably like monarchs—monarchs not of a political territory but of all Catholic Christendom.

The ascendancy of the popes was founded on the religious faith of twelfth-century Europe. The popes had claimed the spiritual overlordship of Christendom since the fifth century, but, for a long time, with little effect. Abuses in the Church had been rife, and the popes had lacked the respect that would grant them an obedient hearing. But monastic reform in the tenth century enhanced popular piety and eventually emboldened the popes. In the 1070s, Pope Gregory VII sought to reverse the tradition of the investiture of bishops by lay nobles. The consequence of a showdown on this issue between Greg-

Innocent II (pope 1130-1143)

ory and the Holy Roman Emperor was a partial victory for the Church, which fueled yet greater religious zeal throughout society. Some, those who bore arms, were stirred by the challenge of the Crusades, the holy wars to liberate Jerusalem from the Muslims. Countless others were moved by a desire to regenerate Christian life.

Reform was desperately needed. Chroniclers frequently lamented over churches that had fallen into disrepair while their priests drank in the taverns; over priests who took no notice of the vow of chastity and were either married or ensconced with concubines; and over illiterate priests who could not construe the Latin Mass. Further up the hierarchy, bishops unblushingly placed their own kin in the most comfortable livings or offered these positions to the highest bidder.

Serious attempts to improve the situation began in the eleventh century, under Pope Gregory VII. The strategy adopted by Gregory and his twelfth-century successors was to bring the Church under stronger, more centralized papal control. A significant step along the road to centralization was made in 1123, when Pope Calixtus II summoned the bishops from all over Europe to attend a great council in Rome. They met at the papal residence in the massively fortified Lateran Palace on the Esquiline, one of Rome's seven hills. The Lateran Council of 1123, the first truly international council of the Church in over 250 years, was one of three to be held during the century. All three addressed Church reform. They issued decrees banning priests from taking wives or concubines, forbade the sale of ecclesiastical goods, declaring this a form of sacrilege, and instituted stricter controls over the ordination of priests and the election of bishops.

Potent as these edicts were, not all were instantly obeyed. Only toward the end of the century did the priests in most of Europe's hinterlands put aside their wives; those in Scandinavia, Spain, and Poland held out against celibacy even longer.

Intent on improving their authority, Gregory and his successors clarified chains of command within the Church. They determined that the bishops of the national churches could be overruled by the pope or one of his papal legates—personal envoys with well-defined and far-reaching powers. They transformed the senior members of the ecclesiastical hierarchy, the cardinals, from purely religious dignitaries into political advisers to the pope. The rules whereby the cardinals elected a pope were precisely defined for the first time.

The individuals named by the cardinals of the day to occupy Saint Peter's throne reflected the Church's new priorities. The twelfth century brought no saints to the papal throne; instead, it gave the Church a succession of gifted administrators, who evolved a system of Church government as enduring as the great cathedrals of the age. The hub of the organization they created was the Papal Curia, the most sophisticated administrative machine that the West had seen since the Roman Empire. Founded within the Lateran Palace at the end of the eleventh century, the Curia employed an army of clerks who came from Rome's monasteries to staff key departments.

In the Apostolic Chamber of the Curia, monks armed with abacus and tally stick eternally struggled to balance the Church's expenditure with its income. The most lucrative source of income was a tax of one penny, called Saint Peter's Pence, which was imposed on every household in devout Christian lands. In the nerve center of the Curia, the Chancery, letters were received from, and sent out to, every corner of Christendom, dealing with every subject that concerned the Church—whether a disputed claim to a parish in the north of England, a complaint from monks over the severity of their abbot, or a request from Armenian bishops for help against the Byzantine Empire.

Adrian IV (pope 1154-1159)

The efficient papal machine, set up to counter abuses within the Church, was soon turned to unforeseen ends. In the course of the century, more and more missives that reached the Chancery came from layfolk desperate for a legal ruling on a dispute concerning property, marriage, or one of a host of other matters. The popes' readiness to offer the Curia as a court of last resort consolidated their already considerable power. But they did not initiate the process. The Christian community looked to the newly reformed Rome, and Rome responded. Its appeal was huge, largely because the popes had at their disposal a body of law more coherent than any other in Europe.

Europe's law was a labyrinth. In the emerging monarchies of the continent, national law was only slowly being forged from a muddle of old tribal customs, traditional rights, and edicts of local lords. Canon law had been equally chaotic, for statements that popes issued often conflicted with their predecessors' edicts or with decrees passed at Church councils. Thus any legal case could become ensnared in a tangle of overlapping principles. Fortunately for the desperate litigants, the vast, creaking edifice of canon law was codified in the early twelfth century, thanks to the efforts of a rising generation of legal scholars from the universities of Bologna and Pavia.

One tool that enabled these scholars to cleave the jungle of contradictions was a system of dialectics expounded by the French scholar Peter Abelard in 1121 in a seminal work entitled *Sic et Non (Yes and No)*. Abelard's method, inspired by the ancient Greeks, was to set contradictory statements side by side, compare their merits, and choose between them. A Bolognese monk named Gratian applied the same logic to the morass of canon law in his influential text, the *Decretum*. The lucidity of his method rapidly made Gratian's *Decretum* the Church's semiofficial legal textbook. It clarified issues ranging from ecclesiastical dress to the proper conduct of marriages and business enterprises—both condemned by the early Church Fathers as distractions from the love of God. While advising against marriage, comparing it to a tempestuous sea voyage, Gratian conceded that it was a lesser evil than adultery. And while usury was to be condemned, Gratian concluded that commerce as a whole could be tolerated.

Armed with the *Decretum,* Chancery lawyers sifted through the complaints of Christendom, both petty and great, for canon law had a bearing on many issues. Judgments from Rome were dispatched to the petitioners by mounted messenger—the Lateran Palace boasted the largest stable of horses in the Western world. Usually the state upheld the pope's ruling, so any litigant who failed to abide by the judgment would be apprehended by a sheriff. By the mid-twelfth century, national monarchs—who resented their subjects' opportunity to appeal to an authority outside the realm—were becoming strong enough to insist that no appeals be made to Rome until the petitioners had gone through a full judicial procedure at home. The Curia accordingly appointed judge delegates to hear cases locally.

Perhaps inevitably, the growing influence wielded by the popes impelled them toward secular politics. And none meddled more energetically in European affairs than the pontiff who saw the century out, Pope Innocent III. When Innocent assumed the crown of Saint Peter, in 1198, the papacy was strong; during his reign it became a juggernaut. His goal was simple: He wished to exercise what the Church termed *plenitudo potestatis*—the fullness of power—the God-given, universal sovereignty of the papacy. As pope, he declared, he stood between God and mortal, higher than all earthly kings. Whatever he saw fit to do, for the perpetuation of Christendom and the eradication of sin, he was justified in doing.

Innocent III (pope 1198-1216)

It was Innocent's avowed desire to promote peace. But he was willing to abandon his usual role if he thought a war would better serve the Church's interests: In one instance, aggrieved by a quarrel with King John of England, he encouraged Philip II of France to invade his neighbor's realm. Innocent forced the kings of Sicily, Aragon, Hungary, and England to acknowledge that they held their kingdoms as papal fiefs. He built up the Papal States, ensuring that the papal monarchy was no longer merely a kingdom of the spirit.

In the hands of Innocent, the papacy reached the apogee of its temporal prestige and power. But there were many Christians who felt that the papacy now conducted itself as an arrogant secular state, rather than the earthly outpost of the Kingdom of Heaven. Some people turned away from the Church, to seek spiritual satisfaction in one of the rising heretical sects. Others contented themselves with satire. Anonymous texts such as the *Gospel According to the Mark of Silver* offered a new set of beatitudes for the age: "Blessed are they that have, for they shall not go away empty; blessed are the wealthy, for theirs is the Court of Rome."

The popes' standing gradually diminished. As kings grew in strength, they made it increasingly difficult for their subjects to appeal to the papacy. Meanwhile, a succession of worldly popes squandered the universal trust that the earlier reforms had fostered. As the popes' spiritual authority declined, so, ultimately, did their power.

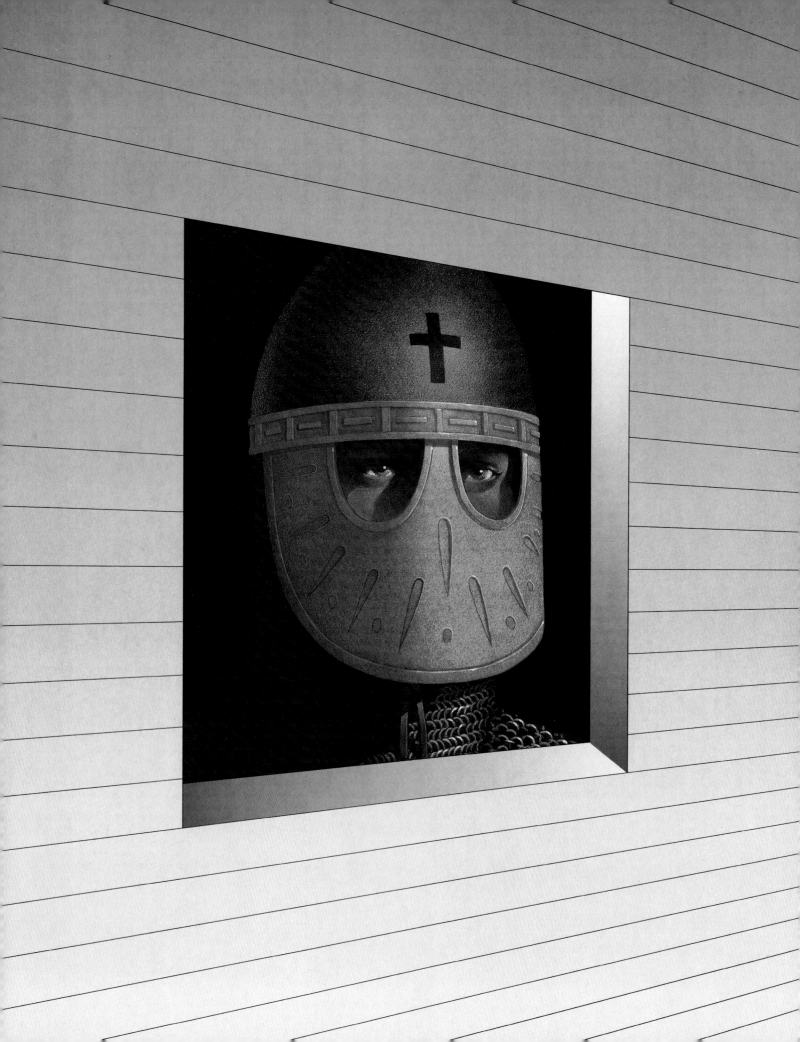

THE CONTEST FOR THE HOLY LAND

2

To the inhabitants of Jerusalem in the autumn of 1095, there seemed no grounds for regarding the future with more than average concern. Muslim, Jewish, and Christian neighbors were carrying on with their lives in relative harmony. Admittedly, Palestine had been trampled by rival Muslim powers for decades, and Jerusalem itself had changed hands three times since 1060: Only the old could remember a time of stable government. But the city was well garrisoned, on a site strong by nature and massively fortified. Nobody would have believed that 2,000 miles away an eminent ecclesiastic was preparing a speech that would soon bring sudden massacre to the city and that for centuries would send armed multitudes marching toward Jerusalem. The age of the Crusades was about to erupt on the unsuspecting East.

Although ignorant of their fate, the people of Jerusalem well knew the passions their city stirred. Jews treasured it as Zion, God's own city, and as the place where King Solomon had built his great temple. Muslims associated it with the prophets who had preceded their founder Muhammad and considered it their third holiest city, after Mecca and Medina. Christians revered Jerusalem as the city in which Christ died and from which, they believed, he was resurrected. On European maps, it was shown as the center of the world. Ever since the fourth century, when Christianity had become the official religion of the Roman Empire and the martyrdom of Christians had ceased, the ardent had sought some other extreme expression of their faith. They had found it in pilgrimage—above all to Jerusalem. There stood what became the most sacred shrine in Christendom—the fourth-century emperor Constantine's Church of the Holy Sepulcher, supposedly built over Christ's tomb. Even after the Muslims captured Jerusalem in 638, they allowed Christians and Jews continued access to the Holy City and its shrines. The pious, penitent, or curious of all three religions journeyed there from three continents.

The crusading movement was inspired by the idea of pilgrimage. Indeed the word crusade did not come into use until the thirteenth century: Before then, people spoke of "the expedition of God," "the business of Christ," or simply "the pilgrimage." But the Crusade conceived in 1095 would be no ordinary pilgrimage. By military might, it would transfer not only Jerusalem but a 600-mile strip of coastal Syria from Muslim to Christian hands, expanding the dominion of the Catholic church, which, thanks to missionary efforts and conquest, already commanded allegiance from Sicily to Scandinavia. The authority of the pope in Rome would extend to an outpost in the East.

The Christian settlers who accompanied and succeeded the Crusaders would lack the manpower to hold their gains securely, however. Edessa, the most exposed of the Christian pockets, would fall to the Muslims in 1144, and the Second Crusade would fail to recapture it. Jerusalem would be lost in 1187, and the Third Crusade would fail to regain it. The Fourth Crusade of 1204, planned with Jerusalem as the objective,

A crusading Italian knight proclaims his holy mission with a cross painted on his steel helmet. A papal call to arms in 1095 sent tens of thousands of men and women from all over Europe on the quest to liberate Jerusalem from the forces of Islam. Motivated by a fervent desire to serve God and by the promise of remission of all their sins, the Crusaders endured dreadful hardships and dangers with scant prospect of earthly reward. For their Muslim adversaries, too, the confrontation came to be seen as a divinely inspired struggle between rival faiths.

would be deflected by chance and greed to the sacking of Constantinople—the Christian capital of the Byzantine Empire. Although Crusades to the East would continue with increasing zeal during the thirteenth century, the Christians would never regain all they had lost.

These Crusades were the first ventures in which the nations of Europe cooperated on a massive scale. It was no accident that the goal that first drew them together was

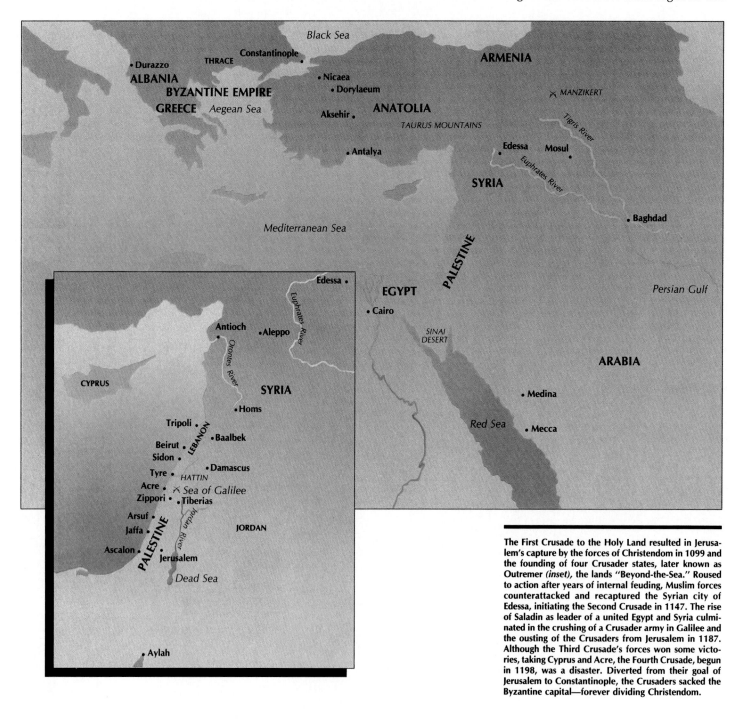

The First Crusade to the Holy Land resulted in Jerusalem's capture by the forces of Christendom in 1099 and the founding of four Crusader states, later known as Outremer *(inset),* the lands "Beyond-the-Sea." Roused to action after years of internal feuding, Muslim forces counterattacked and recaptured the Syrian city of Edessa, initiating the Second Crusade in 1147. The rise of Saladin as leader of a united Egypt and Syria culminated in the crushing of a Crusader army in Galilee and the ousting of the Crusaders from Jerusalem in 1187. Although the Third Crusade's forces won some victories, taking Cyprus and Acre, the Fourth Crusade, begun in 1198, was a disaster. Diverted from their goal of Jerusalem to Constantinople, the Crusaders sacked the Byzantine capital—forever dividing Christendom.

service to God: Religious ardor pervaded twelfth-century Europe, and the idea of the conquest of the Holy Land gripped the imagination and absorbed the energies of generations of European fighting men. From the Muslim side, the Crusades seemed less momentous events; the Eastern Christian states were relatively small and their presence only one factor in a complex political scene. But the attack in the name of an alien faith did ultimately help the Islamic leaders to impose unity and religious orthodoxy in a divided region.

In worldly terms, those who gained most from the Crusades were the trading cities of Italy, especially Venice. The ports of Byzantium and the Levant were key stopping points in the trade between Europe and Asia, and the Christian presence in the East stimulated this commerce. The world was becoming a smaller place.

The start of western Europe's adventure in the Holy Land was timed to perfection. The eve of the twelfth century found the Muslim world divided and quarrelsome. In the decades following the prophet Muhammad's death in 632, his followers had swarmed from the sandy wastes of Arabia in a drive for conquest and conversion. By the tenth century, Islam's sway extended as far as Spain in the west and beyond the Indus in the east, to the Caspian Sea in the north and Egypt in the south. In theory, the spiritual and political head of all Islamic people was the caliph—literally, the successor. But two rival dynasties saw themselves as the true successors of the Prophet: the Abbasids of Baghdad and the Fatimids of Cairo. The Abbasids represented the Sunni—"Lawful"—faith of the majority, which traced its descent from the Prophet's friend Abu Bakr. The Fatimids, harking back to Muhammad's daughter Fatima, were the leaders of the Shia, or "Faction," which over the centuries had absorbed ideas from faiths other than Islam. From Persian Zoroastrianism or from the Christians of the East, they had come to believe in a sacred line of redeemers—for the Shiites, the line was that of Fatima's husband, Ali— who would hide in obscurity for generations before being revealed. Another idea taken up by some of the Shiites was that murder of infidels could be a religious duty.

The Abbasid caliphate of Baghdad had reached its apogee in the ninth century, the Fatimid caliphate of Cairo in the tenth. By the eleventh century, both dynasties had relinquished real power in their realms. In theory, the Abbasids ruled the great swath of land between the eastern shores of the Mediterranean and India. But the Abbasids had lost the initiative to the Seljuk Turks, excellent horsemen and valiant warriors who had originally lived as nomads traversing the steppes of central Asia. From employment as mercenary freebooters on the fringes of Muslim territory, the Seljuks fought their way to overlordship of most of the Sunni lands by 1059. Recently introduced to Sunni Islam, the Seljuks possessed all the zeal of new converts and accorded the caliph great respect. But in worldly matters, he had become the obedient puppet of the sultan, the Seljuk war leader, who happily contemplated the conquest of all Shiites and infidels.

The rich Fatimid realm of Egypt had likewise fallen under military control. Native Egyptian military enthusiasm was scant. The Fatimid army, therefore, contained large numbers of slaves from diverse origins. Like other Islamic societies, the Egyptians purchased boys from pagan tribes, schooled them in religion and the art of war, and then deployed them as crack troops. In Egypt, the slave forces included Turks and Sudanese spearmen, fighting alongside free Berber cavalry from the North African mountains—a quarrelsome mixture. In 1060, a military dispute sparked off seventeen years of civil war between the components of the Fatimid army, complicated by rebellions among Egypt's native Arabs, Seljuk interventions, and raids by the Bedouin from the Sinai Desert. When peace, or exhaustion, finally came, Egypt was in the hands of a dynasty of Muslim Armenians of slave origin who had massacred all of the other contenders. The Fatimid caliph remained, but the Armenians had the title of vizier and the real power.

The land of Syria, encompassing present-day Syria, Jordan, Lebanon, and Israel, had for centuries been flung to-and-fro between the Abbasid and Fatimid powers. It was a mountainous country, defined for much of its length by the Lebanon and Anti-Lebanon ridges, running north-south parallel with the sea; to the east, it petered out into desert waste. But the wide seaboard and the valley between the two ranges were fertile, and Syria's cities were prosperous trade centers. Inland from the Anti-Lebanon Mountains, the oasis of Damascus, fed by snow waters, stood at the junction of the east-west and north-south trade routes. The trade caravans' next important stop to the north was the well-fortified city of Aleppo, its citadel rising from the dusty North Syrian plain on sheer cliff walls. Through the ports of Antioch, Tripoli, Beirut, Tyre, Acre, and Jaffa passed local exports such as sugar and cotton and a share of the lucrative trade in spices from the Far East.

Among Syria's peasants and townspeople, Arabic speakers of mixed Arab and indigenous ancestry predominated, but there were also many Jews, Christians who adhered to the Greek Orthodox rite, and Christians of other persuasions whose views about Christ's divine and earthly natures differed from those of Catholic and Orthodox Christians. These native Christian churches, deemed heretical by Catholic and Orthodox Christians, included Armenians, Maronites—who claimed as their founder the fifth-century saint Maro—and Jacobites, named after the sixth-century preacher Jacob Baradeus. As "people of the Book"—that is, people with a written scripture—the Christians were tolerated by the Muslims, although they had to pay heavy taxes, refrain from riding horses or carrying arms, and show a generally respectful attitude toward Islam. Outside the settled areas, on the Syrian Desert that stretched inland from the mountains, nomadic tribal Arabs roamed.

The civil war in Egypt and the Seljuk intervention left Syria in chaos; cities were held, in no discernible pattern, by diverse Seljuk warlords, local Arab families, Armenian princes, ex-Fatimid governors who had won independence, and miscellaneous adventurers. A few strongholds on the coast remained loyal to Egypt. Jerusalem, after changing hands three times, finally ended up as a possession of the Seljuks. None of this turmoil was particularly intended to disrupt the Christian pilgrimages in the decades before the start of the Crusades; inevitably, however, the hazards of pilgrimage increased.

In the midst of their engagements in Egypt and Syria, the Seljuks managed to deal a mortal blow to yet another great power in the region—the Byzantine Empire. In 1071, the Byzantine emperor marched eastward to confront them. The armies met at Manzikert in Armenia, in the disputed eastern borderlands of Byzantium. The Byzantine army was shattered beyond recovery and the emperor captured. The broad lands of Anatolia in central Asia Minor were left open to the ravages of the Seljuks and of another tribe of Turks, wild and fanatically Muslim, called Danishmends after their leader. Before long, a Seljuk dynasty established in Asia Minor a realm—the sultanate of Rum—which professed itself independent of the Seljuk rulers in Baghdad. The great city of Constantinople seemed in desperate peril from the new Muslim power. And pilgrims heading for Jerusalem faced greater dangers than ever before. The many who made the journey by land now had a devastated and hostile Anatolia to cross before they could reach even Syria.

The loss of Anatolia fell as a fearful blow on a Byzantium already failing in strength. The successor to the eastern half of the Roman Empire, Byzantium was extensive even after Manzikert: It embraced Greece, part of the Balkans, and the remains of its former possessions in Asia Minor. In western Europe, Byzantium conjured images of wealth and luxury. But the splendor of its churches and the artistry of its metalwork and textiles belied the debilitating results of a series of weak emperors' failure to maintain the military machine. The army relied almost entirely on foreign mercenaries.

Beleaguered by its Muslim neighbors, Byzantium possessed no loyal friends in the Christian West. The Orthodox church controlled from Constantinople and the Catholic church of Rome had been drifting apart for centuries—disputing doctrine, competing for converts, and refuting each other's claims to primacy. In 1054, a quarrel

When Alexius I—portrayed here in a twelfth-century mosaic from Constantinople—seized the Byzantine throne in 1081, his empire was torn by civil war and threatened in the east by the Seljuk Turks. He called for help from his fellow Christians in the West, hoping at best for a contingent of mercenaries. Instead, he got an army of Crusaders, who were far more anxious to free Jerusalem from its Muslim occupiers than to alleviate Byzantium's problems. But Alexius was the supreme politician of his generation. After forcing the Crusader lords to swear an oath of fealty, he exploited their presence to serve his own ends without actually committing his own forces to their enterprise. In the long run, however, Alexius's guile achieved little: The Crusades disrupted Byzantium's relations with its Muslim neighbors and helped to widen the rift between the Catholic and Orthodox churches.

over the wording of the Nicene Creed had caused reciprocal anathema and would lead to open schism between Rome and Byzantium. But such was their extremity after Manzikert that the Byzantines appealed to Pope Gregory VII for help.

Gregory found himself caught up in events closer to home and unable to send any troops. However, against the odds, the Byzantines survived unaided. Fortunately, they had been blessed with the subtlest politician of the age, the emperor Alexius, who kept his encircling enemies in a state of discord, and then by a mixture of bluff, bribes, treachery, and skillfully directed force restored the frontiers wherever possible. He spotted a chance when the last undisputed Seljuk sultan in Baghdad died, leaving too many sons and a civil war that might rock the sultanate of Rum. In 1095, Alexius wrote amicably to the pope, Urban II, again requesting aid from Western Christendom. What Alexius presumably hoped to receive was a contingent of professional soldiers, who would serve Byzantium for pay and regain some of the lost territories from the Muslims. The taking of Jerusalem probably did not cross his mind, for it was many centuries since the Byzantines' realm had embraced the Holy City.

From Rome, Alexius's request looked very different. Pope Urban had heard that the Christians of Syria were suffering grievously under the warring Muslims, and he desired to succor them. He was equally concerned to avert the dangers that pilgrims from the West were said to run in those troubled parts. Moreover, the pope—who came from a noble French family—needed no messengers to tell him of the evils that bellicose Western Christians daily inflicted on each other. It seemed to Urban that, if only the knights of the West could be persuaded to direct their warlike vigor against the East rather than against each other, then peace at home would follow. Finally, he dreamed that with Byzantium dependent on Western arms, the unity of Christendom could be satisfactorily restored.

All this might be achieved, thought Urban, by a force inspired by the Church, fighting a holy war. Saint Augustine, writing in the fifth century, had defined how Christians should view warfare. Following Augustine's teachings, Urban considered that warfare might be just, might even be considered an act of love, if its object were to restrain sinners from evil; if it were carried out, under due authority, with a charitable disposition of the heart. The Church still maintained that penance was needed for spilling Christian blood, even in a worthy cause; but a war against such enemies of the faith as the Muslims was a different matter.

Before Urban's time, Spain had been the chief theater of the clash between the Catholic and Muslim faiths. Arabs had overrun Spain in the eighth century but had never quite completed the conquest. From the first generation of Muslim rule in Spain, the Christian statelets that survived in the north had cherished the aim of reconquering the lost lands of the south. This *reconquista* was to take eight centuries. Almost from the outset, the long struggle in Spain had drawn in Christians from elsewhere. In 1085, the reconquista had achieved its first major success, when the city of Toledo, the old capital in the center of the Spanish plateau, fell to the Christians. When Urban decided to answer Alexius's request, the Spanish tradition of a just and sometimes successful war against Islam was one of the elements he could rely on to bring men to his cause.

Another was the tradition of pilgrimage to Jerusalem. Urban considered the Holy City to be the proper objective for the armies of the holy war, rather than the nearer Asian cities that Alexius had in mind. Urban resolved to treat the Crusaders as pilgrims: Like all pilgrims, they would become temporary churchmen, subject to Church courts rather than the law of any land. They and their property would receive the protection of the Church. Urban had no doubts about the rewards the warrior pilgrims could expect. Those who died for the faith had long been promised their reward in heaven. But Urban determined that all those who went to fight the infidel, no matter whether they died or lived, could be confident of complete absolution of their sins and thus certain salvation.

The pope left Italy for his native France, the home of chivalry, a land accustomed to send valiant knights to fight the Muslims in Spain. At Clermont in Auvergne, Urban summoned a council of the bishops and abbots of France. There, on November 27, 1095, he addressed the ecclesiastics and a select gathering of knights in what (judged by its results) was one of the great speeches of history.

He described the sufferings of the Christians in the East, telling in vivid and grisly detail how the Turks "have destroyed the altars that they have polluted with their foul practices. They have circumcised the Christians, spreading the blood on the altars and pouring it on the fonts. And they cut open the bellies of those whom they choose to torment with a loathsome death, tear out their bowels and tie them to a stake, drag them around and flog them, before killing them as they lie on the ground with their entrails all hanging out."

Or some such eloquence: The accounts that survived of Urban's oratory were written years afterward, recording what might, or should, have been said. But the different reports agreed on the gist of his speech: that disaster had overcome Christ's faithful in the East; that the knights of the West should cease their vile private wars

Europe's Other Crusade

This wooden figure of Christ crucified, known as "The Christ of the Battles," is believed to have been carried into battle as a talisman of faith by the eleventh-century Spanish warrior Rodrigo Díaz de Vivar, also known as El Cid. Celebrated as a national hero in the twelfth-century poem *The Song of the Cid,* El Cid personified for the generations that followed him the struggle of Christian knights to end Muslim rule in Spain.

In real life, however, El Cid was not quite the idealist that legend made him out to be: He fought not only for King Alfonso VI of Castile but also for the Muslim king of Saragossa before becoming independent ruler of Valencia in 1094; he died in 1099, shortly before Valencia was recaptured by the Muslims.

During El Cid's last years, the long struggle of the Christian kingdoms of northern Spain to rid their country of the infidel was granted the status of a crusade by Pope Urban II. Knights from France and other countries of Europe flocked to Spain to fight for the Christian cause. But the rival kings of Leon, Castile, Aragon, and Catalonia fought bitterly among themselves as well as against the Muslims. Lack of unity meant that most Christian victories of the twelfth century were temporary. It was not until 1212 that the Muslims were decisively defeated by a crusading army of allied Spanish forces and European knights at the battle of Las Navas de Tolosa. By the middle of the thirteenth century, all of Spain had been reconquered except Granada, which remained in Muslim hands until 1492.

and turn their swords upon the infidels, to avenge and redeem the holy places that were now left desolate; that any who fought in Christ's battle were assured the remission of their sins. The assembly answered Urban with a great shout: *"Deus lo volt"*—God wills it. Thus the First Crusade was launched—the first of hundreds of holy wars summoned by popes over five centuries to combat the seeming enemies of Christendom, whether Muslims or pagans or errant Christians, whether in the East or in Europe. A pope's initiative was crucial for launching a Crusade, since only a pope had the authority to announce the absolution that made all the sacrifices worthwhile. The assembly at Clermont chose Adhemar, the bishop of neighboring Le Puy, to lead the expedition. He was a churchman high in the pope's favor but also with worldly talents, a horseman who could ride in armor like any knight. At Urban's command, Adhemar's knights sewed crosses on their garments, to mark themselves as warriors of the Cross—from which, years later, came the name of Crusade. The churchmen sent preachers out to all the surrounding lands, to carry the news of the pope's holy war and to summon recruits for the march eastward that was to start the following summer. Multitudes listened and took up the Cross. Great lords determined to march with their followers. Some of these magnates had much to lose. Raymond of Toulouse, a noble in his mid-fifties who had spent most of his life consolidating his great estates in southern France, swore never to return to his rich lands, but to live and die in pilgrimage; Godfrey of Bouillon sold the city of Verdun, east of Paris, and mortgaged his estates in order to come up with pay for the soldiers he needed.

Others may have had less exalted motives. Urban had spoken of the shortage of territory in France: "The land you live in is overcrowded and scarcely furnishes food for its own people; this is why you devour and fight one another." To some people, the domains of the infidel lured perhaps as tellingly as the sanctuaries of Christ. But simple desire for others' possessions could hardly lead rational beings to Jerusalem. There was uncultivated farmland even in France, and far more in Germany. And for knights, who were expected to travel equipped with horses, packmules, and servants, crusading was costly; a poor knight could only contemplate the journey if he found a sponsor of some wealth.

The plan at Clermont had envisaged a force armed and trained for war, with experienced military commanders, which would assemble at Constantinople and march to Jerusalem. The preachers that Urban inspired produced this and far more. The Crusade became a popular, as well as a military, movement.

The most famous of these preachers was Peter the Hermit, a brilliant orator and acknowledged holy man, from whose very donkey the cheering crowds pulled hairs as relics. Peter was the proud possessor of a Heavenly Letter, which, he claimed, an angel had given him, commanding him to preach the Crusade to Christ's poor, who would redeem the earth. Pious peasants listened and set off for the Holy Land. They had no horses or armor, but they shod their oxen and crammed their families into their carts, or slung their handful of possessions over their shoulders and walked. There were multitudes: 60,000, said some chroniclers (who had, however, no way of knowing). Among the simple folk were numerous knights, but the bulk of the knightly class was still busy with its preparations. These first Crusaders gathered around Cologne, expecting miracles; there were stories that Charlemagne—the great emperor who had restored the power of western Europe in the eighth century—had risen from the dead to lead the Crusade.

From Cologne, the People's Crusade set out in April of 1096, preceding the armies of the pope. The Crusaders traveled in several bands, of which Peter's was the largest and most disorderly. Hardly had the multitudes started out when their first victims met their fate. Jews were numerous in the trading cities of the Rhineland. Many of the Crusaders could barely grasp the distinction between Jews and Muslims and determined, against the dictates of the Church, to force conversions. A chronicler recorded their refrain: "We have set out to march a long way to fight the enemies of God in the East, and behold, before our very eyes are his worst foes, the Jews. They must be dealt with first." The Jews resorted to prayer and large bribes to the authorities and, at first, secured protection. Then, in May, came the mad count Emich of Leiningen, riding at the head of a rabble too numerous to be resisted. In Worms and Mainz, he threatened the Jews with baptism. Some prudently accepted conversion and lived; those who refused were massacred. In the course of the twelfth century, several thousand Jews perished in similar incidents that accompanied every call to crusade.

Leaving the slaughter behind, the first Crusaders followed the traditional pilgrim route to Constantinople: up the Rhine, down the Danube, and across the Balkans. At each new city, the children among them cried out, "Is this Jerusalem?" There was trouble from Hungary onward; the pilgrims pillaged the country and were attacked in reprisal by the local forces. After a journey of many months, the Crusaders arrived in Constantinople, to be greeted with a cautious welcome from the perplexed emperor Alexius. He ordered the People's Crusade to be fed and sheltered well outside the city walls, and soon arranged for the pilgrims to be ferried across the Bosporus, leaving them to march across the sixty miles of no man's land that separated Constantinople from Nicaea, the capital of Kilij Arslan, the hostile Seljuk sultan of Rum.

In October, in these wilds, the People's Crusade met its first serious enemy. One party, cutoff by the Turks in a hilltop fort with no water supply, endured eight days of thirst. Desperate, they lowered rags into the castle's sewer and squeezed out the liquid that they brought up. At last, however, they surrendered, and some turned Muslim. The Turks sold the others as slaves or used them for target practice. The main body, a little later, marched into Kilij Arslan's ambush and were massacred or enslaved. Peter, who had returned to Constantinople before the disaster, survived.

Meanwhile, the second wave of Crusaders was making its way across Europe. They began to arrive at Constantinople in December 1096; the last straggled in during April 1097. They had traveled by three routes. From Lorraine and the Rhineland, Godfrey of Bouillon and Baldwin his brother led their men by the Danubian road; they were too numerous and well ordered to have trouble with the Hungarians, and besides, they paid for their food instead of plundering. From southern France, the Provençals of Bishop Adhemar and Count Raymond marched across northern Italy and down the Dalmatian coast. Crusaders who hailed from northern France and Flanders traveled

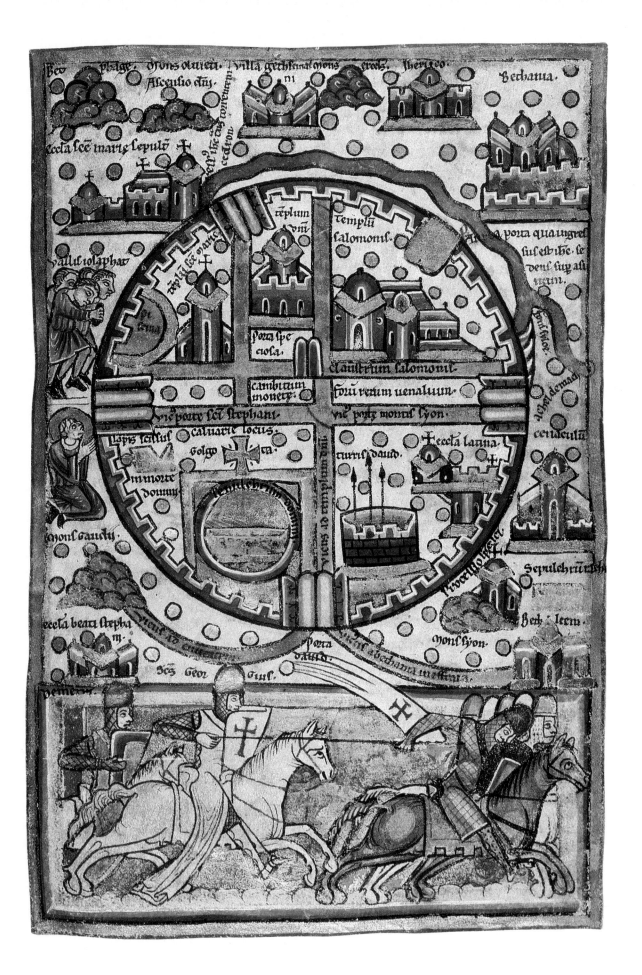

southward to the heel of Italy and took ship across the Adriatic to Byzantine territory. This last army brought to the Crusade some unexpected recruits from among the Normans of Apulia, who were embroiled in civil war. Count Bohemond of Taranto, handsome as a Greek statue, mighty in battle, but far from wealthy, was besieging Amalfi when he heard of the crusading army and its intentions. Seeking both spiritual riches and a domain in the East, he cut up his most valuable scarlet cloak to make crosses for his knights, left Amalfi untaken, and set out for Constantinople.

The forces of these various lords were formidable. The knights, helmeted and clad from head to foot in chain mail, were better protected than their Eastern adversaries, who generally wore tunics of mail, but with soft headgear and leather leggings. As heavy cavalry, trained for a massed charge with lance at rest, with man, horse, and weapon fused into one unstoppable projectile, Western mercenaries were already famous in Byzantium: A knight on horseback, it was said, could have charged through the walls of Babylon. The only Islamic troops who habitually fought thus were the Arabs of southern Spain, who in their long wars with the Christian north had been forced to imitate the enemy or be cut to pieces. The Turks, Arabs, and other constituents of the Islamic armies excelled, rather, as light cavalry; their mounted swordsmen and archers were capable of great mobility and endurance.

The Crusader infantry, which made up seven-eighths of the army, fought with spears, axes, or, most potently, crossbows—which sent bolts clean through shields and armor. The Muslims would note, with reluctant praise, the cooperation on the battlefield between the Western infantry and cavalry, each protecting the other, which gave them a solidity that light horsemen could not match.

To the Byzantines, it seemed that the whole of the barbarian West was migrating to their city, and they doubted the intentions of their unexpected allies. Alexius exploited the Crusaders' staggered arrival. With skill, he kept them divided and dependent on the empire for supplies; so cornered, each crusading lord swore homage to Alexius and promised to hand him all lands gained that had once been Byzantium's. To the Crusaders' surprise, Alexius then excused himself from participating in the venture that he had initiated with his appeal to Pope Urban. Maneuvered into swearing homage to a man who refused leadership, the Crusaders recoiled from the Byzantines. The antipathy was to endure for most of the twelfth century.

By the beginning of May 1097, the last of the crusading force had been ferried across the Bosporus and was marching, together with Byzantine troops, toward the Seljuk capital of Nicaea, over the bones of Peter the Hermit's followers. Kilij Arslan was not there: He had thought that the threat from the West had perished with Peter's enthusiasts and was fighting his Muslim enemies farther east. He could not summon enough troops to defeat the Crusaders when they besieged Nicaea, and the city surrendered to Alexius's envoys. The Crusaders—perhaps 40,000 altogether, knights, foot soldiers, and camp followers—set off southeastward, on to the Anatolian plateau. They marched in two divisions, one a day ahead of the other. Bohemond led the first; the second, led by Raymond of Toulouse, included the forces of Godfrey of Bouillon and of Adhemar of Le Puy.

Beyond the pass of Dorylaeum, almost 100 miles from Nicaea, Kilij Arslan awaited them. On the first day of July, at sunrise, Bohemond's advance guard awoke to find the hills covered with innumerable Turks, howling unintelligible war cries, swirling forward to surround them. The Christians formed a battle line around their camp, against which the Turks skirmished fiercely, shooting arrows from an astonishing range. By the rules of Turkish warfare, victory was in sight; the Crusaders were cutoff and unable to maneuver, and could not resist forever.

But through the growing heat of the day the Crusaders' line held. Around noon, the Turks realized that they had not, after all, trapped their enemy. The second part of the crusading army had marched to the rescue of the first, with Duke Godfrey's troops in the vanguard falling on the surprised Turks like the wrath of God. The reinforced Christian army started to advance, and then the Turks saw that they were caught themselves. Bishop Adhemar had led the Provençals around through the hills and emerged behind the Turkish rear. Kilij Arslan's army fled as best it could, scattering at full gallop. The Crusaders pursued them to the Turkish camp and beyond, killing many. The camp, with its wealth of gold, silver, horses, camels, oxen, and sheep, fell into the hands of the Christians.

Despite their victory, the Crusaders were much impressed by the Turks. "You could not find stronger or better soldiers: if only they had the true faith," they murmured to each other, according to one contemporary chronicle. The Muslims, for their part, were thoroughly dismayed. A Damascene historian began his account of the fateful year with a description of the battle and the Turkish defeat. "When the news was received of this shameful calamity to the cause of Islam," he noted, "the anxiety of the people became acute, and alarm increased."

In the months that followed, the Crusaders pressed on across Anatolia toward Syria. The Byzantine force accompanying the Crusaders had dwindled to a mere token; Alexius and the main Byzantine army were busy in the Crusaders' wake, reestablishing Constantinople's control over the coast of Asia Minor. The Seljuks offered the Crusaders little resistance, but Anatolia was a formidable obstacle in itself, especially in the heat of summer: waterless plains, salt lakes, terrible mountains. Suffering continually, the Crusaders staggered on, leaving their dead beside the roads. Beyond the plateau, they found the great ranges of the Taurus and the Anti-Taurus—former Byzantine territories that had been taken over by the native Armenians in the wake of the Turkish attack on Byzantium. Being Christian, the Armenians welcomed the Crusaders; with the aid of the local people, the Crusaders struggled through the passes. At the end of October, they arrived at Antioch, the greatest city of Syria, a far richer prize than Jerusalem. Most of their horses had died. Four out of five knights would have to fight their next battle on foot or mounted on donkeys.

Antioch should have been impregnable. Its massive walls, reinforced with 400 towers, were a masterpiece of Roman engineering: Their circuit was too great for the city to be blockaded, the Orontes River brought an un-

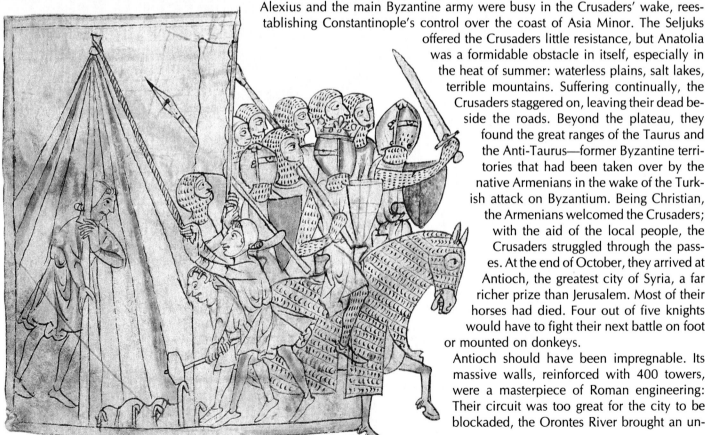

As a company of Crusader knights rides into camp, a work detail pitches a tent in this illustration from an early thirteenth-century French manuscript. While the knights enjoyed the relative comfort of such tents, the common soldiers often had to make do with shelters of brushwood. In addition to the fighting men, a Crusader encampment housed armorers, cooks, laundresses, priests, doctors, entertainers, and sergeants to maintain order. Although many wives went on crusade, accompanying their husbands, marital relations were supposed to be forgone as an act of penance, and women were segregated in separate camps—a regulation honored more often in the breach than the observance.

failing supply of water, and the Muslim garrison was strong and well supplied. Through the autumn and winter, the Crusaders camped outside Antioch's gates, finding that Syria could be almost as wet, cold, and muddy as France; they had no siege engines, and before long, they were short of food. Foraging parties that wandered too far away were assailed by Turks. Despondency spread; many Crusaders slipped away from the misery and famine.

What brought the besiegers victory at last was a combination of their own cunning and a fractured defense. Not only was Syria a patchwork of quarrelsome principalities, but unity had also vanished farther east after the civil war of the 1090s. Now, throughout Mesopotamia and Persia, local princes vied for power.

The two key cities of northern Syria, Aleppo and Damascus, were under rival Turkish princes; a third ruler controlled the powerful state of Mosul on the Tigris. The Muslim governor of Antioch had oscillated in his loyalties too often and too openly between the rulers of Aleppo and Damascus. He appealed to both of them for help, but neither wished to associate with the other. If those contending princes had combined their strengths and marched together to the rescue, the siege of Antioch could have been broken. As it was, the Damascene forces attacked in December, and the Aleppans in February; neither withstood the furious charges of the knights.

The spring came, and with it relief for both parties. In March of 1098, a fleet of ships

A stained-glass window in the cathedral of Chlons-sur-Marne in northeastern France depicts a blindfolded figure, representing Judaism, holding the Crown of Thorns and other implements of Christ's Passion to symbolize supposed Jewish guilt for the death of the Savior. Like other religious minorities in Europe, the Jews suffered terribly at the hands of various crusading armies: The religious fervor fanned by those who preached the Crusades became uncontrollable and led to the wholesale massacre of some Jewish communities. The Church condemned the persecution; many bishops tried to protect the victims, but often their voices went unheard.

from Constantinople arrived on the Syrian coast, bearing pilgrims and food; but, thereafter, the famine became yet more acute. In May, news came that the ruler of Mosul, the terrible Kerbogha, was leading his Persian and Mesopotamian warriors westward to help other Muslims in Syria. As Kerbogha's great army drew near, many Crusaders fled back to Byzantine territory. In Aksehir, halfway to Constaninople, they found the emperor Alexius and his army, and told him of the Crusaders' plight.

Kerbogha's advance was diverted for three crucial weeks. Earlier, when the crusading army emerged from the Anti-Taurus Mountains, Godfrey of Bouillon's younger brother Baldwin had taken a hundred horsemen and ridden eastward along the line of precariously held Armenian principalities. His initiative had been rewarded: The native Christians flocked to his banner, two Turkish strongholds along the upper Euphrates fell, and the Armenian prince Thoros of Edessa adopted Baldwin as his son. Within a month, Thoros died in a riot, and Baldwin emerged as the first ruler of a Crusader state: rich and very near the line of march from Mosul to Antioch. Kerbogha did not like to leave his flank exposed and turned aside to attack Edessa. For most of May, he besieged Baldwin, before abandoning the attempt and returning to his main objective of Antioch, which he reached four days too late.

For meanwhile, Bohemond the Norman had been exploring fresh avenues. He somehow managed to make contact with an Armenian renegade in the garrison of Antioch, the commander of three of the 400 towers. Undaunted by the many defections, Bohemond marched the army away from the city, as if to encounter Kerbogha. Then, on the night of June 2, he returned to keep an appointment with the Armenian commander, who secretly let him pass with his men through the fortifications. The Crusaders streamed in, and by the end of the next day, all Muslims in the city were dead. The narrow streets were nearly blocked by their corpses.

By June 7, Kerbogha's host had arrived, and the Christians were besieged in their turn. They endured misery, hunger, and fear for three weeks; some slipped away over the hills or toward the seacoast. But the spirits of those who remained were dramatically restored. A Provençal pilgrim, Peter Bartholomew, revealed that Saint Andrew had spoken to him in a vision and had declared that a most sacred relic, the Holy Lance, which had pierced Christ on the Cross, lay hidden in the cathedral. After a day's excavation, Peter Bartholomew found an ancient lancehead. Some suspected that he had found no more than he had first hidden, among them Bishop Adhemar who knew much about relics; but many believed and rejoiced. Then Saint Andrew spoke to Peter again, promising victory if the Christians attacked the Muslims.

So on June 28, the Crusaders heard mass, confessed their sins, formed up in six battalions, and marched out under Bohemond's command, bearing the Holy Lance with them. The enemy were far greater in numbers, and some of their troops were excellent. But there was discord within Kerbogha's camp. The princes of Aleppo and Damascus, and the nomadic Arabs of the Syrian Desert, had joined the Muslim army; now they wondered whether a victory for the fierce lord of Mosul would necessarily be in their own long-term interests. The Christians had no such doubts. They advanced resolutely and won a victory more complete than Dorylaeum. Antioch was theirs. That day's slaughter settled events in Syria for several years. The Seljuk power was not destroyed but was seriously dislocated. Thinking only of their own safety, the Turkish princes fled to their cities.

On hearing the news of their fellow Muslims' misfortune in Syria, the Fatimids of Egypt seized their opportunity and advanced to Sunni-held Jerusalem. After six weeks of siege, the Seljuk garrison came to an arrangement: They accepted large amounts of Egyptian silver and marched away. The Holy City was now in Shiite hands again.

Technically, the new ruler of Antioch should have been the emperor Alexius, in whose domains the city had stood. But Alexius had believed the tales of the terrified deserters who fled to Aksehir from Kerbogha and had given up Antioch for lost when he might have come to the Crusaders' rescue. The great victory was above all Bohemond's achievement, and he regarded Antioch as his by right of conquest, choosing to forget his oath of homage to Alexius. The emperor's claim to Antioch was to sour relations with the Western knights for most of the twelfth century and would lead to repeated armed clashes.

During the summer of 1098, typhoid in the city dispatched many, including the charismatic bishop Adhemar. Without his guidance, the great lords were paralyzed with indecision. They lingered in the valley of the Orontes, until at last the common

soldiers threatened to pull down their conquests stone by stone unless the army resumed the pilgrimage to Jerusalem. Eventually, in January 1099, the Crusade moved south again. Bohemond, though, stayed behind in Antioch, the Eastern domain he had coveted and won.

With Raymond of Toulouse as leader, the Crusaders marched up the inland valley of the Orontes, then turned southwest and reached the sea. They were no longer in Seljuk lands. The local Arab rulers were happy to assist the enemies of the Turks and offered guides and food. Without serious opposition, the Crusaders moved south along the coast, passing Tripoli and Beirut, Sidon and Tyre, and Acre. Near Jaffa, they turned inland, among the rocky hills of Judea. On June 7, they came in view of Jerusalem, knelt, and wept. They had been three years on their armed pilgrimage; only one in five had endured till the end was in sight.

But the end was not yet attained. Jerusalem was a major fortress, abundantly provisioned. Such a city could be taken only by furious assault, by treachery, or by a regular siege with all the machinery of war that the Crusade lacked. An assault was tried, with great zeal but without artillery support or scaling ladders; it failed bloodily. Treachery was impracticable; the Fatimids had prudently expelled all Christians from the city. The Crusaders stood baffled, and very thirsty, since the Fatimids had with equal foresight poisoned every well for miles. And news came from Egypt that a great army was gathering to liberate Jerusalem, that a fleet was sailing to blockade the coast of Palestine, and that the emperor Alexius had turned against the Crusade and sought peace with the caliph in Cairo.

Then, just in time, came unexpected help from one of the great merchant cities of Italy—whose leaders, while they may have been calculating on breaking into the Middle Eastern market, were no doubt stirred by the crusading spirit like the rest of Europe. Genoese galleys slipped into the Palestinian port of Jaffa before the Egyptian blockade of the coast was complete. They brought the materials to build great stone-throwing catapults and siege towers—mobile fortresses that could be pushed forward against the walls of Jerusalem.

During the night of July 6, Bishop Adhemar's spirit appeared to one of the Crusaders' number, promising the Christians victory after nine days if they held a fast and made a barefoot procession around the city. The Crusaders obeyed, and a great column wound its way across the rocky slopes, maintaining a distance just out of bowshot from the walls, holding crosses and relics and chanting psalms. In derision, the Muslim garrison, mostly Sudanese and desert Arabs, hoisted crosses onto their turrets; some, in front of the Christians, spat upon the Christians' sacred emblem.

On the evening of July 14, Raymond of Toulouse sent the first tower forward, against a hail of arrows, stones, and the primitive napalm—whose secret was later lost—that the Crusaders called Greek fire. They reached the southern wall but could not gain a footing. Next morning a second tower, commanded by Godfrey of Bouillon, attacked the northern defenses. This time, the Crusaders managed to mount their assault. The defenders could not withstand them.

The Crusaders surged into the city, killing everyone they met. By the next morning, Jerusalem had been comprehensively looted, and many of its inhabitants—both Muslims and Jews—slaughtered. "The horses waded in blood up to their knees, nay up to the bridle. It was a just and wonderful judgment of God," wrote one Crusader.

The first action of the triumphant Crusaders was to troop, weeping with gratitude, into the Church of the Holy Sepulcher and give thanks to God. The second was to

Defenders of Islam

Drawn from many ethnic backgrounds and military traditions, Islamic forces relied heavily on cavalry. About 50 percent of armies from Egypt in the early twelfth century consisted of spear-wielding mailed horsemen *(center)* of Arab and Berber origin. The core of the Seljuk and other eastern Islamic armies was military slaves *(right)*, usually Turks bought in central Asia, who, as mobile horse archers, wore armor often consisting of a lamellar cuirass—of hardened leather in this case—covering chest and back, and an iron helmet worn over a mail coif. After Saladin united Egypt and Syria in 1174, he used both slave and paid soldiers, but he leaned more on Turkic than Egyptian tradition; mounted archers, for example, were prominent in his campaigns. But Saladin armed his forces more than Seljuk horsemen—often in mail *(left)*—so they could meet Crusaders as equals.

Soldiers of the Cross

Although the military equipment of the Crusaders was no more advanced than that of their Muslim opponents, a higher proportion of the Christian forces was protected by armor. The iron helmets and mail tunics worn by most western European knights *(center)* were similar to those worn by the Normans in the previous century, but their kite-shaped shields were larger. They fought with lance and sword, leaving archery to the infantry, such as the German foot soldier on the right, who wears a poor man's armor of horn or hardened leather. Among the Crusaders' Christian allies were the Armenians *(left)*, horsemen whose equipment reflected both Byzantine and Islamic influences. The full suit of mail armor was borrowed from the Byzantine heavy cavalry, while the soft, spurless leather boots were copied from the Turks.

look around in some bewilderment at their conquest and to dispute who should rule it. The half-dozen leaders of the Crusade offered the crown of the new realm to Raymond of Toulouse, but he declared, perhaps from real piety, that he would not be king in Christ's kingdom. Godfrey of Bouillon, when offered Jerusalem, at first declined but then allowed himself to be persuaded into accepting. He chose the title of prince rather than king. Raymond found even this honorific disgusting.

The belated arrival from Egypt of the Fatimid army forced the quarrelsome Christians into reluctant unity, which lasted long enough for the Crusaders to deliver a shattering dawn attack on the Egyptian camp. They won an easy victory and enormous plunder, whereupon many set off home, their pilgrimage consummated. Having attained their goal despite the hardships, the Muslim opposition, and a lack of leadership, they believed that God's intervention alone could explain the triumph.

Raymond remembered his oath never to return from the East but, still piqued by Godfrey's presumption, thought a visit to Constantinople was permissible. Godfrey was left to defend the Holy Sepulcher with 300 knights and 300 infantry. The Crusaders' position was precarious and became more so in the next year, 1100, when Godfrey fell ill and died, and Bohemond of Antioch went campaigning into the mountains against the Danishmend Turks, fell into an ambush, and was captured.

Although Pope Urban had died without hearing of the victory he had inspired, his successor Paschal was equally determined to save Jerusalem. Another great force was assembled; this time the armed pilgrims numbered some 50,000. The reinforcements reached Constantinople in 1101 and were pleased to gain the company of Raymond of Toulouse. In Anatolia, they met with disaster; the Turks had learned from

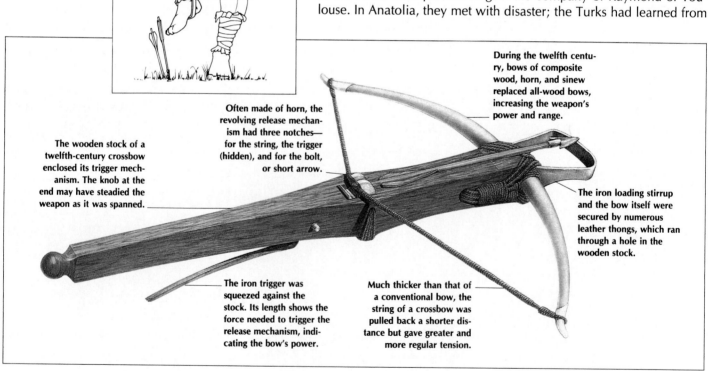

During the twelfth century, bows of composite wood, horn, and sinew replaced all-wood bows, increasing the weapon's power and range.

Often made of horn, the revolving release mechanism had three notches—for the string, the trigger (hidden), and for the bolt, or short arrow.

The wooden stock of a twelfth-century crossbow enclosed its trigger mechanism. The knob at the end may have steadied the weapon as it was spanned.

The iron loading stirrup and the bow itself were secured by numerous leather thongs, which ran through a hole in the wooden stock.

The iron trigger was squeezed against the stock. Its length shows the force needed to trigger the release mechanism, indicating the bow's power.

Much thicker than that of a conventional bow, the string of a crossbow was pulled back a shorter distance but gave greater and more regular tension.

their defeats and avoided close combat. Instead, they dogged the Christian columns toiling in the blazing heat, annoyed them with archery, and waited till thirst and exhaustion broke up their order. Raymond fought his way back to Constantinople, whence he sailed to Palestine and a life of holy war; a few Crusaders struggled through to Syria. But no real help reached Jerusalem by land.

The fledgling Crusader states were saved not by their own strength, but by the extreme disunity of their enemies. To many Shiites or Sunni, the Christians were not the most obnoxious enemies. Any Muslim leader strong enough to threaten the Christians would be seen as an even greater threat to his Islamic neighbors.

The Christians also were fortunate in their leadership. After Bohemond's capture, Baldwin of Edessa took control in northern Syria and was soon summoned south to inherit his brother's throne in Jerusalem. He had none of Godfrey's modesty about declaring himself king, and for eighteen years, he ruled with skill and courage.

For decades, no more great armored columns tried to force their way across Anatolia, but the fleets of Genoa, Pisa, and Venice brought to the East a steady flow of Crusaders, of unarmed pilgrims, and of settlers—both men and women. Through these voyages, the crusading lands became known in Europe as Outremer—Beyond-the-Sea. With the help of the new crusading blood, Baldwin waged a continual war against the surrounding Muslims, with cumulative success. One by one, the cities of Palestine submitted. By Baldwin's death, the kingdom of Jerusalem had a firm frontier along the Jordan and a less certain hold over the sheikdoms farther east. In the south, Baldwin had taken and fortified Aylah—present-day Eilat—on the Red Sea; Sinai remained a land of Bedouins who robbed Egyptians and Europeans impartially. All the western seaboard had submitted, except for the Fatimid fortress of Ascalon and the peninsular city of Tyre—which had almost defeated Alexander the Great in one of the great sieges of antiquity and which continued to defy the Christians until 1124. Baldwin's territory ran north to Beirut. Beyond that, Raymond of Toulouse and his heirs won for themselves the county of Tripoli, which owed some obedience to Jerusalem and reached up to the borders of Antioch. The four Crusader states of Jerusalem, Tripoli, Antioch, and Edessa made up a fragile ribbon of Christian rule stretching 600 miles from the Red Sea to the headwaters of the Euphrates; at their narrowest, the Christian lands measured only some ten miles across.

Meanwhile, Bohemond regained his freedom from the Turks and returned to Italy to enlist volunteers for a new Crusade that would march toward his enemy, the Byzantium of the treacherous Alexius. He met defeat in 1108 at Durazzo—in present-day Albania—and went home to Italy to die disappointed.

Bohemond's nephew Tancred, who became effective ruler of Antioch in his uncle's absence, flung himself enthusiastically into local politics. The Normans and Turks discovered that they had much in common, in courage and chivalry; an Arab chronicler noted with some admiration, "These men used to fight one another and then, after the contest, would meet to dine and talk." By 1108, the alliances were surprisingly mixed. In that year, Jawali of Mosul in alliance with the Christians of Edessa attacked his fellow seljuk Ridwan of Aleppo, who was rescued by his Christian neighbor Tancred of Antioch.

Outremer became a strange fusion of East and West. In all the Christian states, there were never many more than 2,000 nobles and knights, who between them held cities and villages in feudal homage to the great lords of Jerusalem, Antioch, Tripoli, and

With its great penetrating power, accuracy, and ease of use, the crossbow was the most potent weapon deployed by the Crusaders. Used, by the Greeks and Romans, but lost in the ruins of the classical world, it was probably rediscovered by the West during the early Middle Ages—adopted, perhaps, from the Islamic world, whose own forces, however, set greater store by the short composite bows of their horse archers. The Catholic church considered the crossbow to be so dangerously lethal that in 1139 it tried unsuccesfully to ban the weapon's use except against pagans and Muslims. The crossbow's main drawback, literally, was its slowness of loading. Most twelfth-century crossbows were "spanned," or drawn, by means of a stirrup and a double iron hook fastened at one end to the cord and at the other to a strong leather waist belt (inset).

BASTION OF THE WARRIOR-MONKS

Highly skilled in the crafts of war but relatively few in number, twelfth-century Crusaders in the Holy Land built castles to guard their possessions and to serve as centers for fresh conquests. Most were sited at strategic locations.

Belvoir Castle, illustrated here, stood on the edge of a lofty escarpment in southern Galilee, commanding the Jordan Valley and its vital fords *(map, below)*. The Muslims, who captured the castle intact in 1189, knew it as "Star of the Winds," and the Arab historian Abu Shama described Belvoir as being "set among the stars like a falcon's nest."

Built in 1168 for the Knights Hospitalers, a closed order of warrior-monks, Belvoir was one of the first concentric castles in the history of Western architecture, consisting of a square inner stronghold that was surrounded by an outer band of fortifications. The Hospitalers themselves probably occupied the inner stronghold, while their mercenary auxiliaries were housed in the outer structure.

As a defensive system, such a castle had a significant weakness, since if the enemy breached the outer defenses, it could then use them to hold off a relieving force while still besieging the garrison within. In spite of this structural drawback, Belvoir withstood an eighteen-month siege in 1187-1189 before finally being forced to lay down arms and surrender.

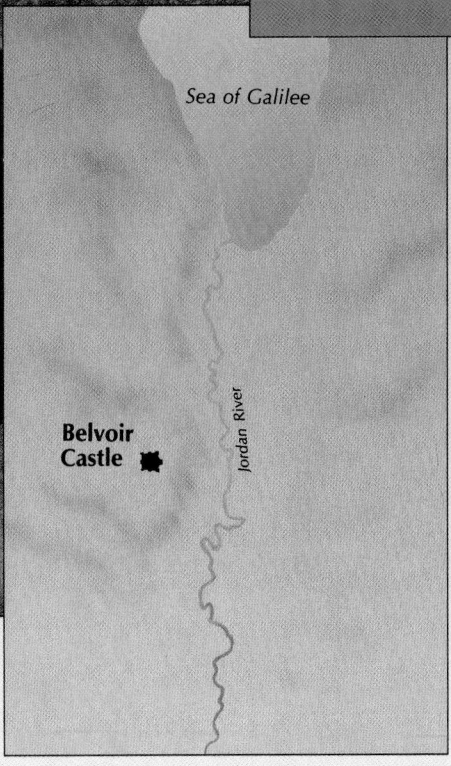

Sea of Galilee

Belvoir
Castle

Jordan River

Edessa. Ranking below these in the feudal hierarchy were the common soldiers of the Crusades and their descendants, together with the colonists who soon outnumbered the Crusaders. Western settlers in Palestine came to total some 140,000. Like the nobles, most of the European commoners came from homes in France or the French-speaking lands of Lorraine, Flanders, or Sicily, but there were contingents from all Catholic lands from Portugal to Norway. The crusading states were the common property of all Western Christendom. To the Muslims, however, all settlers were *al-Faranj*—Franks.

The Franks put their mark on the landscape with a lavish program of church building. Pious Europeans too timid or infirm to crusade themselves sent the funds; indigenous Christians and Muslims, hurriedly trained in the techniques and styles of Western Christendom, supplied the labor. The most splendid new edifice was the recently rebuilt Church of the Holy Sepulcher in Jerusalem, which enclosed the supposed site of Calvary and Christ's burial place, together with the ruins of Constantine's fourth-century church.

The settlers set about ridding all holy places, including Jerusalem, of Muslims. But otherwise, the native Muslims, Jews, and Christians were left little disturbed. In the countryside, natives and Westerners remained apart and their villages were discernible from afar: Native hamlets, of whatever faith, were built in a tight huddle around a well, a mill, and an oven; olive groves and vineyards surrounded the houses. The Western settlers, however, built their villages and towns on a grid pattern, focusing on a church and a courthouse.

In the coastal cities, the various nationalities mingled, but Italian merchants predominated. It was they who provided the shipping to transport pilgrims and warriors and who made their fortunes in the trade on which the wealth of the realms depended. In the trading cities, Venetians, Pisans, and Genoese established communes that were run, virtually independently of the Frankish states, by officials appointed by the mother cities.

Throughout Outremer, only the testimony of a Catholic was deemed fully valid. No native Muslim or Orthodox Christian could hope for a place in the new feudal hierarchy, since an important duty of a feudal vassal was to sit in court and offer his views on the cases; a Catholic voice alone had full weight. But all subjects were ruled with some attempt at justice. While the main civil courts were entirely in Western hands, native courts were allowed to deal with minor cases. The villages were left to govern themselves under their own chiefs, as long as they paid taxes to their new lords. Some Muslims admitted that they were more prosperous under the settled rule of Frankish law than in any land of Islam.

The years passed and took away the heroes of the First Crusade. The next generation of the lords of Outremer were mostly born to the country and felt at home there, although they kept many Western habits that bemused the Muslims. To Eastern eyes, the Europeans—though unquestionably courageous—had no sense of honor or shame at all. They let their women go unveiled and even let their wives talk to other men in the street. The East taught the settlers something: tolerance of the Muslims with whom they traded and hunted when not at war, a taste for olives, grapes, and white wheaten bread—a wonderful contrast to the dark rye bread of northern Europe—perfumes and turbans and fine loose clothing, dancing girls at their feasts and wailing mourners at their funerals. By most Western standards, they lived a life of luxury, funded by taxes on the local peasantry. Yet there was much to the Islamic world that the settlers never perceived. In Muslim society, learned theologians and lawyers advised kings and administered their domains; scholars debated the scientific ideas of the ancient Greeks. Some Eastern learning was now seeping into Europe. But at a time when such Western scholars as Gerard of Cremona and Adelard of Bath were absorbing mathematics, science, and philosophy from Arabic manuscripts, the settlers in the Levant who learned to converse with the Muslims imbibed little of the real culture of the East. Admittedly their contacts were mostly with Turks, who, like the crusading knights, cared less for Arabian learning than for sport and war.

And without their military prowess, the Crusaders would not have survived a decade in the East. By sea alone they were safe. The Turks were not yet proficient sailors, and the people of Syria held that only madmen trusted themselves to the waves. Of the Muslim states, only Egypt possessed a navy, which did not survive an encounter with the Venetian galleys off Ascalon in 1123. But on land, there was never any safety. Outremer lacked natural frontiers, and its immense length made it a nightmare to defend. Minor campaigns followed each other without pause. For defense, Outremer relied at first on the feudal levies of the Western lords, aided by new waves of armed pilgrims and by mercenaries. The native Armenians of the north also made a contribution, and the Maronites of the Lebanese mountains had a good reputation as archers and light infantry, but in general, the Eastern Christians could not be trusted to fight for the Catholics. Urban II had been misinformed about the sufferings of his coreligionists in the East; most of them found the pope almost as alien as the caliph.

As the century drew on, two extraordinary bodies of men began to contribute to the defense of the Crusader states. They were the military orders—the Knights Hospitalers of Saint John and the Knights Templars—who were both soldiers and monks. The orders started in Jerusalem as religious fraternities that cared for pilgrims—the Hospitalers based in a hospice founded by a Catholic abbey in the eleventh century, the Templars in a house adjoining an edifice that was believed to be Solomon's temple. The Templars were knights who included among their duties patrolling the roads and escorting pilgrims between the coast and Jerusalem. From protecting pilgrims, they progressed to protecting the kingdom; they emerged as fully fledged fighting men by the 1130s. The Hospitalers initially had no military connection: They specialized in the care of poor pilgrims when they were sick. But with time, the Hospitalers found the increasingly militant ideology of the Templars too powerful to resist; the Hospitalers took to the battlefield around 1150. Knights in search of salvation came from all parts of Western Christendom to join both orders. Pious lords bequeathed them riches and lands in every country; by the mid-twelfth century, the orders had built castles of their own in Outremer. They lived in austerity and owed entire obedience to their masters; their discipline made them the most formidable armies of Christendom.

Among the Muslims, there was nothing to match the military orders. There was, however, one group that was even more dedicated: the Assassins. From their original headquarters in Persia, these Shiite fanatics established themselves in castles among the hills of northern Syria in the early twelfth century. The exact nature of their religious beliefs is past recovery. All that was known to their contemporaries was that the Assassins, too, owed complete obedience to the master of their order; that they were infinitely skilled in drugs and disguises; and that they fought by preference not on the battlefield but through the meticulously planned murder of enemy leaders.

They first came to the notice of the Crusaders in 1103, when the ruler of the Syrian city of Homs, praying for victory against Raymond of Toulouse, was stabbed as he left the mosque. The Assassins saw powerful Sunni leaders as greater enemies than Christians; to the Crusaders, the Assassins became both a dreaded threat and a potential ally. Most Christian rulers safeguarded their lives by paying tribute. Only the Templars and Hospitalers refused. They were above blackmail, since their masters set no value on their lives. Indeed, after the Templars and Hospitalers became owners of two vast tracts of land in northern Syria, adjacent to the Assassins' stronghold, it was the Assassins who bought off the Templars and Hospitalers with yearly tribute.

Slowly, the attitude of Muslims to the Christians in their midst began to harden. At the beginning, there had been confusion: Some of the Sunni were ready to believe that the Crusaders had been summoned by the Fatimids, to destroy the only true Muslims. But as early as 1105, learned Sunni teachers realized that the Crusade was only a part of the expansion of Frankish power that had begun with the victories in Sicily and Spain, and opined that a united Islam should respond. A few years later, rulers began to dream of a jihad, or holy war, against the infidel—a concept from Islam's early, expansive years, which had fallen into abeyance since the seventh century.

To destroy Outremer, an attacker would need control of Aleppo and Damascus, the two strategic cities of Syria that remained outside Christian hands. In the early years of Outremer, the independent-minded ruler of Damascus often allied himself with the Christians; Aleppo was the object of fierce competition from various Muslim factions and from the Franks.

The stalemate lasted until a new champion arose in the armies of Islam: Zengi, the Turkish ruler of Mosul. Zengi's title was atabeg, or regent; in theory, he was a vassal of the sultan in Baghdad, but with the breakup of the Seljuks' Persian empire, local rulers such as Zengi had as much autonomy as they could snatch for themselves. In 1128, Zengi annexed strife-worn Aleppo.

Zengi was portrayed by Muslim writers of his own era as the first of a mighty trio dedicated to the holy war against the infidel. For the two Muslim heroes who succeeded Zengi, his son Nur al-Din and Nur al-Din's general Saladin, the chroniclers' picture was true enough. But Zengi's stance against the Christians was almost accidental. He was a formidable soldier, but he was not famed for his devotion. Being ruler in Mosul, he was preoccupied mainly with politics in Mesopotamia and Persia. In Syria, he harassed the infidel for twenty years, but he undermined Damascus with even more persistence. In 1140, he besieged Damascus but without success. Deflected from his primary objective, he turned his attentions northward. In 1144, he attacked a Muslim ally of the count of Edessa then, when the count and his army had marched to the rescue, switched his attentions to the city of Edessa itself. Zengi quickly conquered the undefended city and then most of the rest of the state.

Edessa was the first major city of Outremer to be lost, and its fall resounded in the West. A great defeat required a mighty counterblow. In 1146, the king of France, Louis VII, took the Crusader's oath, and an even more influential Frenchman committed himself to the new Crusade. Bernard, abbot of Clairvaux, famous for his eloquence and revered for his sanctity, summoned the French nobles to Vézelay in Burgundy and inspired them to follow their king. The abbot traveled then to Germany and persuaded the German emperor Conrad and his knights that duty required them to fight alongside the French.

MESSAGES FOR THE MILITARY

Heirs to a long military tradition rooted in the Roman and Iranian past, Saladin's Muslim armies used more sophisticated methods of communication than those employed by their Crusader opponents. Beacon fires and smoke signals had been used for a long time in the Islamic world to warn of danger, but Saladin and other Muslim leaders were able to keep in touch with distant military commanders and provincial governors by means of a pony-express service, with riders galloping in relay between various staging posts. By the twelfth century, urgent news could also be sent by pigeon post—a fast but not an infallible system, since it was not unknown for messages that were carried by pigeons to be intercepted by the trained falcons of Crusader hawking parties.

In battle, runners and dispatch riders carried orders from unit to unit. All medieval armies had flags, but in Muslim armies the ensigns were associated with specific ranks, helping a general to locate and rally his troops and serving to indicate the direction of an advance or a retreat.

The Muslims made particularly effective use of martial music as a method of communication, using kettledrums and trumpets to send tactical orders to cease fighting, advance, halt, or retire. During the Crusader siege of Acre in 1191, Muslim drummers continued to pass messages between the beleaguered Muslim garrison and Saladin's troops, who had taken up positions behind the Crusaders. Musicians such as the drummers and trumpeters below also played an important part in encouraging an Islamic army and intimidating its opponents—the Crusaders frequently mentioned the terrifying din that was produced by the kettledrums and horns of an attacking Muslim force.

This Second Crusade, from which so much was expected, failed sadly. The German contingent tried to cross central Anatolia in the autumn of 1147 and met with the same disasters as the expedition of 1101, and the miserable survivors retreated to Nicaea. Three months later, the French, with the few remaining German Crusaders, marched through the fringes of Byzantine territory in western Asia Minor; the Turks and the wild country destroyed the more ill-equipped of the pious pilgrims, but the French king, the German emperor, and some of the knights survived long enough to abandon the march and take ship for Outremer from Antalya, on the southern coast of Asia Minor. When they arrived, still a formidable army, the political situation had changed utterly.

The terrible Zengi had perished before the Crusade arrived. He awoke after an evening's drinking to find his servants finishing his wine; he uttered dreadful threats, then relapsed into slumber, and for their own safety the servants made sure he did not wake again. His sons succeeded him, Saif al-Din in Mosul and Nur al-Din in Aleppo. The Frankish count of Edessa briefly regained his lost capital, but Nur al-Din retook it almost at once. When the Crusaders mustered their forces at Acre in 1148, Edessa looked unassailable. The Crusaders chose instead to try for the rich prize of Damascus. To some of the knights of Outremer, the goal must have seemed foolish: They knew that the ruler of Damascus was the Christians' most loyal ally in Syria. Others, however, were determined to forestall a united Muslim Syria.

The knights of the Second Crusade reached Damascus, took up positions in a well-watered site, and prepared to besiege the city. In their extreme peril, the Muslims

of Damascus realized that ultimately they would prefer the son of Zengi to a Frankish prince. They sent for Nur al-Din, who, though occupied dealing with trouble in the north of his realm, promptly marched his army southward. In their haste to conclude the siege before Nur al-Din arrived, the Crusaders made the error of shifting their point of attack to a spot where the walls were weaker but water was lacking. The walls held up. Parched, bewildered, and despondent, the Second Crusade fell back from Damascus after four days of inconclusive fighting and, on reaching Christian soil, fell apart completely. Nur al-Din hurrried back north, leaving the Damascenes to enjoy a last brief spell of independence.

Although the fiery eloquence of Saint Bernard failed to achieve its objectives in the East, the Second Crusade did yield one triumph in the reconquista of Spain. A force of Dutch and English Crusaders had set sail for Palestine in 1147, intending to travel around Spain and through the Strait of Gibraltar into the Mediterranean. On the way, they passed the Portuguese coast and found King Alfonso of Portugal preparing to attack the Muslim-held city of Lisbon with its marvelous natural harbor. They joined the siege enthusiastically, and with their help, Lisbon was taken by the Christians. More than half of the Spanish peninsula still remained in Muslim hands, but within a few decades, substantial gains by the Christians would tip the balance in their favor.

In the Levant, a new balance was established after the Second Crusade. The Franks took Ascalon in 1153, and all the coast of Outremer was at last safe. Nur al-Din took Damascus in 1154, and all the eastern frontier was threatened. The knights of Outremer looked for safety in a renewed alliance with Byzantium, which, under the emperor Manuel Comnenus, was pursuing acquisitive policies.

Since Nur al-Din did not possess Mosul, his resources were fewer than his father's, but so were his distractions with eastern Islamic politics. Between Nur al-Din and Jerusalem there could be no lasting peace, for Zengi's son was a devout Sunni Muslim and was determined to retake the Holy City. He commanded his subjects' loyalty with his devotion to religion and righteousness: He endowed mosques and created palaces of justice to which all citizens could come with their grievances. In every Muslim city of Syria, he set up schools to provide instruction in the true doctrine and to teach the duty of holy war against the intruding Franks. The teaching found a positive reception because the fall of Edessa had rallied Muslims to the cause of jihad. Nur al-Din commissioned in Damascus a splendid pulpit, to be installed in the great al-Aqsa Mosque of Jerusalem when Allah willed that it should be liberated.

In the middle of the twelfth century, however, the kings of Jerusalem were too strong to be overcome directly. The main conflict shifted to the south, where the Fatimid realm had fallen into chaos. In 1154, a vizier's stepson had murdered the young caliph. In the resulting feuds, successive viziers were ousted or murdered, and total disorder ensued, from which either Christian Jerusalem or Sunni Syria might benefit. Both sent armies into Egypt in 1164 and again in 1167. King Amalric, of Jerusalem, fought in person. The Syrian forces were led by a Kurdish general, a man whose ancestors came from the remote mountains north of Syria but whose family served the Turkish rulers of Syria as soldiers and administrators. The Kurdish general brought his nephew—a young man then known only for his piety, charming conversation, and skill at polo. His name was Salah al-Din Yusuf ibn Ayyub; to the Western knights, he became famous as Saladin.

The fighting was inconclusive and eventually peace was agreed. Egypt paid an

A detail from a stained-glass window at Chartres Cathedral illustrates an episode from the French epic poem *Song of Roland*, in which the French hero Roland *(left)* jousts with the Muslim Moorish king of Saragossa. Although the story is set in eighth-century France and Spain, and was written before the First Crusade was mounted, it was extremely popular throughout the twelfth century, when its heroes were cherished as ideals both by the Crusaders fighting the Muslims in Syria and by their counterparts struggling to oust the Moors from Spain and Portugal.

enormous tribute of 100,000 gold pieces a year to Amalric, and the Franks and Syrians both left the country, except for a Frankish garrison in Cairo.

The Franks—under pressure from the Hospitalers, who expected rich prizes—attacked Egypt again in 1168, without the cooperation of the Templars, who were unwilling to break the terms of the treaty with Egypt. Fiercely resisting, the Egyptians sent to Nur al-Din for help. A Syrian army promptly arrived, and the depleted Frankish forces withdrew without a fight. The Frankish gamble had failed, and its consequences for the Christians were disastrous. The abortive campaign fanned conflicts in Jerusalem and exhausted the treasury. Moreover, by drawing the Syrians into Egypt, it was to give the Muslim front the solidarity that had thus far eluded it.

Only days after the Syrian army's arrival in Egypt, its leaders found themselves embroiled in Egypt's murky politics. Saladin arrested the vizier, an opponent of Nur al-Din. On the Fatimid caliph's orders, perhaps with some promptings from the Syrians, the vizier was strangled and replaced by Saladin's uncle—but the uncle, old and obese, died nine weeks later. Thirty-year-old Saladin succeeded him.

Saladin had placed himself in a deeply ambiguous position. On the one hand, he was a Sunni Muslim and the servant of the Syrian ruler Nur al-Din. Yet he had accepted the post of viceroy to the Fatimid caliph of Egypt, a foreign and heretical power. The Abbasid caliph in Baghdad made his disapproval known. Nur al-Din was justifiably suspicious and confiscated Saladin's lands in Syria. Saladin in turn appropriated Egyptian lands to finance his troops.

Over the next few years, Saladin tightened his hold on Egypt and exterminated the Sudanese guards who were loyal to the Fatimids. Once they were gone, Nur al-Din began pressing Saladin to suppress the Shiite caliphate. A devout Sunni himself, Saladin duly began instating Sunni officials into key posts. On the death of the Fatimid caliph in September 1171, Saladin had the name of the Abbasid caliph pronounced in the prayers in the mosques. Riots were feared, but the Egyptians accepted their transfer to Sunni Islam. Now, at last, Saladin's position was resolved: He governed Egypt as Nur al-Din's deputy, under the notional sovereignty of the Abbasid caliph. In 1174, he brought Yemen into the orbit of the Abbasid caliph as well, when he sent his brother on a successful expedition to conquer the wealthy trading region.

Egypt's capitulation to the Sunni caliph meant disquiet for Outremer, for the Christian lands might now be caught in a pincers movement between Egypt and Syria. King Amalric played for time and sought to arouse Nur al-Din's jealousy of his young viceroy. The king tried also for an alliance with the Assassins, who were alarmed by the fall of the Fatimids and even suggested—undoubtedly with no intention of following through—that they would consider converting to Christianity. But the Templars murdered the Assassin envoys, choosing to forfeit the alliance rather than lose their tribute. And the hope of a quarrel between the two great Muslim leaders vanished in 1174. In May of that year, Nur al-Din remarked to a companion in the orchards of Damascus, "Praise be to Him who alone knows whether we shall meet here in a month's time," and died of a heart attack within two weeks' time.

The heir to Nur al-Din's throne was a minor. Saladin spotted his chance, announced himself to be the child's rightful guardian and marched to Damascus, where the citizens received him enthusiastically. Saladin had little fear that the Franks would invade Egypt while he was away because King Amalric had just died of dysentery, leaving the crown to his son, Baldwin, who was only thirteen and already a leper, weakened and with a short time to live. Thus Saladin, after a few engagements with rival power seekers, made himself master of all Syria, except Aleppo, within a few months. In 1175, the Abbasid caliph set the seal on Saladin's conquests, confirming him as ruler of Egypt and Syria.

Saladin's chief ambition was to reunify Nur al-Din's kingdom, creating a coalition of Muslim states under his own control. He besieged Aleppo repeatedly, and at last, in 1183, the city surrendered. He fought many campaigns in Mosul in pursuit of that

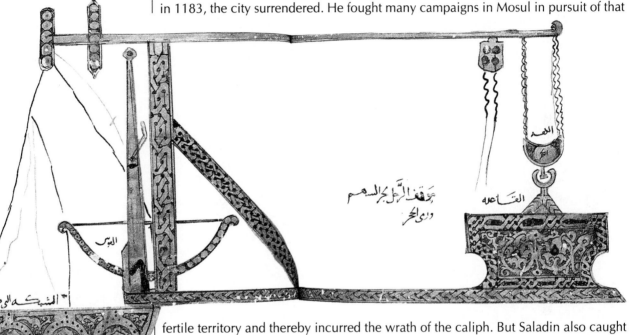

fertile territory and thereby incurred the wrath of the caliph. But Saladin also caught Nur al-Din's passion for holy war and the expulsion of the infidel. He skirmished with the Christians frequently in his first decade as ruler of Syria, but Baldwin the young leper king fought off all of the attacks with immense courage until his death in 1185, and Saladin was able to gain little.

Saladin's strategy was to use the wealth of Egypt to conquer Syria, the wealth of Syria to conquer Mesopotamia, and the wealth of Mesopotamia to conquer Palestine. After his death, his successors, not surprisingly, found an empty treasury. But while he lived, his scheme succeeded, for, like Nur al-Din, Saladin made religion his ally. The wealth of Egypt was used not only for hiring soldiers, but for building mosques and endowing colleges, so that Muslims everywhere were continually reminded of their duty to their religion; and the great princes of Islam, who had in earlier generations fought each other rather than the infidel, were now obliged to join the holy war if they wished to maintain their reputation. Such at least was the story told by Muslim chroniclers who favored Saladin; at the time, others murmured that the victorious campaigns against fellow Muslims argued powerfully for obedience.

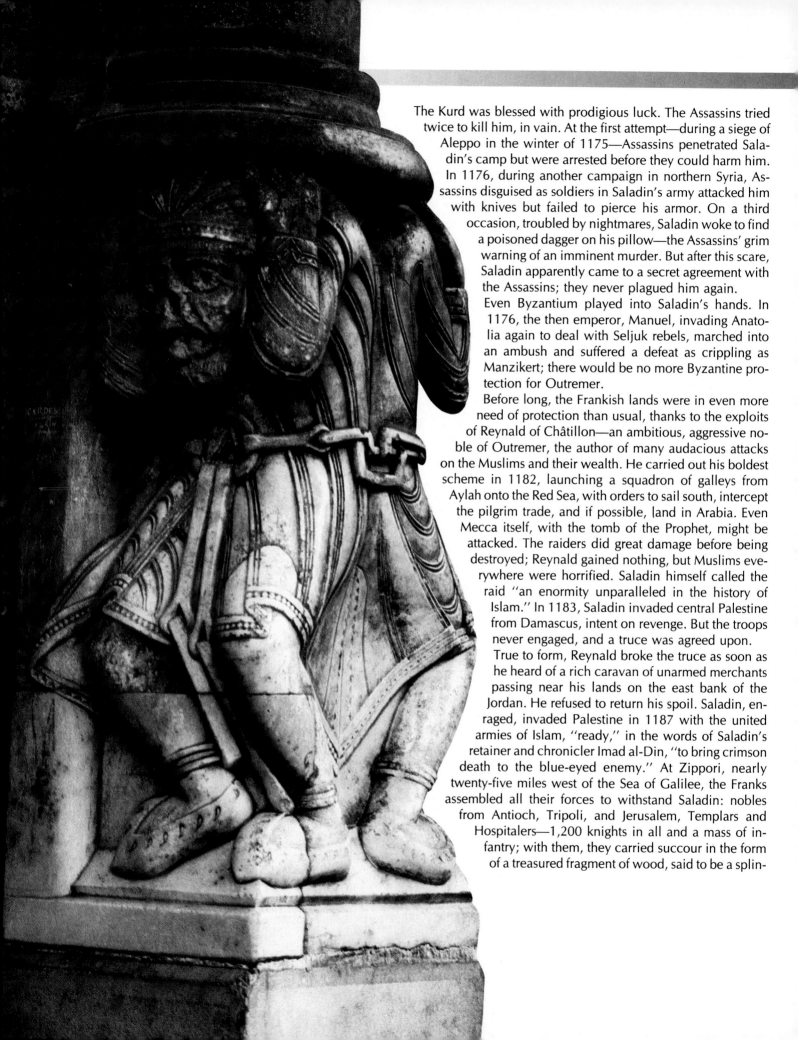

The Kurd was blessed with prodigious luck. The Assassins tried twice to kill him, in vain. At the first attempt—during a siege of Aleppo in the winter of 1175—Assassins penetrated Saladin's camp but were arrested before they could harm him. In 1176, during another campaign in northern Syria, Assassins disguised as soldiers in Saladin's army attacked him with knives but failed to pierce his armor. On a third occasion, troubled by nightmares, Saladin woke to find a poisoned dagger on his pillow—the Assassins' grim warning of an imminent murder. But after this scare, Saladin apparently came to a secret agreement with the Assassins; they never plagued him again.

Even Byzantium played into Saladin's hands. In 1176, the then emperor, Manuel, invading Anatolia again to deal with Seljuk rebels, marched into an ambush and suffered a defeat as crippling as Manzikert; there would be no more Byzantine protection for Outremer.

Before long, the Frankish lands were in even more need of protection than usual, thanks to the exploits of Reynald of Châtillon—an ambitious, aggressive noble of Outremer, the author of many audacious attacks on the Muslims and their wealth. He carried out his boldest scheme in 1182, launching a squadron of galleys from Aylah onto the Red Sea, with orders to sail south, intercept the pilgrim trade, and if possible, land in Arabia. Even Mecca itself, with the tomb of the Prophet, might be attacked. The raiders did great damage before being destroyed; Reynald gained nothing, but Muslims everywhere were horrified. Saladin himself called the raid "an enormity unparalleled in the history of Islam." In 1183, Saladin invaded central Palestine from Damascus, intent on revenge. But the troops never engaged, and a truce was agreed upon.

True to form, Reynald broke the truce as soon as he heard of a rich caravan of unarmed merchants passing near his lands on the east bank of the Jordan. He refused to return his spoil. Saladin, enraged, invaded Palestine in 1187 with the united armies of Islam, "ready," in the words of Saladin's retainer and chronicler Imad al-Din, "to bring crimson death to the blue-eyed enemy." At Zippori, nearly twenty-five miles west of the Sea of Galilee, the Franks assembled all their forces to withstand Saladin: nobles from Antioch, Tripoli, and Jerusalem, Templars and Hospitalers—1,200 knights in all and a mass of infantry; with them, they carried succour in the form of a treasured fragment of wood, said to be a splinter from the True Cross. In July of 1187, Saladin attacked Tiberias by the Sea of Galilee, where the wife of Raymond of Tripoli, one of Jerusalem's foremost nobles, defended the castle because Raymond was with the army at Zippori. To break the siege at Tiberias, the Christian army would have to pass over the waterless, sun-smitten hills of Galilee. With luck, they might achieve this in a long day's march.

Raymond implored them not to: Even if the siege at Tiberias succeeded, his castle could be rebuilt, his wife and children might be ransomed—whereas if the army destroyed itself in Tiberias's defense, the kingdom itself would be in jeopardy. Reynald and the Templars, however, argued for action. Guy of Lusignan, the newly crowned king of Jerusalem, had already been called a coward for standing on the defensive on another occasion, and he was a feudal lord who could not honorably abandon a vassal in danger, however vehemently the vassal protested. He ordered the army to march to Tiberias.

They never reached it. The sun beat down, Saladin's troops harassed the rearguard, and by evening, the army remained far from its goal. Even the Templars could march no farther. There was no water and no sleep in the night. Next morning, the Christian army was driven onto a rocky hill topped by two peaks called the Horns of Hattin. The Muslims set fire to the dry scrub on the hill and attacked from all sides. Raymond of Tripoli led a desperate charge that broke clear through Saladin's regiments and escaped. But the mass of the army staggered to defeat, exhausted inside their armor. The Muslims captured the True Cross. King Guy was one of the last to surrender. Then, in the words of an Arab witness: "The plain was covered with prisoners and corpses, disclosed by the dust as it settled and victory became clear. The dead were scattered over the mountains and valleys, lying immobile on their sides, lacerated and disjointed, with heads cracked open, throats split, spines shattered, bones broken, tunics torn off, faces lifeless, wounds gaping, skin flayed . . . like stones among stones, a lesson to the wise."

Saladin ordered that Guy of Lusignan and Reynald of Châtillon be brought to his tent. He asked Reynald to justify his breaches of faith. The reply showed Reynald at his most arrogant, equating his own position as a mere lord with that of a king. "But this is how kings have always behaved," he answered; "I have only followed the customary path." Saladin was incensed by Reynald's provocation. He offered King Guy a cup of iced water—and with it, by the rules of Eastern hospitality, Guy's life. Guy drank and passed the cup to Reynald. "It is not I who have given you drink," said Saladin, and struck Reynald dead.

After such a victory, there could be little resistance. King Guy was imprisoned. Raymond of Tripoli died—heartbroken, some said, with the shame of the defeat. The great castles of the frontier were stormed or starved out. On the coast, Jaffa, Acre, Ascalon, Beirut soon submitted; generally, Saladin offered very merciful terms. Jerusalem itself was besieged. The commander of the defense knighted all boys of noble family aged sixteen or over; they fought bravely but without hope. Saladin accepted a peaceful surrender. He destroyed the churches with their idolatrous carvings and paintings but spared the Holy Sepulcher. The great pulpit that Nur al-Din had prepared was brought from Damascus to the al-Aqsa Mosque.

Most of the Franks of Jerusalem bought their freedom and escaped, but some could not pay. The historian Imad al-Din exulted: "Women and children together came to 8,000 and were quickly divided up among us, bringing a smile to Muslim faces at their lamentations. How many well-guarded women were profaned, and precious

The likenesses of two chained Moorish prisoners decorate the base of a column in the twelfth-century Old Cathedral at Oloron-Sainte-Marie, in southern France. During centuries of warfare between Christendom and Islam, many thousands of people—civilians as well as soldiers—were captured by the enemy. Normally, they were enslaved, but by the twelfth-century, systems to ransom or exchange captives had been developed. The Byzantine Empire and its Muslim foes traditionally treated one another's prisoners well, and the Crusaders soon adopted some of their attitudes. In Spain, an order of friars was established to negotiate the ransoming of Christians captured by the Moors, while Muslims arranged the release of their coreligionists through the mosques that existed on both sides of the frontier.

ones used for hard work, and pretty things put to the test, and virgins dishonored, and proud women deflowered, and lovely women's red lips kissed, and happy ones made to weep, when Jerusalem was purified of the filth of the hellish Franks." The native Christians made their peace with the conqueror, as they were accustomed to doing, and the towns and villages paid taxes to their new Muslim lords.

But some places remained unpurified. One city of the kingdom of Jerusalem was saved by Conrad of Montferrat, an Italian noble, who chanced to sail into the port of Acre with a company of knights just after the Muslims had taken possession. He had heard nothing of the catastrophe but felt something was wrong, sailed out again, and made for the almost impregnable city of Tyre, which he entered shortly before Saladin arrived. The siege was short and bitter; even when Saladin threatened to execute Conrad's father, who was his captive from Hattin, Conrad refused to surrender. At the start of 1188, Saladin turned away from unconquered Tyre. He may have thought that it could be taken later, along with the states of Tripoli and Antioch; he must have known that refugees from the wreck of the kingdom of Jerusalem would assemble there. It is doubtful if Saladin quite realized what would happen when Europe heard of the fall of Jerusalem.

"Who will give water to my head and a fountain of tears to my eyes that I may weep day and night for the slaughter of my people," cried the pope, Gregory VIII. He summoned the Third Crusade with a great bull that linked the disaster in Palestine to the sins of Christians everywhere and promised remission of sins to all who accepted the call to crusade in a repentant frame of mind. The galleys of Norman Sicily brought a trickle of reinforcements to Outremer in 1188; the next year saw a flood from the north, the start of the Third Crusade. Ships sailed from Brittany, France, Flanders, England, Germany, Denmark; not a coordinated fleet, but small squadrons of local volunteers, knights and barons, and many professional archers and spearmen. They arrived in Palestine to find a new crisis.

King Guy had been released, possibly because Saladin wished the Franks to have a brave and incompetent commander. In August 1189, Guy acted with lunatic courage. He found a few knights to follow him and marched south from Tripoli to reconquer his kingdom, starting with the great port of Acre. The Muslim garrison there was strong, and Saladin could eventually assemble a far larger army to relieve the city, but Guy's move was so unexpected that Saladin's response was delayed. Before the army of relief was ready, the first ships from Europe were disembarking on the beaches outside Acre. In the resulting battles, the Turks discovered that the Christian infantry was dangerous to approach and quite unbreakable. When winter came, the Christians were firmly dug into entrenched camps around Acre, besieging the city and themselves besieged.

From Europe came news that reinforcements were imminent. Frederick Barbarossa, the sixty-seven-year-old emperor of Germany, was marching eastward; Philip and Richard, the quarrelsome kings of France and England respectively, had ceased their old conflict and would come by sea with immense forces. Richard's approach, especially, must have raised the spirits of the besiegers. An immensely strong man, he was known for leading his knights into battle personally, wreaking havoc with a great sword or battle-ax.

For once, the Christian armies would not be short of money. Crusading had always been expensive, but the idealism of the First Crusade had transcended the practical

In this French manuscript of the early thirteenth century, soldiers of the First Crusade are shown besieging the Seljuk Turks of Nicaea in 1097. An attempt by the Seljuk sultan to relieve the city had been beaten back after a fierce battle; to demoralize the defenders further, the Christians lobbed the heads of slain Turkish soldiers over the city walls. Such unsavory tactics were not uncommon. Descriptions of other sieges also mention carrion, offal, and rubbish being thrown into an enemy stronghold to spread disease.

problems. By the last decade of the century, many European families had provided three or four generations of Crusaders, and their coffers had emptied. Popes and monarchs, recognizing the strains, had begun to cast around for means of subsidizing Crusaders. Their schemes came to fruition in time for the Third Crusade. Both Richard and Philip levied colossal taxes to pay for the Crusade. The "Saladin tithe," 10 percent of all movable property from those not going on crusade, was collected in both countries and supplemented with other levies.

Barbarossa had to fight his way across Byzantine territory, for the Byzantines, thinking Saladin invincible, had allied themselves with the Muslims. Barbarossa crossed Anatolia, slaughtering Seljuks by the thousands, and came safely into Christian lands again. Then, in June 1190, disaster struck: In his exuberance, he tried to swim a wide river and drowned, perhaps because of a heart attack. Leaderless, the Germans who had come through so much fell apart; some staggered into Antioch "looking like disinterred corpses," noted a gratified Arab chronicler. For real help, the Crusade would have to depend on France and England. But not until July 1190 were Richard and Philip ready to march. Meanwhile, the double siege went on—the Christian army around Acre and the Muslim army surrounding the Christians.

Its duration was unprecedented: 683 days from start to finish, with the armies always in contact. Outremer was fighting for its life, using every means at its disposal. Muslim observers noted with astonishment Frankish women who fought on horseback in armor and a lady in a green cloak whose archery was much feared by the defenders of the city.

In the summer of 1191, the kings landed. Richard had stopped briefly to take Cyprus from its recently established Greek ruler, a rebel against Byzantium. He improved his finances by taxing the Cypriots at 50 percent and then selling the island to the Templars. Despite a squabble over who should become king of a restored Jerusalem, Christian unity lasted long enough to deliver a series of crushing assaults on the city of Acre, which surrendered in July; Saladin's army withdrew.

As soon as possible, Philip returned to France, whence he profitably attacked Richard's territories. Richard, left in sole command, marched from Acre to Jaffa, on the best line of approach to Jerusalem. Turkish cavalry skirmished all the way, and at Arsuf, Saladin's great host waited in ambush. But Richard the Lion-Hearted was not only the strongest champion in his army, he was also a careful general who deployed his troops with great skill. The lines of spears protected the crossbowmen, who outranged the Turkish archers. When the ambush was sprung, and all the Muslim host committed to battle, the rearguard charged too soon—but Richard took command of it and saved the day. After Arsuf, no Muslim army dared to face Richard again.

Throughout the campaign, Saladin employed the most exquisite manners against his royal enemy. When Richard was unhorsed at Jaffa, Saladin sent a fresh mount with his compliments. When Richard later fell ill, Saladin sent snow to cool his brow. Such courtesies came naturally to Saladin, who, for all his ruthless opportunism, could also display great kindness. While Muslims remembered him for his utter faith in Islam, it was his chivalry that made him a legend among his Christian enemies.

Courtesy did not, however, extend to handing over Jerusalem. Saladin withdrew into the hills of Judea, destroying the country, blocking the springs, making an artificial wilderness. The devoted pilgrims of the First Crusade might have pressed forward regardless; Richard understood logistics and knew that Jerusalem could not be held by the Christians even if it were retaken. Also, he admired the opposition and knew the cost of the war. "You have no more right to send Muslims to their deaths," he wrote to Saladin, "than I have the right to send Christians to theirs."

Several roads might lead out of the impasse. Richard even made the astonishing suggestion that his sister should marry Saladin's brother, who would rule all Palestine, Christian and Muslim alike. Eventually, in the autumn of 1192, a treaty was agreed. The Franks were left in

Founded to protect pilgrims, the Knights Templars adopted the motif of two knights riding one horse as a symbol of their vow of poverty. It appears on twelfth-century seals and in an illustration (right) to the Chronica Majora of English historian Matthew Paris. The knights' shields bear a black-and-white design, which with the red cross on a white ground distinguished the Templars. These warrior-monks did not share a horse, but the tactic of having a cavalryman carry a foot soldier on his mount's crupper to increase an army's mobility was common among their Muslim adversaries.

peace in their coastal cities, the True Cross was restored to them, and Christian pilgrims were allowed free passage to Jerusalem.

Saladin died of a fever five months after the truce. He would be remembered by his opponents as a gallant, pious, and generous soldier, and his story and personality became the stuff of plays and minstrels' songs. A century after Saladin's death, the Italian poet Dante Alighieri introduced Saladin into his poem *The Divine Comedy*, an imaginary journey through the seven circles of Hell, and thence up the mountain of Purgatory to Heaven. Dante located Saladin in Hell; but not, as might be expected for the Christians' worst enemy, in the blazing depths of the Inferno. Instead, the supremely chivalrous Muslim, unable as a non-Christian to enter Purgatory or Heaven, found eternal rest in the peace of the First Circle of Hell, a place otherwise reserved for good men who had had the misfortune to have lived before Christ's birth.

For the Christians, the treaty of 1192 was far more than had seemed possible after Hattin, but it was not what they had hoped for. People of belief had set out to win redemption of their souls by suffering for the city where Christ had suffered for them, not for a compromise peace.

In 1197, Barbarossa's son, the emperor Henry VI, prepared an epilogue to the Third Crusade; learning at last from experience, the great German force intended to journey by sea. But Henry died suddenly. Leaderless again, the Germans were only able to achieve the recapture of Beirut.

In 1198, a Fourth Crusade was preached throughout Europe, summoning Christian knights to fight again in Palestine. Wishing to avoid the depredations of the Turks in Anatolia, the knights planned to travel by sea to Egypt. They approached the Venetians for transport, rashly overestimating the number of Crusaders who would sail. The Venetians duly built a great fleet, the cost of which was to be shared among the Crusaders who traveled on it. When only one-third of the estimated number of Crusaders joined the camp on the Venetian Lido in 1202, the Venetians held out for the original sum promised. They were prepared to postpone the payment until it could be met out of plunder—but on one outrageous condition. The Christian city of Zara on the Dalmatian coast had once been under Venetian dominance but had transferred its allegiance to Hungary. The Venetians required the Crusaders to help them recover the disloyal town. Despite the indignation of many Crusaders, they and the Venetians duly took Zara in 1202. Pope Innocent III promptly excommunicated all concerned, but when the circumstances were explained to him, he lifted the sentence from the Crusaders, leaving it upon the Venetians alone.

Circumstances now conspired to divert the Crusade away from its avowed destination, the Holy Land, and toward Byzantium. The Venetians had built up a good commercial relationship with Egypt and had no wish to be party to an attack; they also harbored a hearty dislike of the Byzantines, who had hin-

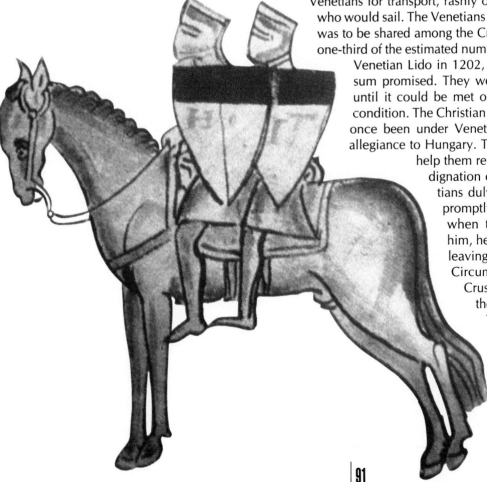

This twelfth-century statue gives a touching glimpse of the personal stories behind the crusading epic. It shows a French lady, Anne of Lorraine, welcoming her husband, Hugh, count of Vaudemont, back from a Crusade after an absence of sixteen years. Most of his family gave him up for dead, but Anne refused to abandon hope. When he finally returned, she commemorated the happy event by commissioning this statue in the Franciscan church at Nancy.

dered, and even murdered, Venetian traders. The leader of the Crusade, Boniface of Montferrat, was friendly with the German son-in-law of an incompetent Byzantine emperor who had been deposed six years earlier.

Rumors reached Innocent that Boniface and the Venetians were hatching a plan to support Alexius, the son of the deposed Byzantine emperor, in a bid for his father's throne. In return for armed support, Alexius promised the Crusaders the funds they badly needed to pay the Venetians. Besides wanting their payment, the Venetians almost certainly expected much commercial advantage to accrue from Alexius's gratitude. Innocent forbade an attack on Constantinople, but his letter arrived after the fleets had set sail from Zara. Had the Crusaders received his message, many might have chosen to pay no attention: They had not forgotten the enmity with which the Byzantines had greeted Barbarossa.

In 1203, the French and Venetians reached Constantinople and installed their protégé Alexius as emperor. At Alexius's request, they settled outside the walls of Constantinople for the winter, to ensure his safety. Their presence was of no avail. Alexius was murdered by a Byzantine patriot who grabbed power himself. The Crusaders found themselves trapped: The Venetians were still demanding their payment, and the only source of funds imaginable was the glittering city of Constantinople, protected by massive walls, which for eight centuries had rebuffed attacks from Bulgars, Russians, and Arabs. The Crusaders took the one route that seemed open to them and stormed the city on April 12, 1204. Constantinople's defenses were less strong by sea than by land, and the city that had withstood so many mighty armies fell to the Christian fleet with ease.

The Crusaders and Venetians looted and burned for three days. Constantine had enriched his capital with the masterpieces of the ancient world: statues of Hercules and Juno, Pallas Athena and Helen of Troy; the Crusaders smashed the marbles and melted down the bronzes to make coins. Nine centuries of piety had filled the churches and cathedrals with jewels and precious metals; the Crusaders led pack-mules to the altars to be loaded with the plunder. The Venetians selected some choice items to adorn their city, including four superb gilded bronze horses made around the third century BC. These steeds, which had once perhaps drawn a pagan sun chariot, were set in place above the portal of Saint Mark's Basilica in Venice.

Then, when the sack was over, the Crusaders erected their own empire in the ruins of Byzantium: an empire Catholic in religion, French in speech, and Italian in its commercial policies. The personal domain of the emperor, Baldwin of Flanders, was to be Thrace and some Aegean islands. Boniface of Montferrat, the leader of the Crusade, received much of mainland Greece, which he held as Baldwin's vassal; the Venetians received the crucial trading posts they desired on the western shores of Greece and certain strategic islands. Innocent III, though appalled by the willfulness of the Fourth Crusade, was nonetheless pleased to establish his spiritual authority over Constantinople. At last, the dream of uniting Eastern and Western Christendom seemed to be very close.

But the Catholic empire of Byzantium proved fragile. The Byzantines regained Constantinople and deposed the Frankish emperors after fifty-seven years, although Frankish lords continued to rule Greece until the fifteenth century. Far from vanishing, the schism between Eastern and Western Christendom was to grow and fester. The Orthodox church could never forgive the attack on its capital and holiest places.

Having been so plundered and dismembered, Byzantium would never regain its former might. For centuries, the empire had served as Christian Europe's bulwark against the Muslims. Now Byzantium's years in that role were numbered. In two centuries, Constantinople would fall to a new Turkish dynasty. Unwittingly, the Crusaders sworn to oppose the Muslims were, by the ravages they wrought on Byzantium, opening the door for Turkish incursions into the Balkans.

From the point of view of western Europe, however, the Fourth Crusade brought many benefits. Italian merchants now had an opportunity to trade directly with the spice and silk routes by way of the Black Sea. By the mid-thirteenth century, the Black Sea ports were more crucial for trade than those of Syria. Even the rapid collapse of the Latin empire left the Italian merchants in place and trading profitably. Venice benefited hugely from its string of trading cities and waxed rich and powerful. The flood of exquisite booty and refugee artisans from Byzantium introduced new levels of sophistication in the arts of the West.

Meanwhile, valiant knights continued to swear their Crusade vows and make the arduous journey east to join battle with the Muslims; indeed, greater numbers would go crusading to Jerusalem in the thirteenth century than in the twelfth. But they would never win victories like those of the First Crusade. Disunity among the Crusaders would continue to dog their attempts, while the growing revenues from international trade would aid the defenders.

The remnant of the kingdom of Jerusalem was to survive a century more; Barbarossa's grandson Frederick II would even regain Jerusalem for a while, by diplomacy rather than force, profiting from the discord among Saladin's successors. The descendants of Guy of Lusignan would rule Cyprus until 1489, and the Venetians would hold the island for a further century. But the attempt to establish a powerful Catholic state in the Levant had failed.

In the East, all the suffering and zealous courage had in the end strengthened Islam. While, to the Syrian leaders, events in Mesopotamia and Egypt signified more than the Christian threat, the calls of jihad had rallied the common people. Ultimately, the Christian presence helped to reunify an area that had been fragmented. By the end of the thirteenth century, the lands under Saladin's fragile dominion would be under the centralized control of the Mamluk sultanate of Egypt. Christian Europe was flexing its muscles, but the Muslim world was discovering new vigor of its own. Indeed, the century of the Crusades saw Islam marching victoriously eastward.

ISLAM COMES TO INDIA

3 "Allah Akbar!" God is most great! "La ilaha Allah; Muhammad rasul Allah!" There is no God but Allah, and Muhammad is His Prophet! From the newly completed Quwat al-Islam Mosque—the name means "Power of Islam"—the cryer's voice rang out over the city of Delhi, calling the faithful to the first prayers of the day. It would be a while before the sun climbed high enough to reveal the rubbled remains of the twenty-seven neighboring Hindu temples that had gone into the making of the mosque or to bring heat to the devout worshipers who knelt facing west within it. Yet, had any of those worshipers looked up to their right, they might have been able to make out in the shadows the flowing Arabic script on the inner lintel of the northern gateway: "In the year 592, this building was erected by the high order of the exalted Sultan Muizz al-Dunya w'al-Din Muhammad ibn Sam, the helper of the prince of the faithful." According to the lunar Islamic calendar, it was 592 years after the prophet Muhammad's flight to Medina; it was also 1195 years after the birth of Christ and the third year of Muslim dominion in Delhi.

The Quwat al-Islam Mosque itself was a prime symbol of that dominion—built by forced Hindu labor, on the site of a Hindu shrine, from the materials of wrecked Hindu temples. And Islamic rule did not stop at Delhi. In the name of the exalted sultan of the inscription, a general from Afghanistan known more briefly as Muizz al-Din Muhammad of Ghur, Muslim generals campaigned throughout northern India. In 1206, just fourteen years after Delhi had fallen, the city would become the capital of an Islamic sultanate ruled by Turks—former slaves of the Afghan invaders—which covered the whole of northern India, from Sind in the west to Bengal in the east. In little more than a century, the Delhi sultanate would briefly extend its rule over the entire subcontinent.

India was no stranger to foreign conquerors. Thanks to well-watered soils and a populace skilled in crafts, it was far wealthier than the more desolate lands to the north. Over the past millennium and a half, Greeks, Scythians from the shores of the Black Sea, and Huns from the steppes of Russia had in turn been drawn to India by its legendary riches. But none had radically altered Indian life. They had imposed their authority for only a little while before their identity was swallowed up by that of their Hindu subjects.

Islam was something new in India; its ways and beliefs would never be submerged. The Muslims brought with them theologians who preached a gospel of monotheism radically different from Hindu beliefs, which espoused a multitude of gods. The abutment of these two cultures would produce a flowering of art, architecture, commerce, and crafts. At the same time, it would open the door to religious conflict and division. With the advent of Islam, the fabric of India changed forever.

When Muslim rule first reached India, Hinduism defined the pattern of the

Carved in the Islamic style by unwilling Hindu masons, stone stalactites and verses from the Koran ornament a section of the Qutb Minar, a 226-foot-high tower built as part of the Quwat al-Islam—Power of Islam—Mosque in Delhi. Elsewhere on the fabric of the mosque, inscriptions lavish praise on its founder, the sultan Muizz al-Din Muhammad of Ghur in Afghanistan, "the ruler of land and sea, guardian of the kingdoms of the world," whose victory over a Hindu army in 1192 laid India open to Muslim conquest.

Toward the end of the twelfth century, India's vast wealth lured conquerors from the Muslim world. Descending from his kingdom of Ghur in Afghanistan, Sultan Muizz al-Din Muhammad swept through the Punjab and inflicted a series of blows upon the indigenous rulers of northern India that culminated in an overwhelming victory at the second battle of Tarai in 1192. In the ensuing decades, the Islamic invaders established an independent sultanate centered in Delhi that imposed its authority on most of northern India. The overlords of the new state were Turkish by ancestry, descendants of the first viceroy, Qutb al-Din, and his son-in-law Iltutmish, who had begun their careers as slaves in the service of the Ghurid court. Their rule was to found an uneasy partnership of Hindu and Muslim cultures.

country's fabric. True, the Buddhist religion, born on the subcontinent in the fifth century BC, still was a presence. But it was a small and introverted one that thrived mainly in the east, with its center at the great monastery of Nalanda, near the Ganges River in present-day Bihar. The great majority of the land's millions of inhabitants were Hindus. An ancient religion—already at least 2,000 years old when the Muslim faith came into being—Hinduism revolved around a vast pantheon of deities and a caste system that theoretically gave each member of society an immutable station in life, one that could be changed only through death and reincarnation. From the highest Brahmans, or priests, through the many warrior and peasant castes, to the lowest street-sweeping untouchables, all castes were bound by a comprehensive set of laws that regulated every aspect of existence. At their strictest, these laws could make life extremely complicated: Brahmans, for example, would take great care over their laundry lest, while drying, the clothes were defiled by the shadow of an untouchable. Tradition decreed that only by following every minute observance laid down for their present caste could Hindus hope to be reincarnated into a higher one in their next existence.

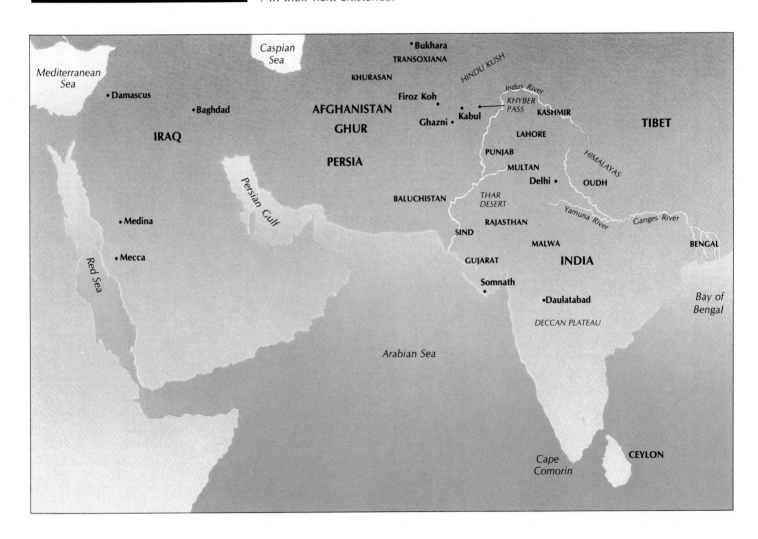

In practice, Hinduism's caste system was only really rigid at the highest and lowest levels of society; in the middle of the spectrum, there was more flexibility. Peasants or herdsmen of quite low status could improve their lot by performing noble deeds—whether building a temple or vanquishing an enemy in war. The order of warrior caste—the kshatriya—included many families of humble origins, who were perpetually skirmishing for a higher place in the pecking order.

This intercaste jostling was reflected on a larger scale by the country itself, in which power relations rarely remained constant for long. For several centuries prior to the creation of the Delhi sultanate, the subcontinent had been dominated by four dynasties. In the steamy south, the Cholas were mighty. In the arid Deccan Plateau of central India, the Rastrakuthras held sway. To the east in lush Bengal, the Palas ruled. The Pratiharas dominated the fertile plain of the upper Ganges and the desert wastes and scrubby forests that stretched westward almost as far as the Indus in present-day Pakistan. But each major dynasty ruled over a jumble of vassal states and principalities whose constant revolts and changing allegiances made boundaries fluid or entirely meaningless.

Meanwhile, to the west, Islamic dynasties waxed and waned. In Islam's early days, the Muslim world had been a single empire ruled first from Damascus by Arabs and later from Baghdad by Persians. But the rift between Sunni orthodoxy and Shiite heterodoxy, present from the earliest years, sundered Muslim unity by the ninth century. As the Baghdad caliphate of the Sunni Abbasid dynasty weakened, different parts of the empire fell into new hands. In Persia, provincial families—some Sunni, some Shiite—took over the reins of authority. Most came to depend heavily on Turkish warrior-slaves purchased as children from nomadic families roaming the steppes of central Asia. Trained in Islam and the military arts, the Turkish slaves in Persian employ were deployed as a faction-free force that could be depended upon to remain loyal to their masters. Those Turks who proved worthy rose to dizzying heights and sometimes intermarried with their overlords. It was through these mobile frontier societies that Persian culture, Turkish warfare, and the Arabic holy books spread into the heart of India in the twelfth century.

But by then Muslims had already made incursions into India for trade and conquest. Arab traders had settled unobtrusively on the south and west coasts of India; Arab soldiers had conquered Sind and Multan, in present-day Pakistan, as early as the eighth century. But there the Arab invaders stopped. Their forces were too sparse to permit further penetration into the heart of the subcontinent and, facing them across the Thar Desert, lurked the mighty Pratiharas and Rastrakuthras.

For three centuries, the Arabs maintained Islamic rule in Sind and Multan. At first, the two regions were governed as administrative provinces of the Islamic empire ruled from Damascus; later, with the weakening of the universal Islamic empire, independent Arab princes founded their own dynasties. Following their usual policy, the Arabs aimed for peaceful coexistence with their conquered subjects. Conversion was certainly encouraged, but in general, the Hindus were allowed to worship as they pleased in their own temples. Indeed, the rulers of Multan actively preserved the temple of the Hindu sun god in the city of Multan as a hostage against possible attack from the Pratiharas. Islam had come to the subcontinent the Arabs called al-Hind, but only, the Hindus liked to think, as a fly on the rump of an elephant, which could be whisked aside at any moment.

A sharper goad was needed to pierce the elephant's hide, and it was applied in the

Painted in metallic pigments on a glazed ceramic dish, this rider wielding a polo mallet symbolizes the horse-borne culture of the Muslim Ghaznavid people who raided India during the eleventh century. By origin, they were central Asian Turks, employed as slave-soldiers by the Persian Samanid dynasty, but in the late tenth century, they gained control of northern Iran—the provenance of this twelfth-century lusterware item—and of Afghanistan, from where they launched their Indian campaigns. Superb horsemen and archers, they fought in the highly mobile cavalry tradition developed by the tribal nomads of their central Asian homeland and plundered almost at will.

eleven century—not from the west but from the north. One of the Persian families that had risen to prominence with the breakup of the Islamic empire was the Samanid dynasty, which from its capital of Bukhara in central Asia controlled the surrounding land of Transoxiana, together with western Afghanistan and Khurasan in northern Iran. The Samanids employed as warrior-slaves a Turkic tribe called the Ghaznavids. Rising to power through merit, Turkish governors came to rule all the outlying provinces of the Samanid empire.

Trust in talented subordinates brought its risks; eventually, the very ability of their slave soldiers proved to be the undoing of the Samanids. Beyond the direct control of Bukhara, the provincial governors soon began to assert their independence, and nowhere did they do so more vigorously than in Afghanistan, a region already settled by migrating Turks, where Samanid control was tenuous at the best of times. Here, around 962, the Turkish general Alptigin rebelled and set himself up as an independent sovereign, with his capital at Ghazni, a small mountain town about 125 miles south of Kabul. The former slaves became the owners of slaves themselves. Alptigin and his successors rapidly built up a formidable slave army, and by 998, Alptigin's twenty-seven-year-old grandson, Mahmud, controlled Khurasan as well as all northern and eastern Afghanistan. A highly competent soldier, Mahmud of Ghazni required only a year to conquer the rest of Afghanistan. In the year 1000, he turned his attentions to the south.

"The whole country of India is full of gold and jewels, and of the plants which grow there are those fit for making apparel, and aromatic plants and the sugar-cane, and the whole aspect of the country is pleasant and delightful. Now since the inhabitants are chiefly infidels and idolators, by the order of God and his Prophet it is right for us to conquer them." So, according to his chroniclers, did Mahmud decide the fate of northern India. And between 1001 and his death in 1030, he turned his words into lethal action, making more than seventeen raids into the unsuspecting country. By this period, the mighty dynasties that had checked the Arabs earlier had all but disappeared, their strength dissipated by constant internecine warfare. In their diminished state, they were no match for the vigorous Turkish armies. The people of the high valleys around the Hindu Kush were the first to feel the brunt of Mahmud's depredations. Though fiercely resisting, the valley inhabitants were defeated. In the years that followed, their experiences were shared by almost all of northwest India—including Multan, which though Muslim, had recently been won over from the Sunni Islamic tradition to the Shiite persuasion. Mahmud's goal was booty, not empire, but many lands he raided fell into his hands after being battered by repeated onslaughts. By 1030, the boundary of the Ghaznavid empire reached the Arabian Sea in the south and, in the east, passed within less than sixty-five miles of Delhi.

The inscribed decoration on this cast-bronze candlestick base illustrates the skilled artisanship of the Ghaznavid court in Afghanistan during the eleventh and early twelfth centuries. In contrast to his harsh treatment of northern India's culture—where his destruction and looting of Hindu temples earned him the nickname "Idol Breaker"—the sultan Mahmud, who reigned from 997 to 1030, made his capital of Ghazni a renowned center of Islamic metalwork, ceramics, architecture, and literature.

The most ambitious of Mahmud's many campaigns was an expedition to the temple of Somnath, located on the shores of Gujarat. Dedicated to the god Shiva, the temple was one of the most revered Hindu shrines and certainly the wealthiest; its endowments included the revenue from 10,000 villages. Wrought silver covered the temple's fifty-six pillars; the chandeliers were of gold. One thousand Brahmans attended Shiva in this holy place, while 300 barbers were maintained to trim the locks of visiting pilgrims, and 350 dancing girls performed continually before the lingam— a huge phallus-shaped idol whose jewel-encrusted surface was washed daily with water brought from the sacred Ganges River, more than 600 miles distant. The deity Shiva, claimed the incumbent Brahmans, was the most powerful of all gods, and it was only his displeasure with other deities that had permitted Mahmud of Ghazni to sack their shrines.

It was a taunt Mahmud could not resist; gathering his army, supplemented by 30,000 avaricious volunteers from central Asia, he set out from Ghazni on October 17, 1024. With the aid of 30,000 camels, he crossed the Thar Desert to arrive at the gates of Somnath the following January. The temple complex was situated in a fort belonging to a local ruler, and the fort's garrison, aided by Brahmans and worshipers, mounted a defense. The fighting raged for three days, the Hindu defenders rushing inside the temple by shifts to receive the blessing of Shiva before returning to perish in the fray. When the battle was over, almost the entire defense force of 50,000 lay dead, and Mahmud stood victorious before the shattered idol.

Mahmud's booty from this single foray amounted to 20 million dinars (almost 3,000 pounds of gold), besides huge quantities of costly hangings, works of art, and precious stones. Of the idol itself, two pieces were incorporated in the steps of a mosque and the rest sent to Mecca, to be trodden underfoot as part of the pavement. It was just one of many such incidents that earned Mahmud the name "Idol Breaker" and according to one chronicler, "so much booty, prisoners, and wealth that the fingers of those who counted them would have been tired."

Mahmud owed his success in part to excellent planning. Always departing around December, in the dry season, he timed his campaigns to coincide with the Indian spring harvest so that there was plenty of food for his soldiers. Having achieved his goals, he would then toil back to Ghazni, his train loaded with booty, before his retreat was cut off by the rivers swollen with the monsoons of June.

But above all, he achieved his conquests through the mobility and professionalism of his army. He maintained a standing peacetime force of about 100,000 men, mostly Turkish slaves, whom he trained and equipped superbly. Crack units included the Dailami, fierce mountain men from around the Caspian Sea, famed for the lethal use to which they put their short, two-pronged spears, and Arab cavalry, known as "daredevil horsemen" after the bravery with which they fought on their tough desert steeds. And in wartime, squadrons such as these were augmented by booty-hunting volunteers from Afghanistan, Persia, even India, whose numbers swelled in direct proportion to Mahmud's fame.

The Indian opposition was virtually identical to that encountered by the armies of the Greek emperor Alexander the Great when he had invaded some fourteen centuries before. The best Indian soldiers came from the kshatriya order of warriors, but the bulk of the army consisted of ill-trained conscripts, snatched from the fields and thrust into military service. Furthermore, since the Indians had no talent for horse breeding and imported mounts were expensive, cavalry formed only a small part of any battle line. Instead, the Indians put their trust in elephants—monolithic and impressive mounts from which a general could get a good view, but easily frightened, and in flight capable of causing more damage to friend than to foe.

The military tactics of the subcontinent are faithfully represented in the game of chess, a seventh-century Indian invention. The king in the original form of the game is mounted on an elephant, but his movements are restricted to maintain his safety: If he is taken, the battle is lost. The infantry to the fore (the pawns) are relatively slow and ill-equipped, their contribution being based on their numbers and nuisance value. The true dynamics of the battle lie with the general (equivalent to the queen in the modern game), his runners (the bishops), and a few cavalry; meanwhile, the flanks are protected by elephants (the castles), which can be moved to the front as the battle progresses.

The Ghaznavids also had elephants, which were admired at a military review by the eleventh-century poet Farrukhi, "One may ask, 'What are those 1,700-odd mountains?' I reply, 'They are the 1,700-odd elephants of the sultan.' " But these were used more for ceremony than warfare. Instead, the Ghaznavids preferred to use their cavalry—harrying, harassing, and tiring the enemy, their mounted bowmen sending showers of arrows into the Indians, before wheeling off, often in feigned retreat. Only when the adversary was disorganized and damaged beyond repair would a decisive, frontal charge be made. For the Indians, the onslaught of the Turks was an unequal fight in which they could only offer numbers and bravery.

As Mahmud drained the Indian countryside of its wealth, Ghazni grew and prospered on the spoils. Markets, bridges, and dams were built, and at the center of the town, Mahmud ordered an exquisitely designed and richly ornamented mosque to be constructed out of local marble and granite. Nor did the sultan stint his own comfort. He left as his legacy a magnificent palace and court whose splendor was a far cry from the steppe tents of his forefathers. The chroniclers spoke of it as incomparable; among them, one Bayhaqi was to report of a palace celebration some years after Mahmud's death, "Everyone on that day who saw that adornment never saw anything

after which could compare with it. I was one of them at the time, and I have never known anything like it." Mahmud had turned Ghazni from a collection of mud-brick dwellings into a glittering showcase of Persian culture.

To complete his transformation from rugged soldier into paragon of civilization, Mahmud became a fervent patron of learning and the arts in the grand Persian style. Adjoining his mosque was a university whose library was enriched by scholarly works looted in his campaigns. His court drew leading literary figures from all over the Muslim world, among them the Persian poet Firdausi and the historian, mathematician, and astrologer al-Biruni, whose home was Khurasan. Of the 400 bards who constantly attended the sultan's court, many were no doubt attracted by his generosity—he is reported to have spent 400,000 dinars on them annually—but others may have come less willingly. A chronicler of the time reported that "whenever Mahmud came across a man or woman who was an expert in any skill, he deported them to Ghazni." And the veiled menace of the Idol Breaker could be seen in a letter to a neighboring ruler. "I have heard that there are at your court several men of learning, each peerless in his science. You must send them to our court so that they may have the honor of being presented there and that we may derive prestige from their knowledge and capabilities."

Amid this splendor Mahmud died, probably of tuberculosis, on April 30, 1030. Before him as he lay on his deathbed were spread the contents of the royal treasury—close to seventy pounds of gems laid in dazzling rows, a mere fraction of the wealth he had accumulated from an empire that stretched almost 2,000 miles from east to west and more than 1,200 miles from north to south.

The central regions of this empire were directly under Mahmud's control, but India, on the periphery, could not have been held thus without impossibly large garrisons. Apart from one brief and unsuccessful attempt at imposing his own civil administration on the Punjab, Mahmud left the Indian princes in place, merely specifying in the peace treaties he imposed on them that they should pay him tribute and occasionally furnish soldiers for his army. Since the tribute was often not forthcoming until

Painted on the inside of a wooden manuscript cover, a Buddha-to-be is shown as a prince who gave away all his possessions, including his house, his kingdom (symbolized by an elephant), and eventually his wife and children. This narrative illustration to an ancient folk tale that celebrates the Buddhist ideal of charity and worldly renunciation was made in Nepal around 1100. In India, the advent of Islamic rule sent Buddhism into rapid decline in its former strongholds of Bengal and Bihar; monasteries were abandoned and sacred texts destroyed. But the religion continued to exist under the benevolent neglect of the kings of the valley of Nepal.

exacted by force, it was hard to distinguish from the booty that Mahmud collected on every Indian campaign.

In the words of al-Biruni, who traveled to India in Mahmud's train, "Mahmud utterly ruined the prosperity of the country and performed those wonderful exploits by which the Hindus became like atoms of dust scattered in all directions. Their scattered remains cherish, of course, the most inveterate aversion toward all Muslims." And certainly the unfortunate Hindus, on whom Mahmud showered his unwelcome attentions, had good reason to hate him: Not only did he impoverish their country, but such acts as the slaughter at Somnath seemed designed specifically to destroy their religion. Yet it is unlikely, even though he had justified his raiding as ordered by his god and prophet, that Mahmud saw himself as a crusader for his faith. He incorporated Hindus into his army and reserved a special quarter for them in Ghazni. To Mahmud, India was quite simply a vast treasure store, whose guardians happened to be Hindu. He had no inkling that his conquest of the Punjab would pave the way for Muslim successors who would come to India not merely to plunder but to rule.

The deer in the outer left hand of this twelfth-century Indian bronze statue is an attribute of the Hindu god Shiva. The inner left hand beckons the devotee to receive a gift; the inner right hand assures him of protection.

The century and a half that followed Mahmud's death saw the expiry of the Pratiharas, the northwestern Indian dynasty that had been instrumental in repelling the Sind Arabs. The vacuum they left was filled not by another great empire but by the Rajputs, former vassals of the Pratiharas. A fierce, quarrelsome people, the Rajputs never united into a single state but remained split into the small kingdoms whose conflicts and rivalries had helped Mahmud greatly.

The roots of the Rajputs had been long forgotten. Conceivably, their ancestors included the Huns who had migrated into India in the fifth century and intermarried with the indigenous Hindus. The Rajput leaders, members of the kshatriya caste, claimed warrior status by descent from mythical progenitors forged by fire on Mount Abu in southern Rajasthan.

Each Rajput kingdom mirrored the others in its organization. At the top was the king, or *maharajadiraja* (great king) as the newly independent rulers styled themselves, who controlled a bevy of vassal princes. Vassals from the periphery of the realm would pay their ruler tribute in exchange for autonomy within their regions. At the realm's core, the king had a right to a share in the produce from all land, although unlike the feudal monarchs of Europe, he was not considered the ultimate owner of the land itself. The king distributed produce from the land to subsidiary rulers, religious institutions, and even merchant guilds, by means of grants. Usually such grants were made on pieces of cloth or bark—the art of papermaking only reached India in the twelfth century—but for religious grants, they took the form of copper-plates, that the donor's pious act might survive in people's memory. In return, all save religious institutions were obliged to provide the king with a fixed number of soldiers.

This bronze statue of Ava-lokitesvara, a Buddhist divine figure dedicated to the relief of human suffering, is seated in the classic pose of adoration, the palms of his hands pressed vertically together in front of his chest.

The Language of Hands

In India's Hindu and Buddhist traditions, the arts of sculpture and dance have adopted closely related symbolic languages. Just as a performer reveals the meaning of a dance through ritualized movements, so the statue of a deity conveys messages through the attitude of its body. The god's posture, the arrangement of the limbs, and the gestures of the hands all convey to the worshiper precise meanings that can be readily understood at a glance.

A few of the many traditional hand positions are shown and interpreted here and overleaf. Such poses were often associated with particular deities, who might additionally be identified by their dress or by the objects they held. This code not only helped classify the Indian pantheon—the deities of which are known in various and contrasting forms—but also imparted to their representations in art a compelling otherworldly grace and serenity.

A typical grant from twelfth-century Gujarat required the recipient not only to maintain law and order and collect revenue for his monarch, but also to supply 100 foot soldiers and twenty cavalry for his lord's army.

So long as the conditions that accompanied the grant were followed, the vassal had virtual autonomy within his region and could promulgate his own laws. In one instance of a religious grant, these laws were so comprehensive as to cover offenses ranging from murder to idle gossip. But vassals who were disloyal could expect not only to surrender their possessions but also to be put to such menial, humiliating tasks as sweeping the king's stables.

Besides collecting land revenues, the Rajputs grew rich from taxes on merchants. India was a noted producer of spices, ivory, and cloth of every quality. The ninth century traveler Sulayman described Bengal cotton as "so fine and delicate that a dress made of the material may be passed through a signet ring." The metal industry was also highly developed, producing articles that ranged from massive beams for construction work to swords wrought so finely that, in the words of a writer admiring a company of Indian soldiers, the lustrous finish of the sword blades "looked like ants creeping on the surface of a diamond."

Mahmud's depredations had stifled trade, but in the more settled period that followed his death, goods once more moved around the subcontinent. The merchandise was carried in large and splendid caravans, which were heavily guarded against brigands. A drum would be beaten around town before a caravan's departure, and then it would set off, a snorting, yawning line of camels, buffaloes, mules, donkeys, and oxen, above which swayed the peacock feathers decorating the merchants' white umbrellas. The magnificence of the occasion was often tarnished by the poor state of the roads. One frustrated traveler recorded, "as a result of the impassability of the road from water, thorns, and mud, 2 miles seemed like 800."

Despite such handicaps, India's trade with the Islamic world and the European continent was flourishing too, accompanied by an increased use of gold coinage—a currency that Europe itself would scarcely be able to afford until the thirteenth century. The two land trade routes—used for compact, high-value goods such as spices and silver—were across the Khyber Pass into Afghanistan or through the desert of Baluchistan into southern Iran. Heavy commodities such as cloth traveled westward by ship. In Gujarat, there was a flourishing boatbuilding industry, which succeeded despite a ban on the use of nails. (A common Hindu belief of the time held that any extraneous iron might attract the ship to magnetic rocks.) But Arab shipping

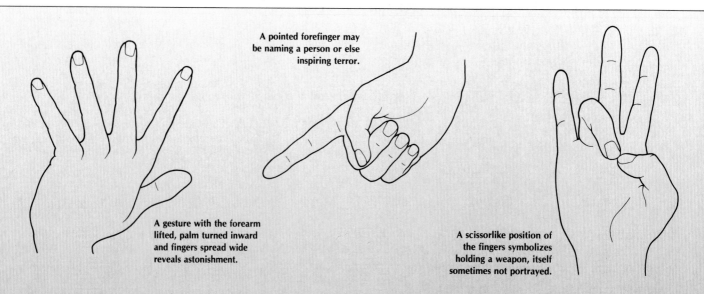

A gesture with the forearm lifted, palm turned inward and fingers spread wide reveals astonishment.

A pointed forefinger may be naming a person or else inspiring terror.

A scissorlike position of the fingers symbolizes holding a weapon, itself sometimes not portrayed.

handled the bulk of the sea trade, and Arab merchants continued to make converts to Islam along India's western shores.

The growing prosperity fostered by trade produced discord among rival Rajput kings avid to match each other in wealth and status. Fighting became so much a way of life that an elaborate code of chivalry came into being. The antiquated battle techniques that the Ghaznavids had encountered persisted in an ever more ritualized form. The strict laws governing warfare decreed, among other provisions, that a warrior could only fight someone of equal rank and before battle must taunt the enemy with boastful expressions. Under such circumstances, set battles invariably disintegrated into a melee of unconnected private duels, and war itself became a muddled and protracted affair. At one siege, victory was delayed for several months because the attackers had politely allowed food supplies to get through.

Along with chivalry in warfare, northern India idealized generosity and romance. Wandering minstrels sang of legendary heroes and their amorous exploits; one monarch supposedly kept a retinue of 3,300 bards to set his valor to verse. The spirit of the time was reflected in the rulers' pastimes, one of which was organizing mounted duels—ponderous and gargantuan versions of western Europe's tournaments, in which the nobility, perched atop elephants, would fight to the death. In Kashmir, this sport became so popular that one twelfth-century king killed almost all of his best warriors in its pursuit.

While the Rajputs attended to the niceties of chivalry, the Ghaznavids were fighting for survival. None of Mahmud's successors matched his prowess as a leader, and the Ghaznavid empire slowly began to disintegrate. To the east, their territories were nibbled away by the Rajputs, while to the west, they faced a considerably greater threat in the form of the Seljuks—Turks originating, like the Ghaznavids themselves, in central Asia, who had become mercenaries to the Persian ruling class and then taken over the reins of power themselves. In the mid-eleventh century, the Seljuks wielded power throughout Persia and were taking control of parts of Afghanistan. For another century, the Ghaznavids clung to the tattered remnants of empire, but with all their attention on their borders, they failed to notice a growing danger from within.

In 982, a Samanid historian had laconically remarked of the small province of Ghur in western Afghanistan, "from here come slaves, armor, coats of mail, and good arms." It was also the home of good warriors, as Mahmud had discovered in 1020, when he had been hard put to subdue and convert the pagan Ghurids to his own

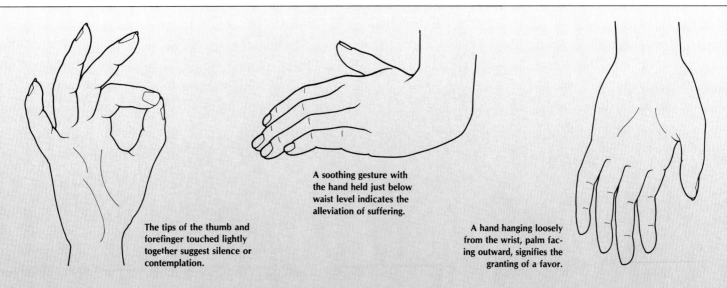

The tips of the thumb and forefinger touched lightly together suggest silence or contemplation.

A soothing gesture with the hand held just below waist level indicates the alleviation of suffering.

A hand hanging loosely from the wrist, palm facing outward, signifies the granting of a favor.

Sunni Muslim faith. The ancestors of the Ghurids were Persians, not Turks like the Ghaznavids and the Seljuks. For many centuries, the Ghurids had lived unremarked by other peoples in their mountain fastness, but by the early part of the twelfth century, they had begun to flex their muscles. The Ghaznavids no longer counted for much. By now the Seljuks were also past the height of their power, threatened by the belligerence of other Turkic peoples. The Ghurids began to buy Turkish warrior-slaves and built up a formidable army. Before long, Ghurid society was a complex blend of Persian and Turkish elements.

In 1150, to avenge the death of his brother at Ghaznavid hands, the Ghurid leader Ala al-Din Husayn marched on Ghazni. Overstretched and weakened by border

Rising in tiers of elaborately carved marble to a central pendant, the domed ceiling of the thirteenth-century Tejpal Temple, on Mount Abu in Rajasthan, provided an ornate setting for sixteen statues of Jain goddesses of wisdom. The Jains were members of a minority religion founded in India around the sixth century BC; one of their binding precepts was the avoidance of injury to all living things. In the early years of the Delhi sultanate, the Muslims harassed the Jains and destroyed some of their temples. But in Rajasthan the Rajputs, a powerful warrior people, protected Jain shrines and thus ensured the continuance of the tradition. The Jains soon entered a more tranquil era. Later Muslim rulers dealt tactfully with them because they included some of the wealthiest traders and most powerful bankers in the subcontinent.

wars, the Ghaznavids were no match for the Ghurids, and the capital fell almost without a fight. Ala al-Din's revenge was severe. All male inhabitants were killed, the women and children carried off into slavery. The remains of all the Ghaznavid kings—save Mahmud and his two sons, who were respected as great Islamic rulers—were torn from the ground, their tombs destroyed, and the town then put to the torch. For seven days the glittering palaces and mosques of Ghazni burned, until scarcely a trace was left of Mahmud's great city, and Ala al-Din entered history as Jahansuz, "the World Burner."

The Ghaznavid king had fled to the Punjab following his defeat, but even with this threat out of the way, Jahansuz did not revel in his conquests long. Shortly after the sack of Ghazni, he was defeated and imprisoned by the Seljuks. For the next twenty years, the original Ghaznavid territories became the center of a bitter squabble among the Seljuks, the Ghurids, and the Punjab-based remnants of the Ghaznavids. It was not until 1173 that the matter was finally settled, when Ghiyas al-Din, the World Burner's nephew, expelled the Seljuks from Ghazni, set himself up as sultan, and appointed his younger brother Muizz al-Din Muhammad as his deputy.

It was the beginning of an extraordinary partnership. In an age of fratricidal strife, Ghiyas al-Din commanded the absolute loyalty of his brother. Remaining in his capital, Firoz Koh, northwest of Ghazni in present-day Iran, Ghiyas al-Din sent Muizz al-Din forth to extend the Ghurid territories. It was a charter that few rulers of the time would have dared afford a near relative, but one that Muizz al-Din fulfilled. While Ghiyas al-Din defended his realm in the north and west against the Turkish threat, Muizz al-Din continued to serve his brother faithfully, even though the territories Muizz al-Din captured would easily have enabled him to set up a rival kingdom.

India's wealth drew Muizz al-Din, as it had drawn Mahmud. More insistently than Mahmud, Muizz al-Din voiced his ambitions in the language of religion. He proclaimed holy war against the infidel Hindus and by this ploy succeeded in attracting soldiers and binding them to him; Islamic piety infused his repeated campaigns, although Muizz al-Din was not above making alliances with Hindus.

He swept into India, taking Shiite Multan in 1175 and Sind in 1182. By 1186, he had captured Lahore and the Punjab, sending the last Ghaznavid ruler in chains to Firoz Koh. His next move ended disastrously on the plain of Tarai, near Karnal, when in 1191, he was overwhelmed and almost killed by the superior numbers of a coalition of Rajput clans led by Prithviraja, the king of Delhi. The Rajputs had come together against a common enemy for almost the first time in their history.

But Muizz al-Din was not to be put off so easily. Returning to Ghazni, he assembled a force of 12,000 horsemen and, in 1192, came back for revenge. The two armies met again at Tarai. Choosing an early hour one morning when Prithviraja's forces were conducting an elaborate ritual to ensure success, the Muslims attacked. Muizz al-Din employed Turkish tactics, ordering his men to harry the flanks of the Hindu army, avoiding hand-to-hand conflict, and feigning retreat to draw out the enemy. Caught in the showers of Muslim arrows, the Indians found themselves at a loss, unable to employ the man-to-man fighting at which they excelled and unable to pursue the elusive horsemen without dangerously exposing themselves. The one-sided battle of attrition continued until the mid-afternoon when, judging the Hindus to be sufficiently weary, Muizz al-Din charged their center with the flower of his cavalry.

It was a rout. Exhausted and undisciplined, the Indians were swept away by the unexpected charge, in which perished not only Prithviraja but also his brother.

ROUT OF THE RAJPUTS

Hindu domination of northern India ended on the plain of Tarai, about sixty miles north of Delhi, in the dry season of 1192, when Sultan Muizz al-Din Muhammad of Ghur, at the head of a Muslim army, decisively crushed a Hindu coalition led by the Rajput chieftain Prithviraja.

The two forces had met in the same spot the previous year, only for the Muslims to be defeated by the Hindus' superior numbers. Now, with a force of some 12,000 infantry and mounted archers, Muizz al-

Din returned to the plain seeking victory.

The battle commenced in the early morning and proved to be a triumph of mobility over mass. Following centuries-old tradition, the Indian army of at least 100,000 men adopted a static battle line, consisting mainly of large numbers of ill-trained infantry. Poor horse breeders, they had few cavalry, depending instead on imposing but unwieldy war elephants, which were deployed as mobile shooting platforms. Although archers were counted among their ranks, the Rajputs preferred the glory of single combat in which warriors could demonstrate their prowess with sword and lance.

Against this inflexible foe, Muizz al-Din adopted classic Turkish cavalry tactics. Sending out four companies of mounted archers, he instructed them to harass the Hindu ranks but to avoid hand-to-hand fighting. After loosing their arrows at the Indians, the Muslim archers wheeled away in feigned retreat. Indians who gave chase were cut down; the ranks of the warriors that held their ground were decimated.

For many hours, the Muslim archers charged and volleyed, supplied with fresh arrows from their camp at the rear. Then, at last, reckoning the Hindus to be too weak to effectively retaliate, Muizz al-Din ordered his elite cavalry corps of professional slave-warriors to charge. The Muslim soldiers swept the disorganized Indians from the field, killing Prithviraja. The way to Delhi was now open.

According to a Muslim historian, "one hundred thousand groveling Hindus swiftly departed to the flames of hell," and despite the bombast, the victory he described was certainly momentous, one that broke the back of Rajput power and gave Muizz al-Din northern India to the gates of Delhi. Prithviraja's son, the new ruler of Delhi, was obliged to pay tribute to the Muslims.

Faced with Shiite rebellions on his western border, Muizz al-Din was forced to return to Ghazni, appointing as viceroy his most trustworthy officer, Qutb al-Din Aybak. Of Turkic central Asian origin, Qutb al-Din had been bought as a slave and trained by the governor of Nishapur in Khurasan and, on the death of his master, had passed into the hands of Muizz al-Din. The name Aybak meant literally "Moon-face"; the Turks used it to denote fair skin and comeliness. Of Qutb al-Din's appearance the chroniclers said little, save that he had suffered an accident that deprived him of the use of one of his little fingers. This deformity did not prevent his being an expert horseman and archer, and he quickly rose to prominence in the Ghurid forces. Military expertise aside, he also impressed his master with his lavish generosity, which in later years would earn him the nickname Lakh-baksh, "Giver of tens of thousands."

Qutb al-Din's first concern was Delhi. Strategically positioned at the gateway to the fertile plain between the Ganges and Yamuna rivers, Delhi represented the key to control over this part of North India. It had been settled as early as 1400 BC, and the remnants of several ancient capitals in the immediate vicinity testified to its importance. Now, though ruled by a tributary prince, it remained a potential nucleus for Indian patriotism, and during the winter that followed the battle of Tarai, Qutb al-Din ousted the Hindu prince. Qutb al-Din immediately set about making his presence felt. All Hindu temples were demolished. Work began forthwith on the Quwat al-Islam Mosque and the Qutb Minar, a huge victory tower that would symbolize Muslim dominance in India.

Delhi became Qutb al-Din's headquarters. Over the next ten years—with the help of Muizz al-Din, who returned periodically from Ghazni—he launched a series of campaigns that brought almost all northern India under his control.

While Qutb al-Din was occupied in the north, it was another great Turkish soldier, Ikhtiyar, who carried the scimitar of Islam to eastern India. Though an able warrior, Ikhtiyar had initially been hampered in his rise through the ranks by his unprepossessing appearance. It is said that his arms were so long he could touch his calves without bending. While this was the legendary Hindu sign of a great hero, it was repugnant in Muslim society. Yet Ikhtiyar had served well under two of Muizz al-Din's minor generals and, as a reward, been granted land in Oudh, the northern province that straddled the Ganges and Yamuna rivers. Raids to the east brought him more riches, and by 1192, he had attracted enough supporters to form his own army.

In that year, he marched on Bihar, took its capital, Odantapuri, and in the process sacked the ancient Buddhist monastery of Nalanda, killing all the Buddhist monks, who put up only a feeble defense. The city was rich in plunder, among which was the monastery's fabled library. But the only people who could interpret the books were dead; as mere curios, the mysterious tomes were packed up with the other booty and transported to Delhi in the summer of 1193. Ikhtiyar received a rapturous reception there. He returned to Bihar laden with Qutb al-Din's generosity and the grant of all his conquests, past and future, as his personal fief.

Encouraged by his success, Ikhtiyar thought of extending his rule to the eastern

HE VICTORY MOSQUE

Begun in 1195, during the reign of the Muslim viceroy Qutb al-Din, Delhi's Quwat al-Islam Mosque *(overleaf)* was symbolically located on the site of a Hindu temple. By 1230, the mosque was overlooked by the Qutb Minar *(right)*, by far the tallest edifice in the city, built as a victory monument commemorating the Muslim conquest of northern India. The Qutb Minar may also have served as a minaret from which to sound the call to prayer.

Most of the complex was constructed piecemeal from twenty-seven Hindu temples that were demolished to provide materials for the project. Sharing the Muslim detestation for human images, Qutb al-Din ordered the Indian builders to deface representations of the Hindu pantheon. In their place, he commanded inscriptions offering praise to Allah and eulogizing his titular master, Sultan Muizz al-Din Muhammad. Yet in raising this monument to a foreign dynasty and an alien god, the local masons unconsciously enshrined indigenous Hindu elements, creating a style of architecture that was neither wholly Islamic nor purely Indian.

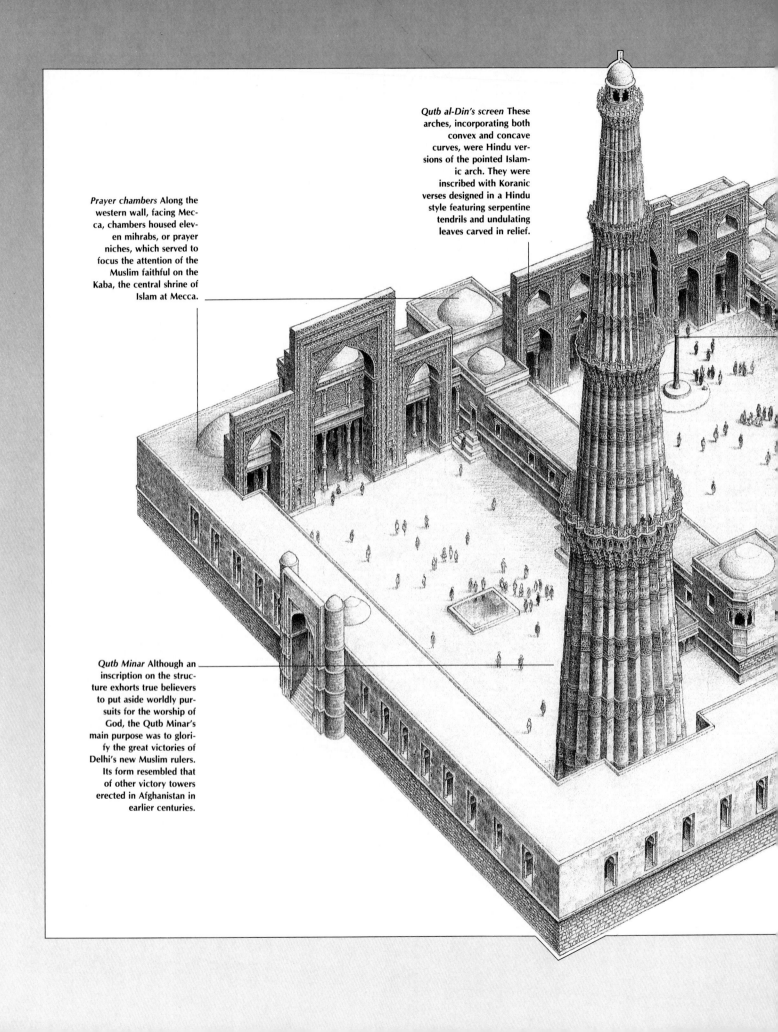

Prayer chambers Along the western wall, facing Mecca, chambers housed eleven mihrabs, or prayer niches, which served to focus the attention of the Muslim faithful on the Kaba, the central shrine of Islam at Mecca.

Qutb al-Din's screen These arches, incorporating both convex and concave curves, were Hindu versions of the pointed Islamic arch. They were inscribed with Koranic verses designed in a Hindu style featuring serpentine tendrils and undulating leaves carved in relief.

Qutb Minar Although an inscription on the structure exhorts true believers to put aside worldly pursuits for the worship of God, the Qutb Minar's main purpose was to glorify the great victories of Delhi's new Muslim rulers. Its form resembled that of other victory towers erected in Afghanistan in earlier centuries.

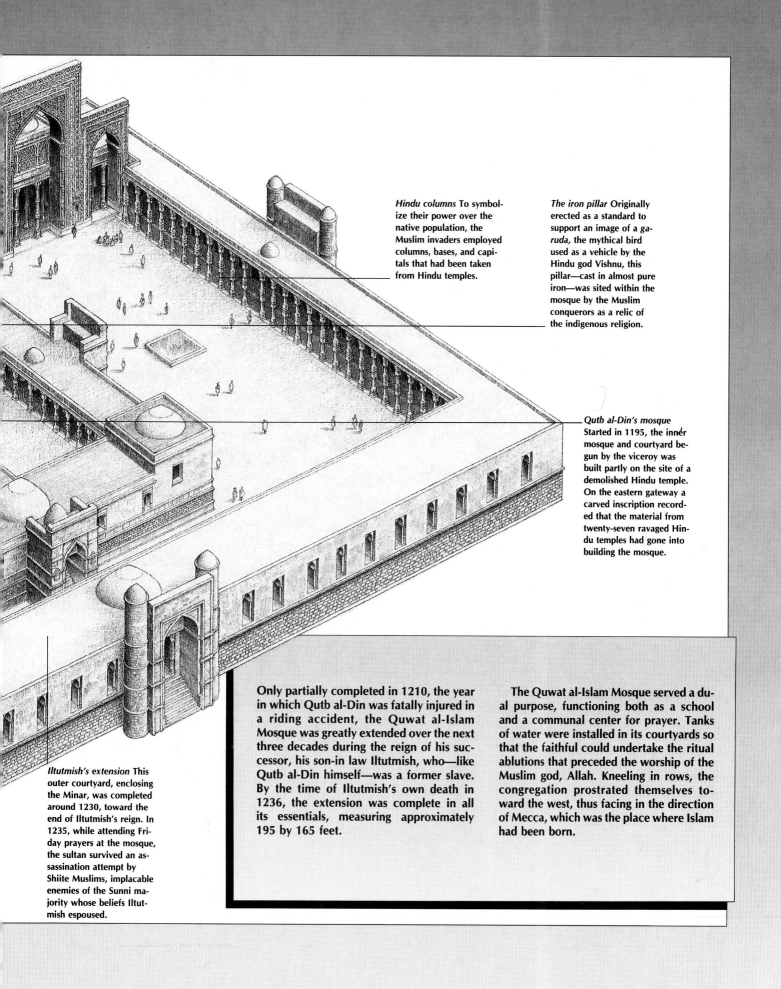

Hindu columns To symbolize their power over the native population, the Muslim invaders employed columns, bases, and capitals that had been taken from Hindu temples.

The iron pillar Originally erected as a standard to support an image of a *garuda,* the mythical bird used as a vehicle by the Hindu god Vishnu, this pillar—cast in almost pure iron—was sited within the mosque by the Muslim conquerors as a relic of the indigenous religion.

Qutb al-Din's mosque Started in 1195, the inner mosque and courtyard begun by the viceroy was built partly on the site of a demolished Hindu temple. On the eastern gateway a carved inscription recorded that the material from twenty-seven ravaged Hindu temples had gone into building the mosque.

Iltutmish's extension This outer courtyard, enclosing the Minar, was completed around 1230, toward the end of Iltutmish's reign. In 1235, while attending Friday prayers at the mosque, the sultan survived an assassination attempt by Shiite Muslims, implacable enemies of the Sunni majority whose beliefs Iltutmish espoused.

Only partially completed in 1210, the year in which Qutb al-Din was fatally injured in a riding accident, the Quwat al-Islam Mosque was greatly extended over the next three decades during the reign of his successor, his son-in law Iltutmish, who—like Qutb al-Din himself—was a former slave. By the time of Iltutmish's own death in 1236, the extension was complete in all its essentials, measuring approximately 195 by 165 feet.

The Quwat al-Islam Mosque served a dual purpose, functioning both as a school and a communal center for prayer. Tanks of water were installed in its courtyards so that the faithful could undertake the ritual ablutions that preceded the worship of the Muslim god, Allah. Kneeling in rows, the congregation prostrated themselves toward the west, thus facing in the direction of Mecca, which was the place where Islam had been born.

coast and thence over the Himalayas to Tibet. Accordingly, in about 1202, he mustered a small force of 2,000 horsemen and marched on Nadia, capital of Bengal. Ikhtiyar moved rapidly—so rapidly, indeed, that he left the main body of his army behind and arrived at the gates of the city with only eighteen men. Reports had already reached the city of this long-armed invader, causing most of the wealthier inhabitants to take preemptive flight; yet astonishingly, Ikhtiyar and his men were mistaken for horse traders and granted free entrance. Perhaps nobody expected the conqueror to arrive with so small a force. The king, Lakshman Sena, had remained in his capital, whether from confidence or sloth, and was at his midday meal when the raiders arrived at the palace gates. Drawing their swords, Ikhtiyar and his men stormed the palace, cutting down guards and bystanders without discrimination. Although Lakshman managed to escape through a back door, the invaders gained a tenable defensive position to which they clung until the greater part of the army arrived to relieve them.

It was as decisive a victory as Tarai, and it gave Ikhtiyar all Bengal. Setting himself up as governor, he ruled in the name of the sultan, minting coins that bore Muizz al-Din's name. But while nominally a Ghurid vassal, his wealth and his distance from Delhi made him virtually independent. With this newfound power, he at last had the means to subjugate Tibet, and in June 1205, he set out with an army of 10,000 to realize that ambition.

The expedition was ill-fated. Faced with the rigors of winter and a scorched-earth defense by his opponents, his men were reduced to eating their own horses and forced to retreat. On the journey home, the local population destroyed a bridge to cut off Ikhtiyar's retreat and forced him into battle. Ikhtiyar's troops were defeated and slaughtered, and Ikhtiyar himself only survived by swimming the river to safety. He returned to Bengal in 1206 with a pitiable force of 100 men. It was the biggest defeat sustained by the Muslims to date, and one that broke Ikhtiyar. Later that year, he was killed by a rival's knife.

Yet his rule was to have profound effects on the region. The sacking of Nalanda marked the end of Buddhism as a major Indian religion. Secluded in their monasteries, the Buddhist monks had long since lost touch with the laity and, as early as the eighth century, had been in popular disrepute. Their presence had been maintained, however, by the patronage of the eastern kings, who did a lucrative trade with the Buddhist countries of Southeast Asia. With the advent of Islamic rule and the consequent loss of royal support, most monks migrated to Tibet, where the religion continued to flourish.

Because of the kings' commitment to Buddhism, a sizable minority of the lay population of Bengal had been Buddhist. But the establishment of Islamic rule in Bengal led to the conversion of most Buddhists to Islam in the course of the thirteenth century. Hindus also accepted conversion: Islam appealed especially to the region's many impoverished, low-caste agrarian workers. Ultimately it was Ikhtiyar who was responsible for the strong Muslim presence that thereafter was a major factor in the politics of Bengal.

Ikhtiyar typified all that brought the Muslims success in India. Rising through merit from a lowly beginning, he was an archetypal product of the Turkish slave

Decorating a page from a fourteenth-century manuscript of the Persian national epic, Firdausi's *Shahnama*, or *Book of Kings*, an illustration shows the Sassanian king Bahram Gur winning his crown by ordeal. Most likely created in India for one of the land's Islamic rulers, the manuscript represents the fusion between Persian and indigenous traditions, with the naive, naturalistic style of Indian art applied to a Persian fable. In Firdausi's text, the king battles with two lions—the symbol of Persian royalty; here the artist has substituted his own, indigenous concept of majesty—two raging tigers.

system. His military genius was founded on sound training in tactics and rigorous discipline. Ever the opportunist, he was a true soldier of fortune, whose success attracted a swarm of adventurers to India.

On his ignominious return from Tibet in 1206, Ikhtiyar is reported to have asked wonderingly, ''Has any misfortune befallen Sultan Muizz al-Din that my fortune has turned so bad?'' His concerns were well founded. Having succeeded his brother in 1202, Muizz al-Din became engaged in a constant struggle to hold together his new empire, and on March 15, 1206, he died on the banks of the Indus, probably murdered by members of a Shiite faction that he had persecuted seven years before. In the aftermath, the precarious unity of the Ghurid territories collapsed. A quick succession of rulers followed Muizz al-Din, but as in the Samanid empire, real power had devolved to the regional generals: On his master's death, Qutb al-Din declared himself sultan of the Indian provinces. But he did not enjoy his new realm long, for in the early days of November 1210, his horse fell during a game of polo; the pommel of the saddle crushed his chest, and he died soon after.

In the ensuing power vacuum, the sultanate almost collapsed under the quarreling of regional governors, until in 1211, Qutb al-Din's son-in-law Iltutmish fought his way to the throne. Born in central Asia, Iltutmish had been sold into slavery by his brothers, who according to chroniclers of his reign, were jealous of Iltutmish's consummate beauty, virtue, and intelligence. Such a paragon was he that his master refused to sell him to Muizz al-Din himself, even for a vast sum; Muizz al-Din accordingly decreed that nobody else in Afghanistan should have the opportunity of buying Iltutmish. Qutb al-Din, on one of his trips back to Afghanistan, sought and gained permission to purchase the legendary slave and take him to India. Under Qutb al-Din, Iltutmish rose rapidly, progressing from chief of Qutb al-Din's guards to his chief huntsman and then to provincial governor. Qutb al-Din gave Iltutmish his daughter in marriage and, after Iltutmish had shown valor in battle, finally granted him liberty. Once he had succeeded his father-in-law, Iltutmish proved himself an able and popular leader. His status was recognized in 1229, when he was confirmed as sultan by the caliph of Baghdad.

By that time, Iltutmish had successfully consolidated his position, defeating a handful of Turkish governors who disputed his rule and containing an underswell of Rajput rebellion. But outside his territories, on the other side of the Himalayas, there lurked a more serious threat—the Mongols, under their ruthless leader Ghengis Khan. Of steppe ancestry, like the Turks, the Mongols used the same horse-borne tactics but added a strength and sav-

agery that swept all before them, and by 1221, the Mongols were already at the Indus. Iltutmish averted a full-scale invasion, but although the invaders quickly found fresh lands to conquer farther west, they maintained a presence in Sind and the Punjab that proved a constant thorn in the side of the sultanate.

With the threat of the Mongols always present, it was more than ever necessary for the sultanate to guard against internal rebellion by Hindus, and Iltutmish set about reinforcing the Muslim rule instigated by Qutb al-Din. Although he was technically a vassal of the Baghdad caliph, like all Muslim rulers, the sultan was effectively an independent sovereign, bound only by the Sharia, the divinely sanctioned law of Islam. The sultan ruled with the advice of the ulama, Muslim doctors of law and theology, who salved his conscience by reinterpreting religious theory to meet secular fact. Suicide, for example, was deemed a crime under the Sharia, but no action was taken against the families of those Hindu women who flung themselves, according to custom, on their husbands' funeral pyres. Polo, horse racing, and gambling, theoretically forbidden, were in reality tolerated.

Among other things, the Sharia stipulated the possible sources of a monarch's wealth: tax on agricultural produce, tax on non-Muslims, one fifth of the booty taken in battles against the infidel, and a tax on Muslims, to be used for the general good of the community. The amount of all these taxes tended to vary with the whim of the sultan and amenability of the ulama, but undoubtedly the most important was that from agriculture, which supplied not only money but men.

The sultanate was divided into provinces, each ruled by a Muslim governor responsible for administration and tax collection. In return for a share of the revenue, the governor was obliged to supply the sultan with a quota of soldiers. In addition, the sultan could award land grants to his soldiers in lieu of pay or for good service. These grants varied in size from a village to a province and carried with them the duty to provide men for the sultan's army. In theory, the land itself was not granted, only its revenue, and the grants were not hereditary. But in practice, existing grants were rarely revoked, and to all intents and purposes the grantee owned the land.

The new system of land tenure did not depart dramatically from the arrangements under the Rajputs. Indeed, away from the immediate vicinity of the towns, Hindu life remained virtually unchanged, and only the highly mobile Muslim army provided the population with a reminder that they now worked for different masters. The oil to keep the machinery running was provided by Hindu administrators who, though disdainful of the foreign ''barbarians,'' learned Persian, the language of bureaucracy throughout the eastern Muslim world, and retained their traditional niche.

Iltutmish died in 1236, and a series of weak descendants succeeded him. For three decades, the court was riven by intrigue, and the Muslims' central authority counted for little. Then in 1265, the last descendant of Iltutmish died, and an eminent slave named Balban seized power. Balban ruthlessly eliminated all opposition, whether Hindu or Muslim. In the twenty-two years of his strong reign, the seeds sown by Qutb al-Din and Iltutmish came to fruition, and Muslims and Hindus began truly to integrate. Three centuries earlier, al-Biruni had written: ''The Hindus believe that there is no nation like theirs, no kings like theirs, no religion like theirs, no science like theirs. Their haughtiness is such that if you tell them of any science or scholar in Khurasan or Persia, they will think you both an ignoramus and a liar.'' Now, at last, Hindu insularity was crumbling.

Foremost among the reasons for this integration was the rapid urbanization of northern India. Everywhere, small towns sprang up, complete with mosques and markets, administrators' homes and thriving artisans' quarters. Initially just small fortified settlements from which the Muslims could enforce rule, they rapidly became centers of commerce and local government where ethnic differences merged, and from which Muslim influences seeped into the Hindu countryside. The art of paper-making, which had reached the Arab world from China in the eighth century, found a ready reception in India. The Persian irrigation wheel—a bullock-powered device for raising buckets of water in a continuous sequence—now swelled the yield of Indian crops. Metalworking, at which the Indians had always excelled, was enhanced by the introduction of fine Muslim filigree techniques. Elegant lusterware in the Persian style graced the tables of the wealthy, and Hindu cuisine was enriched by the introduction of kebabs and yogurt-based dishes.

Nowhere was the urban revolution more apparent than in Delhi. Once a small, provincial Rajput town, it was now an imperial capital, which ever since Qutb al-Din had started the construction of the Qutb Minar had been the nucleus of sultanate government. Here the Turkish governing class spent the wealth it had accumulated, attracting artisans, entertainers, students, servants, and soldiers. (Every soldier in the sultanate had to appear in Delhi for an annual review.) Some 20,000 beasts of burden were used to ferry a continual supply of provisions into the city. A Hindu-dominated moneylending business thrived; commerce boomed, and local industries ranged from arms manufacture to the training of dancing girls. All elements of Indian society met here, from mystics and merchants to brokers and bawds. The four-story houses of the rich rubbed shoulders with the low, thatched shelters of the poor, and grand litters carried the wealthy through noisy streets congested with the lower castes. The complaint to the governor of the city made by one sleepless resident painted a good picture of the town's vibrant bustle: "The life of the humble petitioner, which had been pretty uncomfortable before owing to the loud, all-night prayers of the mystics living on either side, had finally become unbearable owing to the opening of a tavern on the opposite side of the street, with a grocer-boy thrown in to enliven the social landscape and help the sales." It was big, sprawling, ugly, and uncomfortable, yet for all its faults the citizens loved it, calling it Hazrat-i Delhi, Revered Delhi, or simply Shaher, The City.

With this urbanization came a large number of converts from Hinduism to Islam, mostly low-caste artisans, who saw an opportunity for advancement in a religion that espoused equality. Whereas previously they had been forced to live apart from other castes, they could now enter the towns, change their jobs, and mingle freely with all. Those who converted were often more interested in economic benefits than theological niceties. Elephant handlers, weavers, and butchers, whose services were in demand among the new rulers, became Muslim almost to a man. Sweetmeat makers, on the other hand, preferred to stay where the money was—with the Hindus, who besides consuming large quantities of sweets also offered them to the gods.

Yet economic factors were not the only reason for conversion: One group of Muslims in particular succeeded in presenting the Hindus with a face of Islam with which they could identify. These successful missionaries were the Sufis, isolated groups of mystics, sometimes regarded as near heretics by orthodox Muslims. Some of the Sufis were gentle and pacific, others made their reputations as fearsome warriors who slaughtered Hindus. From the last decade of the twelfth century, Sufis

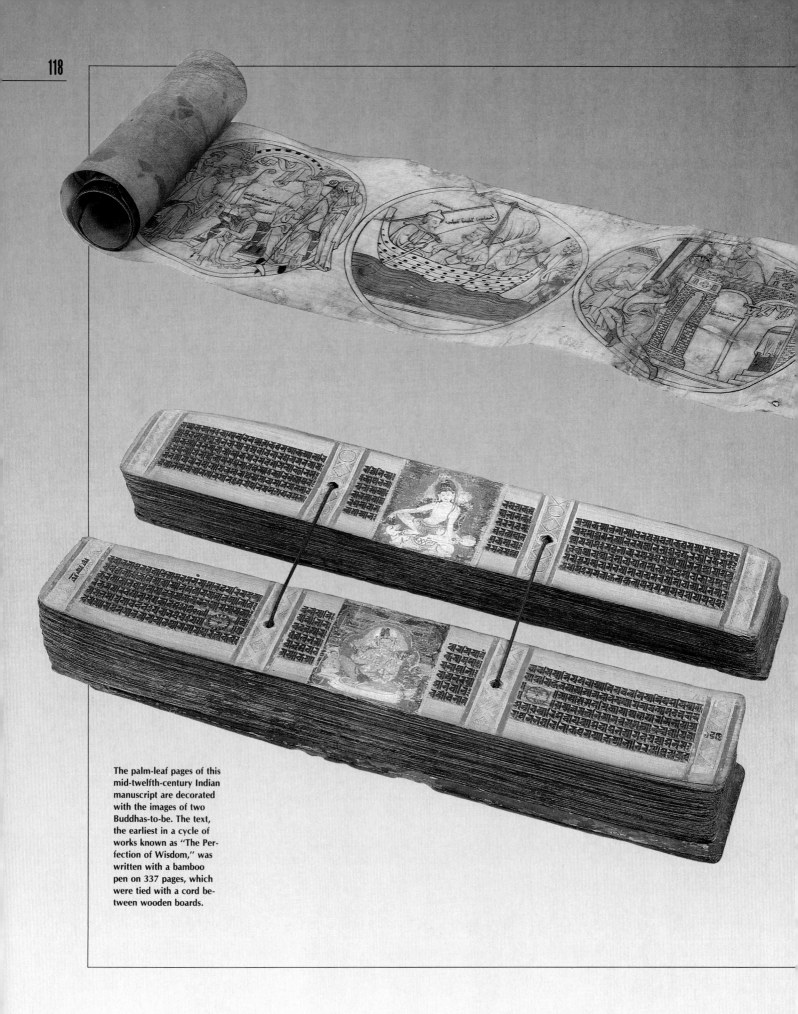

The palm-leaf pages of this mid-twelfth-century Indian manuscript are decorated with the images of two Buddhas-to-be. The text, the earliest in a cycle of works known as "The Perfection of Wisdom," was written with a bamboo pen on 337 pages, which were tied with a cord between wooden boards.

BOOKS IN VARIED GUISES

The drawings in this English scroll produced around 1200 illustrate scenes from the life of Saint Guthlac, who lived as a hermit in Lincolnshire at the beginning of the eighth century. Made of parchment, the scroll is nearly ten feet long.

Once they had developed written languages, cultures throughout the world were challenged with discovering a solution to the problem of how to present a text of some length in a manageable and portable form. By the twelfth century, the solutions adopted were many and highly ingenious.

Although paper had been used in China from the second century BC, knowledge of its manufacture did not reach India and Europe until the twelfth century AD. The alternative materials on which medieval texts were written included such diverse choices as parchment (made from treated animal skins), silk, birch bark, and—particularly in India and Southeast Asia—palm leaves *(left, below)*.

In China, some Buddhist texts were printed with inked woodblocks on a series of sheets of paper, which were then joined and folded concertina fashion *(below)*. In twelfth-century Europe, artisans were producing books in a form that would remain basically unchanged for centuries: Leaves of parchment were stitched together and then bound between wooden boards that were covered with leather. But the simpler continuous scroll, in use throughout much of Europe and Asia for centuries, was still widely employed in Europe for certain texts, such as genealogies and the lives of saints *(left, above)*.

Accordion-folded, the continuous pages of this twelfth-century Chinese book were made from paper printed with inked woodblocks. The text is part of a catalog to the Triptaka, the canon of Buddhist scriptures, compiled in AD 597.

spearheaded the spread of Islam in the Indian countryside and built religious colleges outside many small towns. Often Sufis formed into bands of fakirs, literally mendicants, who preached a close adherence to the words of the Prophet and performed trance-inducing rituals to achieve spiritual union with God. This devotional asceticism found a ready welcome in India, where it fitted into a recognized tradition: The Sufis were seen in much the same light as the Hindu spiritual teachers, gurus. Furthermore, their insistence on equality, as originally preached by Muhammad, brought them into far closer contact with the artisans and cultivators than did the pronouncements of the distant ulama, and it was the fakirs more than any others who brought Islam to the Hindus.

The traffic of ideas, however, was not purely one-way. There was a good deal of intermarriage at the top of the social scale. Important Muslim families chose Hindu princesses as brides for their sons; the Hindu women would live within the Muslim households and would be permitted to continue their Hindu worship if they did so discreetly. At lower levels of society, the two populations remained more aloof, but the Muslims took to Indian spices and, eventually, some deeply ingrained Hindu customs. Caste distinctions, theoretically unknown in Islamic society, began to develop, with the highest caste comprising the Turks, Arabs, Afghans, and Persians, followed by upper-caste Rajput converts and finally artisan converts from Hinduism, who were divided into "clean" and "unclean" occupational classes.

Though not averse to this limited assimilation, the leaders of both religions, the ulama and the Brahmans, tried to maintain a rigorous distinction between religious practices. They were largely successful, but they could not prevent some changes from creeping in. The religions met most intimately at the tombs of Sufi holy men, often found in the center of the religious college set up by the departed Sufi. Around the tomb, the Muslim followers of the Sufi would pray and read the Koran. But the reputation of the Sufis—especially those mighty in battle—also attracted Hindus. Even though the Sufis' prowess had been directed against Hindus, it was still revered. While the Muslims treated the departed Sufis as saints, the Hindus came to venerate them as gods. Women, especially, worshiped these figures of power, who were credited with the ability to cure barrenness. The Hindu devotees of the Sufi were not usually permitted within the college, so they left offerings of sweet-smelling flowers such as marigolds outside the walls to propitiate the dead hero.

While Hindus and Muslims drew closer in such small ways, the Delhi sultanate peaked and then declined. The empire's greatest moment came in the early fourteenth century when the sultan Ala al-Din briefly extended his rule over the entire subcontinent from the Himalayas to the far south. Successive rulers were to try and emulate his conquests, but all found it impossible fully to control the territories under them. One later sultan even went to the measure of moving his court, and a large part of the population of Delhi, almost 700 miles south to Dalautabad to control the Deccan, but security in the south merely led to unrest in the north, and the experiment had to be abandoned. By the late fourteenth century, the Deccan, the Punjab, Malwa, Gujarat, and Bengal had all assumed independence, some under Hindu, some under Muslim rule. The sultanate that survived was a withered stalk of its former glory, with a mixed achievement to look back on. Under the Delhi sultanate, the Muslims adjusted to a Hindu world, the Hindus to their alien rulers, but much stood in the way of a fusion of cultures, let alone of religions. India now supported two major faiths, which, far in the future, would turn explosively against each other.

Belief in an existence beyond the grave was almost universal in the twelfth century, when disease, famine, and war made lives unpredictable and short. Each of the great religions had its own vision of the life that followed death, but most assured the good of a reward in heaven and the wicked of torment in hell.

Not all images of heaven were the same: Muslims anticipated lush gardens, where the blessed reclined on cushions, attended by beautiful maidens; virtuous Christians looked forward to the rarefied delights of spiritual bliss in the presence of God, while most Hindus and Buddhists envisaged pleasurable, though temporary, resting places for a person in the cycle of rebirths on the route to enlightenment—a state the Buddhists called nirvana.

The various hells, likewise, differed, although roaring flames were a common theme of several religions. The Christian hell was forever; the Muslims believed that God, in his mercy, could choose to end the torment. Hindu and Buddhist hells, like heaven in these religions, were definitely not permanent.

For some faithful, the chances of entry to heaven appeared to improve significantly during the twelfth century. Christian thinkers reduced the fear of an eternal hell by elaborating the concept of purgatory, whereby mortals destined for union with God could do penance for their sins; after a finite period of suffering, they would attain heavenly joy. "Just as a vessel, cleansed from rust and well-polished, is placed in the treasury," wrote the Christian monk Ordericus Vitalis in the 1130s, "so the soul, purified from the stain of every sin, is led to paradise."

In war-torn Japan, as well, many Buddhists found consolation in a newly interpreted tradition that made it appear as if nirvana was more readily accessible to everyone. The extended cycle of lives—including numerous heavens and hells—through which a Buddhist frequently progressed on his path to enlightenment could be avoided entirely if a devotee relied on the infinite compassion of Amida Buddha, a legendary mortal who had gained full enlightenment and was working to help all beings achieve the same. "Namu Amida Butsu," intoned believers—"I take my refuge in Amida Buddha."

In the afterlife, the followers of Amida were thought to take up residence in the Pure Land, where one could gain enlightenment under the supervision of Amida Buddha himself.

The teeming bas-relief at right—part of an explicitly imagined sculpture of the afterlife decorating a church doorway *(inset),* at Conques in southern France—shows the vivid reality with which twelfth-century Christians envisaged the Day of Judgment. The figures at the right of the bottom row represent newly dead souls awaiting their fate. Demons seize the unfortunate wicked and thrust them into the eager jaws of hell. The just, however, receive their reward in the company of the patriarch Abraham *(near right),* seen here embracing two small figures, while on the sloping roof overhead, the dead arise at the sound of the last trump. Above them appears the figure of Christ—returned to earth as a stern, but humane, judge—who welcomes the blessed to eternal bliss with a raised hand.

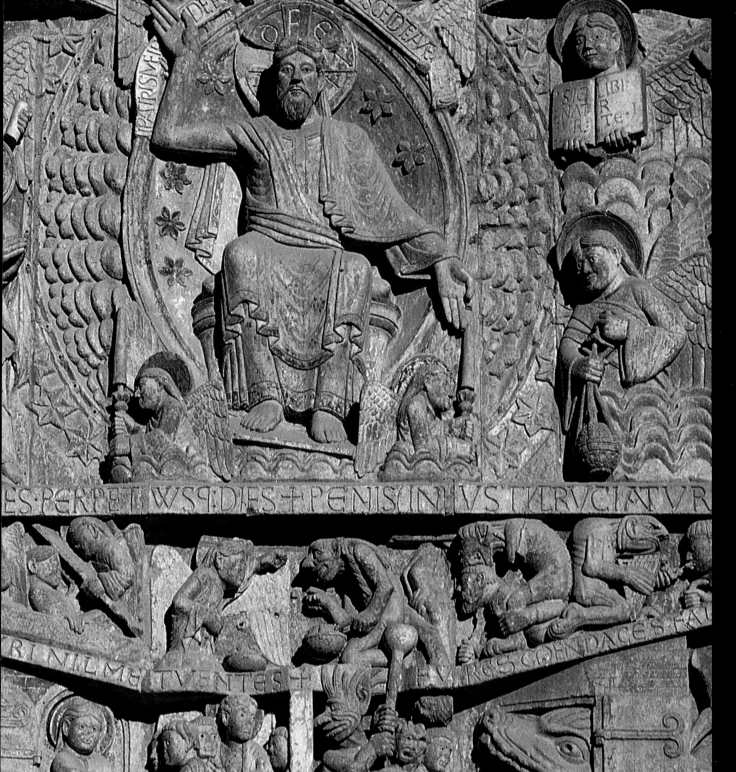

Shown in a detail from a thirteen-foot-long triptych painted on silk *(above)*, musical handmaidens of Amida Buddha prepare to escort a believer to the Pure Land—a realm held to lie somewhere in the west. The cult of Amida, who had been worshiped in China since the fifth century, had reached Japan around the year 1000 and had attracted a wide following by the twelfth century. A whole category of paintings, known as *raigo-zu,* depicted the descent of this benevolent savior to earth to welcome the newly dead.

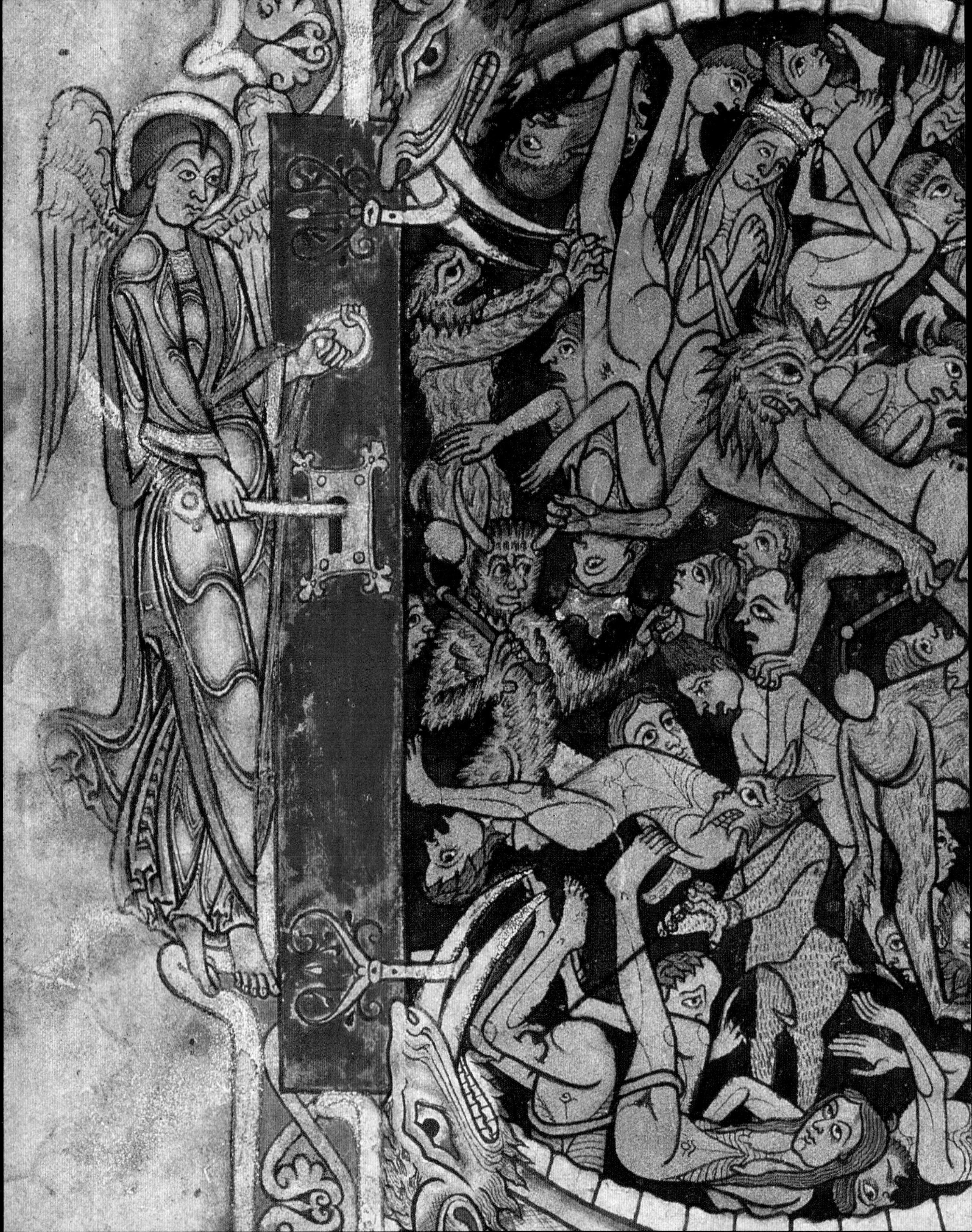

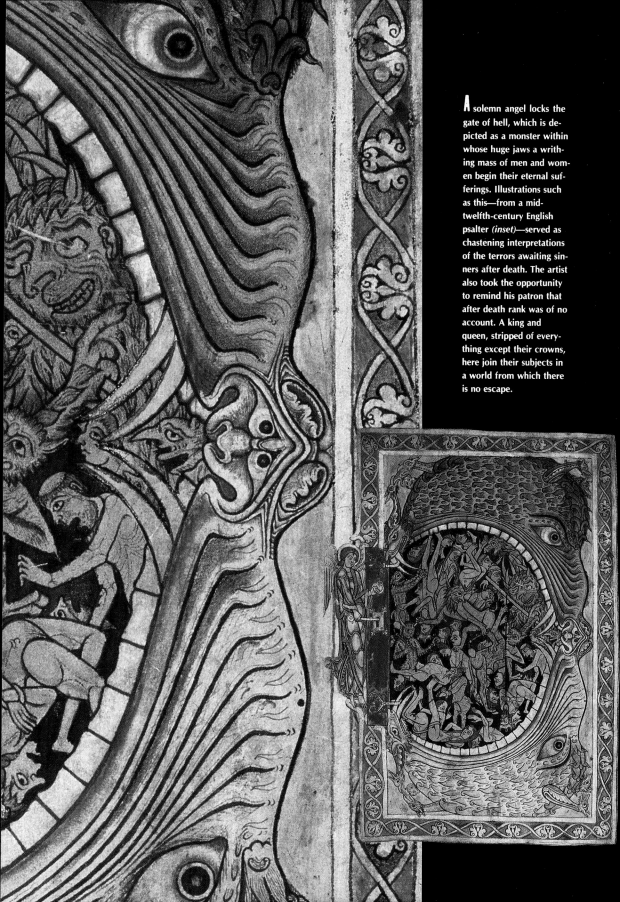

A solemn angel locks the gate of hell, which is depicted as a monster within whose huge jaws a writhing mass of men and women begin their eternal sufferings. Illustrations such as this—from a mid-twelfth-century English psalter *(inset)*—served as chastening interpretations of the terrors awaiting sinners after death. The artist also took the opportunity to remind his patron that after death rank was of no account. A king and queen, stripped of everything except their crowns, here join their subjects in a world from which there is no escape.

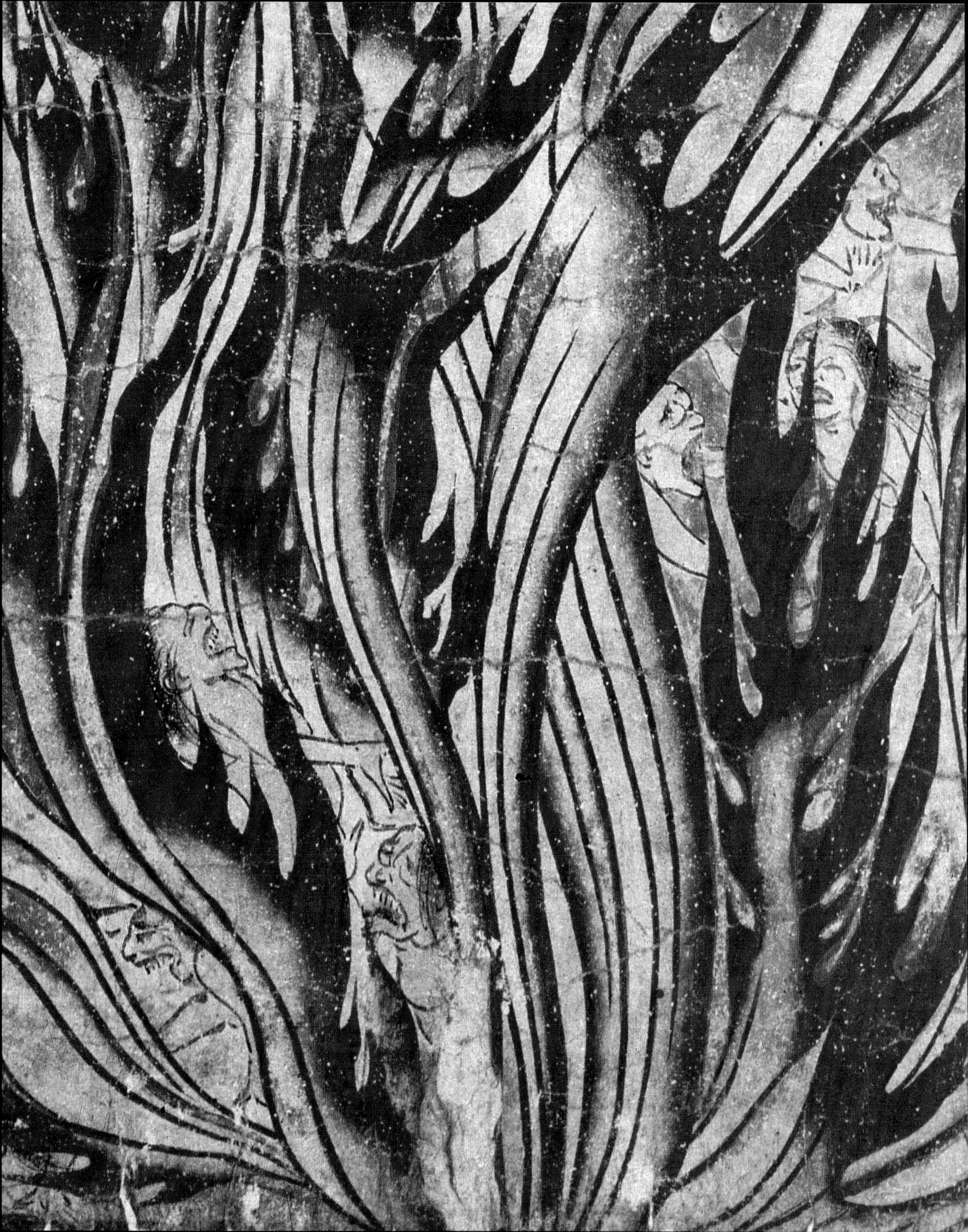

Pursued by a club-wielding demon, a sinner plunges into the Hell of Smoke, Fire, and Fog, as imagined by a Japanese artist of the late twelfth century. There were several Buddhist hells, including the Hell of Crushing and the Hell of Howling, each reserved for specific offenses. Here, the sufferers have all broken a fundamental precept by inducing the faithful to drink alcohol. Their one consolation amid the flames is that the torment is not eternal; they will enter many more states and eventually experience the bliss of enlightenment.

TEMPLE STATES OF ASIA

Early in the twelfth century, work began on one of the world's most extraordinary building projects. Deep in the agricultural heartland of Cambodia, thousands of artisans and slave laborers toiled for more than three decades to create a temple complex of unparalleled magnitude: a center of worship covering an area of over 300 acres with a stupendous temple and an intricate array of soaring towers, galleries, pavilions, cloisters, and sculpted colonnades. Eventually to be known as Angkor Wat, meaning "the city that has become a temple," it was (and remains) the largest religious structure on earth.

Ever since the seventh century, the Khmer people of Cambodia had been energetically and devotedly building temples far and wide across their kingdom. But Angkor Wat had special significance. Its construction coincided with a golden age in mainland Southeast Asia, a century of prosperity and power during which the Khmer established an empire that embraced all of the area of Cambodia, together with parts of Laos, Thailand, and southern Vietnam.

The Khmer's architectural ambitions were not slaked by Angkor Wat. By the late twelfth century, they were constructing an entire city designed as an expression of faith. This walled and moated metropolis, which would be known as Angkor Thom (Great Capital), extended over three and a half square miles.

Simultaneously, religious architecture was flourishing on an unprecedented scale in the neighboring Burmese state of Pagan, which stretched for over 600 miles from the mountains of southwest China to the Bay of Bengal. This kingdom, too, rose to its zenith in the twelfth century. Then, as rapidly as it had risen to prominence, Pagan declined into obscurity.

The Cambodian empire was only a little more enduring than Pagan. In the fifteenth century, the enormous temple complex of Angkor Wat, together with nearby Angkor Thom, was abandoned to the tropical jungle. Meanwhile, other less ostentatious Southeast Asian states endured and prospered.

The vast mainland region between India and southern China had long comprised scores of states, great and small, as had the myriad islands that make up present-day Indonesia and the Philippines. Trade was the mainstay of most of the states sited on the islands, on the coast of the mainland, or beside a major river. Those states located in the interior lowlands of the mainland depended very largely on rice farming. The only state of the region that had a truly mixed economy was in Java: There, both rice growing and trade flourished.

For traders and rice growers alike, water was an element critical to prosperity. On the mainland, rushing streams carved routes for traders through the mountains in the north, and great lowland rivers and lakes—generously fed by seasonal rains brought

Wearing an expression of benign contemplation, the most powerful of Cambodia's Khmer rulers, Jayavarman VII, is portrayed as a living embodiment of the Buddha, part man and part divinity. In real life, however, Jayavarman was renowned more for his ruthlessness and his grandiose building program than for godlike serenity. His thirty-year reign witnessed the extension of Khmer dominion over much of mainland Southeast Asia and was accompanied by a massive scheme of public works, including temples, hospitals, and roads, more than 100 wayside hospices and—the king's greatest monument—the new capital of Angkor Thom, crammed with palaces and shrines.

by the monsoon winds—flooded annually to bring life and fertility to the plains. In the archipelago to the south, the islands were threaded by narrow straits and channels that allowed sea passage for vessels sailing between east and west. The typhoon winds that brought devastating storms to other parts of the tropics rarely touched these equatorial islands, and the calm seas encouraged trade.

Trade brought the disparate communities of the region into frequent contact. The hunters and gatherers and the slash-and-burn farmers of the remote islands and the mainland jungle highlands traded forest produce for the rice of the more sophisticated farmers of the upland valleys, who in turn took this produce, and the ores they panned for and mined, down to the lowlands. These lowland kingdoms passed the goods to one another's markets or to the port entrepôts handling overseas trade.

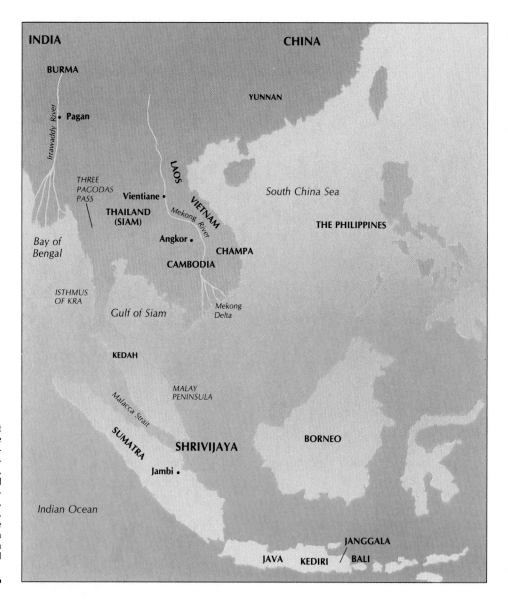

Of the four great powers in twelfth-century Southeast Asia, two were inland states sustained chiefly by rice grown on rich and well-watered soils; two were maritime and depended heavily on trade. Angkor, in Cambodia's hinterland, was the capital of the Khmer empire, which, in its late twelfth-century heyday, enveloped most of the area of Cambodia, southern Vietnam, southern Laos, and Thailand. The kingdom of Tambadipa, centered in the city of Pagan in the Burmese plain, stretched at its zenith from the frontiers of China to the Bay of Bengal. The trading state of Shrivijaya spanned a key passage for shipping, the Malacca Strait. Shrivijaya vied for business with the twin states of Janggala and Kediri in eastern Java.

Since the beginning of the Christian era, the ancient trade networks of Southeast Asia had formed a key link in an international chain that tied the Mediterranean, the horn of Africa, and South India to the court of China. Few traders, before the Portuguese erupted into the Asian seas in the sixteenth century, had ever traveled the entire distance. Goods were passed from hand to hand along the lengthy route, enriching a number of great entrepôts along the way. The coastal states of Southeast Asia gained more than most. Not only did the region's forests and mountains produce some of the most highly prized spices, incense, precious stones, and metals, but its strategic position astride the major sea route between India and China guaranteed prosperity to its ports.

International trade reached even the outermost islands of the archipelago, where local pearls, nutmeg, and sandalwood were exchanged for highly valued metals such as copper, tin, and iron. Other desirable imports were goods that lent prestige to the rulers of these small island states—great bronze drums from northern Vietnam, jades from China and southern Vietnam, beads of glass and semiprecious stones from India. But, far more significantly, new ideas came with the foreign traders who, riding the variable monsoon winds, often found it necessary to remain several months in the kingdoms they visited.

Indian traders were the ones who, from the fourth century AD on, had made the most profound impact. Indeed, almost all of the peoples of Southeast Asia—with the notable exception of northern Vietnam, overshadowed by China—had come under India's cultural and religious influence. Both Hinduism and Buddhism had spread along the sea routes to the Malay Peninsula, Sumatra, Java, and Borneo, and to the major ports of the Mekong Delta. Religious teachings were also carried overland—through Burma and down the Three Pagodas Pass into the Bangkok plain and beyond. At the same time, many states were influenced by Indian mythology, law, literature, architecture, and sculpture.

But there was no straightforward proselytism. Like so much that came to Southeast Asia, religious doctrines were adapted to suit local needs. For example, Hinduism, with its pantheon of gods and picturesque cosmology, was accepted by many kingdoms, but the rigid caste system that led to the stratification of Indian society was eschewed. Indeed, in those states where Hinduism took hold, it was invariably mixed with Buddhist teachings and with local ancestor and spirit cults.

Buddhism took even stronger hold in Southeast Asia, where it entered in various forms. Some of the kingdoms opted for Theravada—Doctrines of the Elders—Buddhism, the form of the religion perhaps closest to the original teachings of the Indian philosopher Siddhartha Gautama in the sixth century BC. All Buddhists believed in rebirth after death, but Theravada Buddhism focused on the eventual release from the cycle of rebirth and the subsequent attainment of nirvana, a state of total enlightenment. It emphasized, too, the importance of charity, especially to the Sangha—the congregation of monks who made up the Buddhist church—since through charity one gained merit, thus increasing prospects of a better condition in the next life and moving one step closer to the ultimate goal of nirvana. On the other hand, some of the Southeast Asian kingdoms came to favor Mahayana—Great Vehicle—Buddhism, a later form of the religion that stressed the immediate goal of enlightenment in the present time through the intercession of saints and the practice of asceticism. But in Southeast Asia, Buddhism, like Hinduism, was blended with indigenous religious concepts; Mahayana doctrine, especially, involved esoteric knowledge and secret ritual practices. It also absorbed many ideas from Hinduism, including a Hindu-style pantheon of gods.

Thus almost all the states of Southeast Asia developed hybrid religions, part Indian, part indigenous. In the larger kingdoms, rulers sought links with the world of the gods, spirits, and ancestors through both local and Indian symbols of divinity. And these monarchs overlaid their native traditions of kingship, architecture, and art with ideas imported from India.

According to both Hindu and Buddhist philosophy, the universe comprised a circular, central continent ringed in turn by six concentric circles of land, each one

Working side by side, members of a Javanese community gather the rice harvest, some reaping the crop with small bamboo-shafted knives, others pounding and winnowing the precious grain. Steamed in cauldrons, rice was the staple diet of all villagers. Java's fertile volcanic soils produced more than one crop annually, and the surplus was exported to outer islands in return for spices and sandalwood, which in turn paid for Indian textiles and Chinese ceramics. Apart from its dietary and economic importance, rice was imbued with an almost mystical significance—the very symbol of purity, honor, and hospitality throughout Southeast Asia.

separated by an ocean, with the outer one enclosed by a wall. In the center of the universe rose a cosmic mountain, Mount Meru, around which revolved the sun, the moon, and the stars; and on the summit of the mountain stood the paradise city of Indra, king of the gods, surrounded by eight guardians at the cardinal points. In various parts of Southeast Asia, capitals were built in conformity with this image—a huge central temple representing Mount Meru and, where climatic conditions allowed, moats or canals symbolizing the primordial seas.

Not only did cities resemble the mountain at the center of the universe, the ideal state was also held to reflect the cosmic pattern. In fact, the geography of most

Southeast Asian states did conform fairly closely to the mythical Mount Meru. Each major state was surrounded by lesser satellites held in orbit within the sphere of influence, or gravitational pull, of the center. Beyond the margin lay similar rival centers and their satellites. Such states had no precise boundaries: They were defined by their capitals, which exercised jurisdiction over the surrounding territory and human energy. In the early twelfth century, for example, the Khmer's capital of Angkor controlled satellites in the plains and uplands of Thailand and the mountains of Laos, but Angkor's control over some of these mountain regions was spasmodic.

Often such external control by the capital city would be established by forming alliances with local rulers or provincial communities some way from the center of the sphere of influence. In return for supporting the state's monarch, the local chiefs enjoyed greatly enhanced status; their people were assured of protection by the state's army and a share in the prosperity of the state. A kingdom's hold over areas located some distance from the capital was therefore by indirect rule through tributary relationships. Direct rule was only exercised in the state's core, the land found in the immediate environs of the capital.

Indian beliefs defined the role of the king and the organization of his government in the states of Southeast Asia. The throne was thought to represent Mount Meru, and the king was identified with the Hindu gods or, in Buddhist countries, with one of the bodhisattvas, saintlike aspirants to Buddhahood who, by indefinitely postponing their own nirvana, were able to help others on the way to enlightenment. The king was supposed to have four primary queens—corresponding to the four cardinal points—as well as four secondary queens, and four chief ministers.

In Pagan, Angkor, and the other Southeast Asian states, elaborate state ceremonial accompanied these exalted notions of monarchy. The royal court was expected to re-create a world of the gods, a heaven on earth, not merely through the exercise of power or justice but also through great spectacle and public drama. The state was a theater in which the capital was a stage, the king and all his princes were the leading players, the priests were the directors, and the mass of people served as supporting cast, stage crew, and audience. Through the ritual of these performances, the king was thought to absorb power and to legitimize his position. He also undoubtedly awed the lower orders with his magnificence.

The day-to-day administration of the Southeast Asian states was normally in the hands of a court elite, a professional civil service. But the king remained the hub of state organization and the fountainhead of all authority. His rule was absolute, though often far from tyrannical. Since his power always depended in large measure on the health of the state's economy, he himself often took an active role in the development of trade and productivity.

But, above all else, the king's role was perceived as being of a spiritual nature. Although religious teachings varied from one state to another, they all incorporated one common Indian belief: The next life was determined by the deeds a person performed in the current existence. However, one's own deeds were not the only factor that weighed in one's fate. The king was credited with the power of improving

This bronze lamp (above) and these three bells (opposite) were made in eastern Java, which in the twelfth century produced much sophisticated metalwork. The lamp and the left-hand bell probably formed part of a Javanese Buddhist temple's ritual furnishings. The lamp was designed to burn coconut or animal oil. Flames at each corner of its reservoir illuminated an image of Ganesha, the elephant-headed god, credited with the power to remove hindrances. The bell is crowned with a sacred wheel symbolizing triumphant passage through the region of the ideas of the Buddha. No doubt this bell served a ritual purpose, its chimes punctuating the chanting of the liturgy. The two other bells had a practical function: They hung from the necks of cows or goats, aids to locating the beasts if they wandered.

his subjects' future existences by the actions he himself decided to undertake.

In Buddhist states such as Pagan, the king might donate large tracts of land to the religious establishment in order to guarantee satisfactory reincarnation and ultimate nirvana, both on his own behalf and that of his subjects. But in both Hindu and Buddhist states, the most meritorious means of accumulating merit available to royalty was temple building. Every monarch felt obliged to construct a temple complex when he ascended to the throne; very often he felt a strong compulsion to construct a temple greater than those erected by his predecessors. As a result, starting in the seventh century, temples began to mushroom all over Southeast Asia, eventually numbering in the tens of thousands.

By the twelfth century, there were four centers that had become dominant in Southeast Asia. Tambadipa (identified by the name of its capital, Pagan) directly controlled the rice-rich bowl of Upper Burma and held by means of force the Mon kingdom of Lower Burma. Its great rival was the Khmer kingdom of Kambujadesa (also known by the name of its capital, Angkor), which occupied most of the area of Cambodia, much of Thailand and southern Laos, and periodically, the kingdom of Champa in southern Vietnam. Beyond the mainland, the other great kingdoms were the twin states of Janggala and Kediri in East Java and the coastal power of Shrivijaya, located on the Malacca Strait.

Of these states, Java was historically the most distinguished and, as the one kingdom combining agricultural wealth with a booming foreign trade, the most economically sound. For a while, in the eighth century, Java had been powerful enough to raid mainland territory, including Cambodia, the homeland of the Khmer people. At that time, the Javanese capital had been located in central Java, fairly remote from the sea and hence from convenient foreign trade. The rich volcanic soils of the island, abundantly watered by the monsoon, had yielded a surplus of rice, which was put to monumental ends: It fed armies of laborers who, in the eighth century, built numerous great temples, including the vast Buddhist shrine of Borobudur in Java's central plain.

In the tenth century, the seat of government was moved eastward to gain proximity to the sea. Java's prosperity soared as a result of political changes in China, India, and the Middle East, all of which led to increases in international trade. Java's rice was in demand, but even more avidly sought were nutmeg

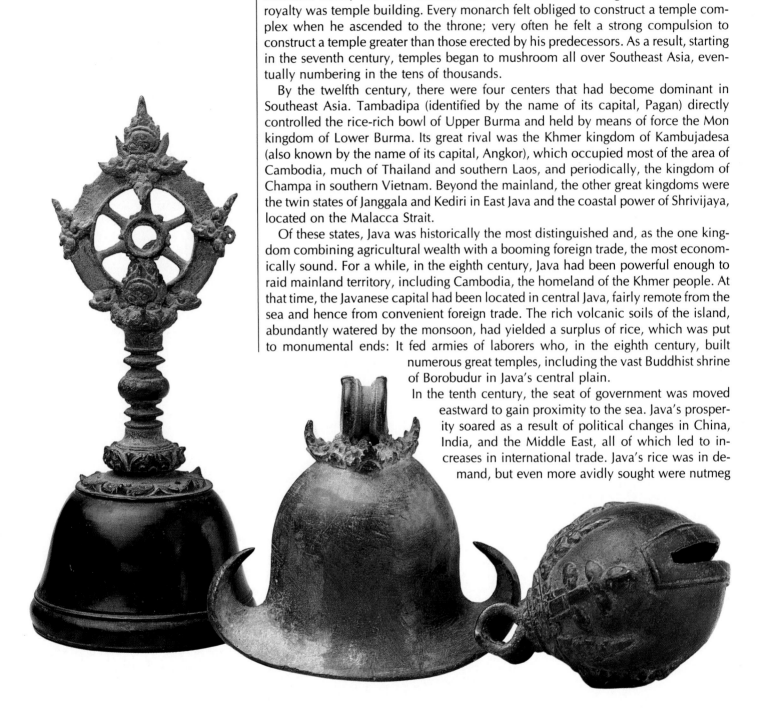

Carved in stone, the Javanese queen Dedes poses in the guise of Prajnaparamita, Buddhist goddess of wisdom. Women played a vital role in Java, controlling much of the trade in markets and often inheriting property in their own right. But few women were more influential than Dedes, widow of a regent in the kingdom of Janggala, who by marrying the lowborn usurper Ken Angrok, "he who upsets everything," legitimized his coup. Ken Angrok went on to defeat the king of neighboring Kediri in battle; with Dedes, Ken Angrok founded the Singosari dynasty that united the two kingdoms of eastern Java under one rule in 1222.

and cloves from the Moluccas—islands northeast of Java that fell within the Javanese sphere of influence. From the eleventh century on, black pepper—previously a monopoly of South India—began to figure as a major Javanese export.

In 1045, East Java was divided to form the coastal trading state of Janggala and the interior state of Kediri. While Kediri was renowned for culture—it nurtured the golden age of classical Javanese poetry—Janggala was much wealthier, and in the early thirteenth century when the two kingdoms were recombined as Singosari, the area of the former Janggala remained dominant.

The kings of Janggala and Kediri were not so much despots as patrons, leaders in time of war, and important figures in local religion. Although the king and nobility had rights over a proportion of the harvests and over a certain amount of unpaid labor from each village, local communities were relatively free to regulate their own social and economic lives.

Twelfth-century Janggala and Kediri probably had the most sophisticated economies in all Southeast Asia. Certainly they were the only states where coinage of silver and gold as well as Chinese copper currency circulated throughout the land. Elsewhere, money was restricted to the ports, while taxes were calculated in terms of goods or labor; but in Java, tax demands were expressed in money terms—and anything from land and houses to rice, tools, and toys could be bought and sold for cash. Indeed, most of Java's considerable wealth was expended on consumer goods, with Chinese porcelain being in especially strong demand. Now that Java's surpluses could buy foreign luxuries, Javanese religious feeling was no longer expressed in temple building, which virtually came to a standstill.

In this period, as for centuries before, Java's greatest rival was Shrivijaya. While Java kept a grip on the sources of spices and sandalwood, Shrivijaya controlled the main sea route between India and China, and prospered from trade in goods from distant lands: Egyptian glass, African frankincense and myrrh, Indian swords and cotton. Neither state ever managed to gain control of the other's trade, but they were forever trying to do so.

Shrivijaya reached the zenith of its wealth and power in the eleventh and twelfth centuries. Its capital at that time was probably a port that stretched for almost two miles along both banks of the Batang Hari River in southeast Sumatra. It was a semiaquatic city: Most of the population lived in tiled or thatched stilt houses on the marshy shore, some on rafts actually on the water. The state had other prosperous ports on Sumatra and in Kedah on the Malay Peninsula. But, as a rival to Java, this state was at a distinct disadvantage because it lay in the wet equatorial belt, where the jungle was dense, the coasts swampy, and the soils of the interior mostly poor and acidic. The bulk of the population made their homes in or close to the ports, the rest living in farming and trading villages strung out at intervals along the lower course of rivers in Sumatra and the Malay Peninsula. These villages and fields belonging to Shrivijaya rarely spread more than a mile from the banks of the rivers. The jungle-clad lowlands and the mountains beyond the riverine settlements belonged to other peoples who traded with Shrivijaya's populace but went their own way. Unlike fertile Java, Shrivijaya was never able to produce surpluses from the land and was compelled to exploit its strategic maritime position in order to survive.

Inevitably, this trading state was particularly exposed to the religious and cultural influences coming from India and China. It probably adopted a form of Mahayana Buddhism, and in the twelfth century especially, a number of temples were built on

Sumatra and on the west coast of the Malay Peninsula. But Shrivijaya's kings and aristocrats were more concerned with sea power than with leaving their mark on the landscape. Their subjects were too few to embark on great labor-intensive projects. And much of the state's revenues were expended for immediate political ends. Allies had to be paid off, local armies maintained, and foreign contacts lavishly entertained. Wealth flowed very fast through the hands of Shrivijaya's rulers. As a result, Shrivijaya was never noted for temple building on the spectacular scale achieved by Java. In the twelfth century, such wild extravagance was to be left to the two great states of mainland Southeast Asia: Pagan and Angkor.

Just as East Java and Shrivijaya were traditional rivals for power in maritime Southeast Asia, so the kingdoms of Pagan and Angkor were the principal contenders for supremacy on the mainland. In the twelfth century, both states had large conscript armies and fiercely expansionist policies, and they often clashed along the present-day Burma-Thailand border. But this mountainous region between their territories consistently proved an effective natural barrier, and neither state was ever able to command the frontier heights for long.

Originating in the high country east of Tibet, the Burmese-speaking people of Pagan had filtered south from the fifth century onward to settle as a loose confederation of tribes in agricultural areas of Upper Burma. There they cultivated rice in the vast, fertile plain of the Irrawaddy River. As well as being experienced farmers, they were skilled horsemen and archers, and during the eleventh century, they united under a powerful king, Anawrahta, to form a single state centered in the capital of Pagan, on the left bank of the Irrawaddy River. Soon afterward, they invaded and occupied all of Lower Burma, where a major state had long been established by the Mon people. The Mon rulers were subsequently deported to Pagan, together with some 20,000 monks, artists, and artisans.

The conquest of the Mon had some curious results. Culturally, for a time, the conquerors became the conquered. The Mon language became the main language at the court in Pagan, and through the influence of Mon monks, the Burmese melded their traditional spirit worship with Theravada Buddhism. This process was further advanced by Kyanzittha, one of Anawrahta's many sons and his most outstanding general. After succeeding to the throne in 1084, Kyanzittha consolidated the whole of Burma under one central authority and wholeheartedly embraced Mon culture together with Theravada Buddhism.

By the time of his death in 1113, Kyanzittha had extended the frontiers of his kingdom to include most of present-day Burma aside from the northwest coast. However, this wise and effective monarch failed in his lifelong attempt to forge real unity between the Burmese and Mon peoples. Although the royal family intermarried with the Mon, their Burmese subjects despised the people from the south and would not admit them into society. During the reign of Kyanzittha's successor—his half-Mon grandson, Alaungsithu—the cultural influence of the Mon at Pagan diminished sharply, vanishing almost completely by 1174 when a new king, Narapatisithu, took his place upon the throne.

This was a watershed in Burmese history. The Mon tongue was eclipsed by Burmese as the language of literature and stone inscriptions. The weighty Mon style of architecture—derived from early Indian Buddhist temples hewn into caves—was rejected in favor of a loftier, more light-bathed Burmese style. More important, the Mon form of Theravada Buddhism was replaced by a version that was brought from

CITY OF SHRINES

Piercing the blue haze above the plain of Pagan, more than 2,000 Buddhist temples and stupas were erected as the crowning glory of Burma's Tambadipa kingdom. Each type of structure fulfilled a different purpose, the temples crowded with worshipers, the stupas—inaccessible to ordinary citizens—serving as repositories for relics. Every one of the structures was lovingly decorated, with the employment of a variety of techniques.

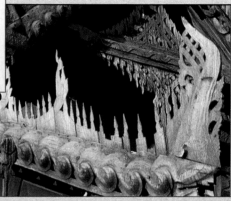

Each of the seven tiers of the four wooden pagodas surrounding the Shwezigon stupa in Pagan was fringed with elaborately carved wood.

Stucco was molded to make this frieze portraying a mythical demon that was believed to provide protection for any building adorned with its image.

Gold leaf was applied every few years to the Shwezigon stupa's dome. Elsewhere in Pagan, gold leaf was used to highlight carvings and paintwork.

Like most of Pagan's stone monuments, the Gawdawpalin Temple was painted with whitewash, both decoration and protection from the elements.

Ceylon by reformist monks. This version placed particular emphasis on the performance of acts of charity.

In other parts of Southeast Asia, various schools of Hinduism and Mahayana Buddhism were court religions, more or less imposed upon the populace. In Pagan, however, the new Buddhism became a genuinely popular faith. People of all ranks of society sought to accumulate merit by donating a part of their wealth—money, property, land, produce, livestock, and most commonly, labor—to the Buddhist establishment; and the kingdom's social and economic order was very much dependent on the people's cooperation, which their religion instilled in them as a duty.

Typical of the interior decoration of Pagan's religious buildings, this mural of a demon adorns a wall in the Myinkaba Kubyauk-gyi Temple, founded by a scholar prince in 1113. Wall paintings helped disseminate the Buddha's teachings to a largely illiterate congregation, serving as visual sermons on the scriptures. They were first sketched in charcoal, then colored with pigments imported from as far afield as India, China, and Ceylon.

Pagan had a more enveloping society than Java or Shrivijaya. The civil service answering to the hereditary royal family supervised the frontiers, planned the great temples and monasteries, and in the center of the state, oversaw the details of agricultural production. But any despotic notions that the Pagan kings harbored usually foundered on the shortcomings of the administration. Systems simply did not exist to direct the state from above; the peasants owned land, farmed it as they pleased, and cooperated informally to maintain their all-important irrigation channels. They were, however, required to pay taxes or provide seasonal labor for the state in lieu of taxes—and it was this labor, together with that of pious volunteers, that realized the construction of Pagan's innumerable temples.

In Pagan, as in other Southeast Asian kingdoms, state ceremonial figured prominently in the nation's life. A king would arrive for his coronation in a lavish procession, accompanied by a royal white horse and white elephant. (Both animals were tokens of kingship borrowed from India, the white elephant being an especially potent Buddhist symbol since it represented Buddha himself.) Once seated on his throne, the king was surrounded by bearers of the royal regalia—a white umbrella, a magic sword, a yak-tail fan, a crown, and sandals. Eight holy maidens administered holy water and adjured the king to rule in a just manner. Then the king intoned a magic formula reputed to have been uttered by the Buddha at birth: "I am foremost in all the world. I am the most excellent in all the world. I am peerless in the world." Finally, the king poured a libation of water from a golden ewer and meditated on the three jewels of the state religion—the Buddha, the law, and the congregation of monks that constituted the Sangha.

For all the pomp and ceremony, the king of Pagan was by no means a complete autocrat. His principal duty was to accumulate merit on behalf of the state as a whole. All the rulers of this kingdom were extravagant patrons of religion, making a great public show of their charity, piety, and concern for the people's welfare. Indeed, any king who failed to do so lay himself open to charges of being unfit for office and invited a palace coup. This burden of duty spurred an ever-mounting program of temple building. During Pagan's golden age, beginning in the late eleventh century, some 3,000 to 4,000 temples and shrines were erected in the twenty-five square miles of the capital, the greatest number going up during the reign of King Narapatisithu.

Some of these buildings were architecturally outstanding. For example, the Ananda Temple, Kyanzittha's masterpiece in the Mon style, was conceived as a solid mass in which vaulted corridors led to four dark central chambers in each of which a gigantic statue of the Buddha was illuminated by a shaft of natural light to achieve the maximum theatrical effect. Altogether, the temple contained 1,400 terra-cotta and 1,600 stone sculptures, including 80 reliefs depicting the progress of the Buddha to enlightenment. The great temples of Sulamani, Htilominlo, and Gawdawpalin ex-emplified the Burmese style, with their great light-admitting doorways, brightly colored interiors, and sense of space and height.

By the late twelfth century, Pagan had become a powerful, prosperous, and cultured state of 1.5 to 2 million people living in a country that stretched from the borders of China to the tip of the southernmost peninsula of Burma. Never had its military might been greater, its agriculture more productive, its temples and monasteries more affluent. Yet, in none of these respects could it quite equal the success of its rival, the Khmer kingdom of Angkor, beyond the mountains in the southeast.

The Khmer had been an important force in Southeast Asia for even longer than the Burmese. The origins of the Khmer lay not in a single tribe but in a large linguistically related group of peoples, the Mon-Khmer, who had settled over a vast area between Burma and the China Sea in prehistoric times. Attracted by fertile, annually flooded lands, they had concentrated their settlements in the valley of the Tonle Sap—the great central lake of Cambodia—and close to the major rivers, especially the Irrawaddy, the Menam, and the lower regions of the Mekong.

As early as the first century AD, a Khmer prince had seized control of the lower Mekong basin. But for hundreds of years, the kingdom he created was plagued with power struggles. Later the Khmer of the Mekong basin fell under Javanese influence. It was not until the year 802 that the anarchic Khmer communities of the middle Mekong and great lake region were united to form a powerful new state loyal to one divine ruler. By this time, the Khmer had fallen under the spell of Hindu ideas. Under the new state religion, the principal object of worship—and the symbol of the king's supernatural connections—was the lingam, a sacred stone pillar shaped like a phallus, which represented the creative power of the Hindu god Shiva. But the Khmer never completely gave up their ancient tradition of ancestor worship. The temples they built from the seventh century onward, while exploiting magnificent Indian forms, were always dedicated to the ancestors of the builder and were usually also tombs, intended to house his own remains.

In the tenth century, the Khmer founded their great capital of Angkor in the alluvial plain between Tonle Sap Lake and the sacred Mount Mahendra, traditional home of the ancestor spirits. Around the city, they built colossal reservoirs to feed an urban network of canals representing the six primordial seas of the universe.

From their new capital, the Khmer army—a mighty force composed of archers, a cavalry of lancers and charioteers, and a royal regiment of elephants, numbering many tens of thousands strong—burst out to make the kingdom so extensive that it was no longer identified by its capital, Angkor, but by a national name: Kambuja or Kambujadesa, which honored Kambu, a mythical personage from whom the Khmer of that time believed themselves to be descended. Eventually, this name would evolve into Cambodia.

From the middle of the eleventh century, the Khmer state controlled the largest territorial empire in Southeast Asia—all of Cambodia and most of present-day Laos, Thailand, and South Vietnam. But in this relatively underpopulated region, the most valuable and significant gain from its conquests was not territory but human energy: Countless thousands of prisoners who were set to work to build fortifications, temples, and irrigation systems. In the process, society grew more urbanized, the bureaucracy more centralized; and at the dawn of the twelfth century, the kingdom began an age of extraordinary prosperity, one that paralleled and ultimately surpassed the golden age of Pagan.

The key to the Khmer's prosperity was the exceptionally high yield of their rice fields. In Cambodia as a whole, it rained for only half the year, during the monsoon season, and in the region of Angkor, the rainy season was even shorter. But the annual flood of the Mekong inundated such an enormous area of land that it was a relatively easy matter for the peasant farmers to hold back the water for their paddy fields. At least one, often two, rice crops could be produced every year. Part of every crop had to be given as tax to the king and part to the local temple. Even so, the rice yield was more than sufficient to feed the population. With the surplus, the enormous slave-labor force was fed.

Although rice cultivation was the mainstay of the Khmer's economy, they also grew millet and other crops, and tended groves of banana, orange, and pomegranate trees. Moreover, they offered for sale a variety of exotic products that attracted foreign merchants, especially ones from China. Most of these goods were the natural products of the mountain forests, brought to the lowlands by hill tribes: cardamom grown in the Cardamom Mountains; rare scented woods, resin, and beeswax; rhinoceros horn and elephant ivory; and, above all, the flashing and iridescent feathers of Cambodian kingfishers.

Because of their brilliant sheen and coloring, the feathers of kingfishers were more highly prized than any other goods on the Chinese market; for centuries they had been fashioned into blue and green tiaras that were virtually mandatory headgear for the bride at a Chinese wedding. Consequently, the birds were netted in vast numbers at forest pools by Khmer hunters, who used a caged female kingfisher to attract the male. In return for such jungle novelties, Chinese merchants brought to Angkor the goods of their more advanced industrial economy: gold and silver ware, paper, pewter, porcelain, mercury, saltpeter, lacquered or copper plates, iron pots, umbrellas, wooden combs, and flower-patterned silks.

The Khmer's prosperity first peaked in the reign of Suryavarman II, who came to the throne in 1113 and ruled for most of the first half of the twelfth century. It was under his aegis that work began on the huge, sprawling temple of Angkor Wat. The temple was set at the end of a triumphal avenue, and its architecture was the consummate artistic expression of a society that had reached maturity. Its scale and symmetry were breathtaking, but perhaps its most staggering feature was the relief sculpture decorating every terrace, gallery, pillar, and buttress. The tapestry of stone depicted scenes from Hindu epics and scenes of Khmer military victories.

Requiring an estimated 455 million cubic yards of building materials—most of them probably transported by rafts over the vast network of rivers and canals from quarries at least twenty-five miles away—Angkor Wat was a stone microcosm of the Khmer cosmology. The five gilded towers of its central temple symbolized the peaks of Meru, the cosmic mountain; its outer walls marked the edge of the world, and its surrounding moat the ocean that lay beyond. But besides representing the world mountain of Indian metaphysics, it probably served as the funerary temple of Suryavarman II, his ashes being placed in the central tower. Like all Khmer kings, Suryavarman was obsessed with power not just during, but also after, his lifetime.

Ostensibly, Suryavarman's reign was a glorious one. It saw the creation not only of Angkor but also of numerous other temples, both near the capital and in distant provinces, for all the provincial aristocracy felt the need to reinforce their power by building edifices as grandiose as they could afford. The king's ambassadors were dispatched to the imperial court of China. The armies of Suryavarman II achieved notable victories in renewed wars against the kingdom of Champa in southern Vietnam.

But the cost to the kingdom was very high. The king's extravagant public works and military expeditions emptied the exchequer; not long soon after his death, in about 1150, the fortunes of Cambodia were dramatically reversed.

The authority of the monarchy was now seriously weakened by a succession of power struggles between rival claimants to the throne. Villagers and ambitious regional lords rebelled. Then the frontier defenses started to crumble. In 1177, the Cham, traditionally a seafaring people, sailed up the Mekong to the Tonle Sap and eventually overran Angkor itself. Temples and sanctuaries were ransacked for their gold and treasures; the entire capital was laid to waste.

Remarkably, this catastrophe marked not the end of Khmer power but a time of renewed glory. After four years of anarchy, royal authority was reestablished by Jayavarman VII, a cousin of Suryavarman II. He routed the Cham invaders in a great naval battle, regained the capital, and in 1181, was crowned king at Angkor. His reign, which extended into the next century, saw the Cambodian state rise to even greater heights of achievement and dominion. The Khmer now produced more rice and built more temples than they ever had before. By the turn of the thirteenth century, some 4,000 temples were scattered across the land. The late twelfth century also saw the Khmer empire expand still further. Most notably, in 1190, the king's avenging army overwhelmed the kingdom of Champa. The ruler of the Cham was brought as a captive to Angkor, along with a multitude of prisoners who were to be employed on Jayavarman's stupendous building program, the most ambitious one undertaken in the history of the Khmer people.

Dressed in the costume of a Burmese prince, this gilded temple guardian protected one of the four shrines of Pagan's Ananda Temple, built in 1105 by King Kyanzittha. Pilgrims would pass the stucco-coated birch statue on their way to offer prayers, flowers, and incense before images of the Buddha. Although the guardian's function was to repel evil, whether in spiritual or human guise, he was carved with a calm smile hovering on his lips; Buddhist teaching enjoined all to suppress their emotions and remain placid no matter how provoked.

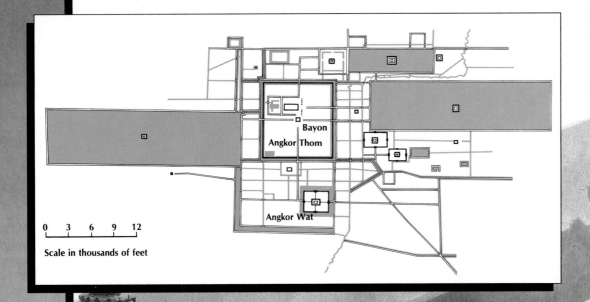

(inset)

Bayon

Angkor Thom

Angkor Wat

0   3   6   9   12

Scale in thousands of feet

ANGKOR'S MARVEL

The largest sacred structure in the world, the temple of Angkor Wat covers more than 300 acres yet occupies only a tiny fraction of the Angkor complex *(inset)*—a royal city and religious center laid out over some 135 square miles. Founded early in the twelfth century and dedicated to the Hindu god Vishnu, the temple became a Buddhist shrine. Pilgrims of both faiths worshiped there, approaching it down a wide causeway more than a third of a mile long, symbolizing the rainbow bridge to heaven. Entering the temple enclosure through gateways guarded by seven-headed serpents, visitors came to the steeply terraced central shrine, surmounted by five gilded towers representing Mount Meru, home of the gods. Everywhere the temple's sandstone fabric was decorated with relief carvings, some depicting demons, deities, and beasts, others showing scenes of the Khmer in peace and in war.

Before he ascended the Khmer throne, Jayavarman VII had embraced the doctrines of Buddhism. Now, as king, he established Buddhism as the dominant religion of the Khmer empire. The figure of a bodhisattva became the personification of the king's divine connections in place of the royal lingam of Hindu times; and, in the style of contemporary rulers in Pagan, Jayavarman determined to seek merit for himself and his realm by the construction of greater and greater monuments to the Enlightened One.

The most ambitious project of Jayavarman's reign was the building of a new royal capital adjacent to the old one. This was Angkor Thom (Great Capital), which in terms of audacity and scale could only be rivaled by nearby Angkor Wat. Surrounded by a 295-foot-wide moat, Angkor Thom could be approached only by a long causeway bordered by two rows of eight-foot-high stone figures and by balustrades in the form of a rearing naga, a many-headed cobra. The capital was guarded by a great wall, eight miles long, which was pierced by five magnificent gateways, each fifty-nine feet high. The gates were adorned with carvings of elephants and lotuses, and surmounted by towers bearing four enormous faces of the Buddha.

Within a second, inner wall lay the royal apartments, variously roofed with lead or yellow pottery tiles, and the offices and residences of the high priests, nobles, cour-

At the center of Angkor Thom stood the Bayon, a huge Buddhist temple decorated with friezes in relief depicting scenes of life in the Khmer empire. The detail below shows Khmer palace servants cooking a banquet in the open air—the sort of feast celebrated a dozen times a year on religious holidays. The preparations are taking place under an awning stretched between trees teeming with monkeys and peacocks. On the right of the frieze, two men grill meat held in cleft sticks over a bed of charcoal. Next to them a pig is lowered into a cauldron as an assistant blows vigorously to fan the flames. To the left, a cook pours rice into a boiling pot, while another adds to a pile of baskets, and a third fills clay jars. Bustling among these figures, waiters carry trays laden with bowls of rice to the feasters.

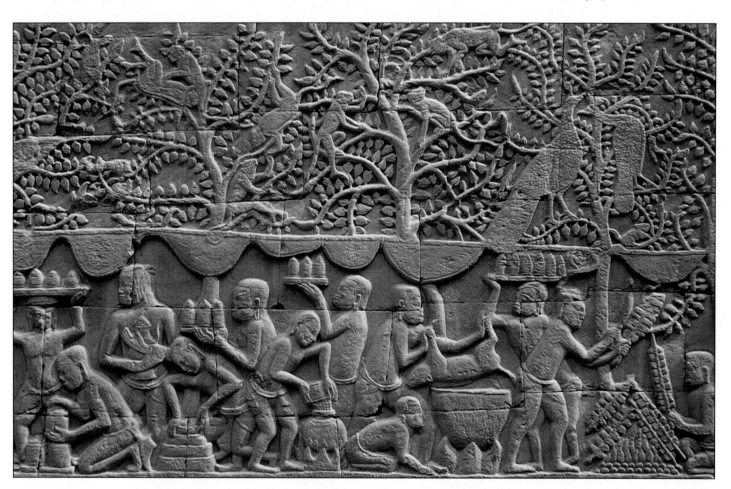

Some of the Bayon friezes commemorate the victories of the temple's founder, Jayavarman VII, whose campaigns against the Cham empire extended Khmer power into present-day Vietnam. A Khmer warrior *(immediately above)* thrusts his spear into the eye of a Cham opponent. In the scene at top, a company of Khmer foot soldiers rush forward, their spears raised. One of the infantrymen *(far right)* wears a jacket of flowered cotton to mark his superior rank; the rest fight seminaked. Though not depicted here, paintings of animals whose ferocity the soldiers hoped to emulate often decorated their bodies. Mounted on an elephant among the infantrymen, an archer prepares to shoot. Elephants, in addition to their role as mobile shooting platforms, were used to punch through an enemy's defenses.

tiers, and generals. These stately buildings lined a grand central square, scene of the pomp and pageantry of an imperial capital: religious ceremonies, military reviews, and state occasions with massed bands and spectacular parades.

In the middle of the city rose the king's new temple-mountain, the Bayon, whose soaring gold-leaf tower, surrounded by scores of lesser towers, marked the very heart of the Khmer empire. A vainglorious extravaganza of statues and bas-reliefs, the Bayon in its own era surpassed even Angkor Wat in prestige. The Bayon housed an immense statue of the Buddha. And on its fifty-four towers were carved 200 huge, faintly smiling faces—ostensibly faces of the Buddha but bearing more than a passing likeness to the king himself. They peered down from every direction, so that wherever a person walked in the city, an image of the omnipresent Buddha gazed after him. In addition, the temple boasted more than half a mile of bas-reliefs that, unlike those of earlier temple-mountains, depicted the everyday lives of contemporary Khmers.

Besides building Angkor Thom, Jayavarman VII sought religious merit through acts of charity. While his first wife worked to improve the lives of the people (she took in and resettled hundreds of poor young girls who had been abandoned), the king himself was preoccupied with the health of his people—so much so that one stone inscription recorded: "He suffered from the sickness of his subjects more than from his own; for it is the public grief that makes the grief of kings and not their own."

During Jayavarman's reign, more than one hundred state hospitals were in service, some of them as far away as northern Thailand and Laos. According to inscriptions

that may or may not have exaggerated a trifle, each hospital was served by a staff of over one hundred people, including two doctors, two pharmacists, fourteen male and female nurses, two cooks, two rice pounders, two clerks, and sixty general assistants.

Jayavarman VII also advanced the Angkor civilization by the building of roads, bridges, and rest houses. Previously, communications in the Khmer empire had been poor; for the most part, upcountry travelers had to make their way by crude jungle tracks. Jayavarman had three main roads constructed—one leading northwest through the Dangrek Hills to the town of Phimai, another heading from Angkor Thom toward Champa on the Vietnamese coast, a third connecting Angkor with Kompong Thom, about sixty miles to the southwest. These highways involved some impressive engineering: Along the Kompong Thom road, for example, the Khmer built twenty-two stone bridges, the largest of which, the Spean Praptos, was designed with twenty-one arches to cross over a deep ravine. And all of the highways had numerous rest houses, sited at intervals, to provide shelter and sustenance for the weary traveler.

Angkor's empire in its twelfth- and thirteenth-century heyday included huge tracts of tropical rain forest where elephants and tigers roamed and village life was rudimen-

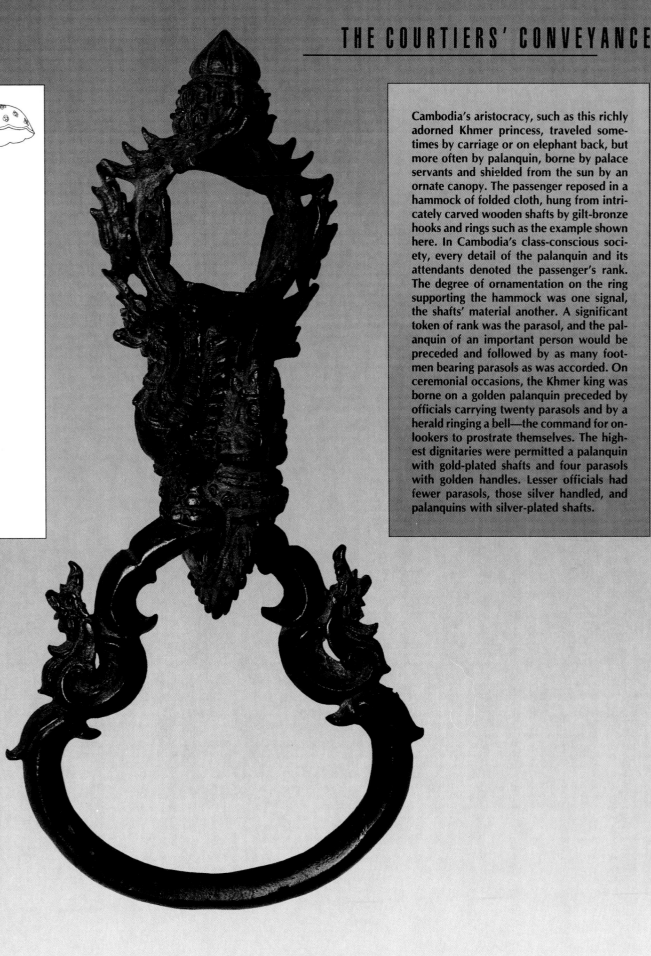

Cambodia's aristocracy, such as this richly adorned Khmer princess, traveled sometimes by carriage or on elephant back, but more often by palanquin, borne by palace servants and shielded from the sun by an ornate canopy. The passenger reposed in a hammock of folded cloth, hung from intricately carved wooden shafts by gilt-bronze hooks and rings such as the example shown here. In Cambodia's class-conscious society, every detail of the palanquin and its attendants denoted the passenger's rank. The degree of ornamentation on the ring supporting the hammock was one signal, the shafts' material another. A significant token of rank was the parasol, and the palanquin of an important person would be preceded and followed by as many footmen bearing parasols as was accorded. On ceremonial occasions, the Khmer king was borne on a golden palanquin preceded by officials carrying twenty parasols and by a herald ringing a bell—the command for onlookers to prostrate themselves. The highest dignitaries were permitted a palanquin with gold-plated shafts and four parasols with golden handles. Lesser officials had fewer parasols, those silver handled, and palanquins with silver-plated shafts.

tary. The Angkorean heartland, however, was now a well-developed agricultural zone. From the lofty towers of Angkor Thom, the king of Cambodia could survey a carefully planned landscape extending as far as the eye could see—a gentle, sloping plain dotted with temples and settlements, and marked out like a checkerboard with a vast network of rivers, canals, and flooded rice fields.

Here, in and around the metropolis, at least half a million people—perhaps a quarter of the total Khmer population—lived by farming, and by fishing the abundantly stocked waters of the Mekong and the great lake of Tonle Sap to the south. In Angkor, as in Pagan, no one knew hunger. Every free citizen had at least one or two hectares to cultivate, and except for the unpredictable intrusion of disease or conscription for military service, life was not harsh.

The gap between poor and rich was nonetheless great. In Angkor's social pyramid the hereditary king stood at the apex. Beneath him was a ruling elite of hereditary royal priests whose families made up a provincial aristocracy. The prominent families of the provinces had in the past been kings in their own right, and even in the twelfth century, they felt they had rights over the Khmer throne—which they exercised principally by marrying their daughters to the king. The priesthood was itself graded: The royal chaplain came near the top, with assorted scholars, astrologers, poets, and ritual sacrificers further down. It was from the ranks of the priesthood that the professional civil service, the daily administrators of the affairs of state, were drawn. The priests enshrined the power of the king, enforced the laws, and kept out all pretenders to power from the lower orders.

A long way below the priests came the trade guilds of craftworkers and skilled artisans; and below them were the army officers and village heads who commanded the local militia in the provinces and who, in time of war, were expected to place their peasant forces at the disposal of the army. Then came the overwhelming majority of the Khmer population: the farmers who cleared the forests, tilled the land, cultivated the rice, and after the harvests had been gathered in, paid labor service to the king by helping to build great temples, palaces, and public works.

The peasants, however, were not quite the lowest of the low. Beneath them were three categories of slaves. There were prisoners of war from campaigns in Burma and Champa, and in the small Mon and Thai states; primitive tribespeople rounded up in raids in the forests and mountains; and native-born Khmers, temporarily enslaved in punishment for misdemeanors or as a way of paying off debts. Slaves usually labored at the most arduous and unsavory jobs, such as the building of temples and aqueducts. However, many also filled specialized roles, whether as cooks, librarians, gardeners, dancers, scribes, flower collectors, or musicians. Some Khmers voluntarily accepted slavery as an expression of religious sacrifice: These volunteers were normally assigned to temple maintenance.

In theory, the king exercised absolute power over this social pyramid. Indeed, he was extolled in court literature as a man who excelled all others in all ways—as a veritable superman credited with the strength to lift ten wrestlers simultaneously. In reality, however, his possession of the throne depended on the support of the regional lordly families, especially those related to his mother and his principal wife. Occasionally, a king might be overthrown in a palace revolution, but never by someone outside the ranks of the aristocracy. Always the new monarch came from the ruling class of priests.

Despite the king's vulnerability to aristocratic rivals, he remained inviolate in the

Armed with nets, pots, and spears, Cambodians mount a nocturnal fishing expedition on the great lake of Tonle Sap, near the Mekong River. The size of the catch was determined by the rhythm of the seasons, since each year as the summer monsoon flood waters receded, Tonle Sap became an enormous natural trap—a squirming stew of carp, gudgeon, and tench. Working mainly by night, the fishermen used torches made from palm leaves to lure the shoals toward the dugout canoes.

eyes of the ordinary people. A godlike figure, he left his Angkor palace on ceremonial occasions accompanied by cavalry, massed bands, princes and ministers of state on elephants, and thousands of palace maidens, some armed with shields and lances, others brandishing flaming torches or candles and bearing utensils of gold and silver. The king's wives and concubines, shaded by gold-flecked parasols, rode in chariots, in howdahs on elephant back, or in litters borne on men's shoulders. The king himself, surrounded by troops of soldiers, stood on the back of a magnificently caparisoned elephant whose tusks were sheathed in gold; as the king passed by, the crowds knelt down and touched their foreheads to the ground.

The courtiers shared much of the king's magnificence. The aristocrats who dwelt within Angkor Thom employed at least one hundred slaves per household and dined from gold and silver tableware. Their wooden residences, roofed with tiles, were furnished with rugs imported from China, with skins of tiger, panther, or deer, with bronze thrones, low tables, and embroidered curtains. Carved friezes of floral designs decorated the walls, and vases of flowers scented the air. The aristocracy swathed their bodies in Chinese silks and brocades, dressed their hair in elaborate chignons, and perfumed themselves with sandalwood or musk.

Zhou Daguan, a Chinese envoy, resided in Angkor for one year in the late thirteenth century and kept a copious record of his experiences. He saw Angkor just after its peak, but his observations were often highly prejudiced, for, like most Chinese, he viewed all foreigners as barbarians. He did, however, acknowledge that Khmer court life was refined and sophisticated.

Peasant life was infinitely simpler; Zhou judged it to be somewhat primitive. Both men and women wore only a simple rectangle of cloth wrapped around the waist and became deeply tanned by the sun. They lived in stilt houses walled and floored with bamboo slats and thatched with palm leaves. Recording his impressions of a typical Khmer home, Zhou wrote: "The ordinary people have a house, but without table, bench, basin, or bucket. They simply use a clay pot for cooking rice and make the sauce on an earthen stove. They bury three stones for the hearth and help themselves to dishes by using the shell of a coconut as a ladle. The rice is served on Chinese plates of earthenware or copper, and they help themselves to the sauce with leaves of which they make small cups. For spoons, they use smaller leaves that can be thrown away when they have finished. For sleeping, they use only bamboo mats, and they also sleep on the floorboards."

For the peasants, social life centered around the communal meal. Zhou described this repast as "simple," although he went on to describe a varied and appetizing diet. The staple foods were rice and fish—perhaps gudgeon, shad, carp, eel, or shark—supplemented by pork, venison, prawns, shellfish, turtle, vegetables, and fruit. There were also alcoholic drinks made from fermented honey, sugarcane, rice, and leaves.

The ordinary people had plenty of diversions. Snake charmers, storytellers, minstrels, and dwarfs provided endless entertainment on the streets of towns and villages. Elephant, hog, and cock fighting were always popular spectacles. Individual sports such as boxing, wrestling, and archery had many adherents, as did various team activities, including ball games and a form of polo. Moreover, every month saw a public gala or major religious ceremony, and the New Year in October was celebrated with a two-week-long festival climaxed by a firework display.

Another social pleasure—almost mandatory in Cambodia's sticky climate—was bathing. There were no bathhouses in Angkor, but freshwater pools and moats and canals were all about, and in this aquatic civilization it was usual for almost everyone to make at least one weekly excursion to a nearby river. This was a joyful occasion and a picturesque scene: The lotus blossom flourished in the pools of Angkor, and exotic birds such as rosy pelicans, bronze ibis, and purple heron stalked the riverbanks. But Zhou did not entirely approve. So much bathing, he felt, was surely bad for the health. Worse, the women "have no shame about leaving their clothes on the riverbank and going into the water."

Zhou considered Khmer women to be very passionate and Khmer society to be dissolute. Girls, he reported, were allowed a premarital liaison with their future husbands, and married women felt entitled to be unfaithful if their husbands were away from home for more than ten days—as often happened in time of war. "I am not a spirit," a neglected wife would say. "How then may I sleep by myself?" On the other hand, as Zhou reported, if a wife were caught committing adultery, her husband could lawfully crush her lover's legs between two stone blocks until the lover had agreed to hand over all his possessions in compensation.

Marriage remained a highly respected institution, for sexual union was seen to have a social purpose far beyond purely personal pleasure. It was regarded as a symbolic rite necessary to ensure the continuing fertility of the land as well as of the population. Responsibility in this respect weighed especially on the prowess of the king. Every night, whether he liked it or not, one of his palace courtesans would come to his bedchamber. Any failure to comply with this amorous routine would have been considered fatal for the well-being of the nation.

The Khmer Potter's Craft

While the richest Khmers prized translucent Chinese porcelain, the merely affluent acquired less refined, but inventive, glazed wares by local potters. Made from coarse materials, built up in coils or thrown on a wheel, the pots were often shaped as stylized animals and colored with copper or iron oxides for a green, brown, or black surface. Owls, elephants, and rabbits—such as at right—were favorite subjects. The Khmers linked elephants with kingship and warfare, but the forms of owls and rabbits were simply liked. Cats were also portrayed; popular pets in Southeast Asia, they killed rats in the rice barns.

Large pots by Khmer potters stored water, grain, and oil; small pots held powdered mineral lime, which was chewed with betel leaves, a stimulant producing a sense of well-being.

At the time of Zhou's stay, the king of Cambodia had five wives—"one for his private apartment and the other four for the four points of the compass. As for his concubines and girls of the palace, I have heard their number estimated at between three and five thousand, divided into several classes." In addition, a royal troupe of dancing girls was permanently on call, retained mostly to reenact stories or scenes from the Hindu epics in the presence of the royal family.

According to Zhou, the noblewomen, especially those of priestly families, occupied a prominent place in Khmer society. Not only did they marry kings; some, by force of their personality and intellect, achieved positions of state in their own right. Never venturing outdoors without a shaded palanquin or a parasol of red Chinese taffeta, the ladies of the aristocracy preserved the paleness of their complexions: "white as jade," Zhou called them.

The Chinese envoy was less complimentary about Khmer women of the lower orders. "The women here age very quickly," he observed, "probably because they marry and have children before they are old enough. At twenty or thirty, they look as old as Chinese ladies of forty or fifty. But then it is they who do the work, who attend to commerce. If a Chinese upon arriving here takes a wife, it is, among other things, to profit from her commercial aptitudes. Each day the market opens at six and closes at noon. There are no little shops in which people live, but they use a kind of straw mat, which they spread on the ground. Each has her own spot. I have heard tell that they pay the authorities for their pitches. In the smaller transactions, the payment

This elephant vessel has the rounded form of much Khmer pottery. The opening is in the center of the howdah that rests on the beast's back.

is rice, cereals, and Chinese objects; next are cloth goods; and for large transactions, gold and silver are used."

Overall, from his male perspective, Zhou viewed Angkor with some favor: "Rice is plentiful, women easy to find, the houses easy to manage, property easy to manage, and business good." But, he stressed, there were darker sides to Cambodian life. Certain household slaves—aborigines captured from the mountain solitudes—were treated rather like animals by their Khmer owners. Tropical diseases were rife; Zhou mentioned leprosy, but cholera, typhoid, and malaria were also probably common. The forests beyond the civilized center of the realm were full of perils: crocodiles straying from the swamps, leeches, tigers, wild buffaloes, and bandits.

At the time when Zhou was committing his judgments on Angkor society to paper, the great civilization of Pagan was crumbling; Angkor itself was under threat, although it would not really succumb until the fifteenth century. Both cultures owed their disintegration partly to their architectural extravagance, which left very little money in the treasury to defend the state against foreign attackers. But the downfall of the two great temple states was due in even greater measure to fundamental weaknesses in their power structures.

In Pagan, the flaw was the hold the Buddhist church possessed over the monarchy. The kings of Pagan, responding to the Buddhist emphasis on generosity, persisted in giving huge tracts of land to the Sangha who—unlike private individuals—were not

These two jars take the form of a pair of whimsical cats—the one frowning, the other wearing a mischievous grin.

subject to taxation. Thus the kings sacrificed large sources of revenue that were needed to fuel the military. Occasionally a king, recognizing his exposure, would accuse the Sangha of becoming worldly and take back some of the land that had been granted. But the kings were also thwarted in their budget-balancing efforts by tax-dodging individuals who would pretend to donate land to the Sangha while secretly arranging that it should reach the hands of a particular monk; when he died, the land would revert to the original owner.

In 1270, Kublai Khan, the Mongol emperor of China, sent three ambassadors to Burma to demand homage. When his envoys failed to return, he launched a series of retaliatory raids that culminated in all-out invasion and the occupation of Pagan in 1287. Thereafter, although many of its finer brick-built temples and pagodas survived, the once-mighty capital soon became a mere village.

It is unlikely that the kingdom of Pagan, even at the height of its military power, could have resisted the armies of Kublai Khan. But the Chinese invasion accelerated the disintegration of a state already faced with rebellion by the Mon of Lower Burma and by rival chieftaincies in the north. Unlike Angkor, which was dependent on the support of powerful regional families, the Pagan state tried to keep its Burmese empire strictly under central control. When the capital was lost, the entire state fell apart.

In Angkor, as in Pagan, the economy was seriously weakened by the twelfth-century spending spree on new temples. While the Khmer were preoccupied with building, a new threat was growing on their western frontier. The Thai, a dynamic highland people driven south by the Chinese, had crossed the mountain regions of Laos and Upper Burma and were expanding their territory in the region of the Menam basin, which had long been under Khmer suzerainty. In 1431, after two centuries of intermittent fighting, the Thai overran the Cambodian heartland; the following year the great capital of Angkor was abandoned to the jungle.

Even before the final onslaught, Khmer civilization had been gravely weakened by civil war. Angkor's fundamental problem lay in the division of power among so many regional lordly families, all with royal connections. In about 1430, the death of a Cambodian king had resulted in a fierce contest for the succession and the defection of many powerful nobles and priests. When the Thai invaded, the capital had already lost its authority over its outlying provinces; and after the fall of Angkor, Cambodia plunged into total chaos as long-running dynastic struggles continued to undermine all attempts to rebuild the state.

With the eclipse of first Pagan and then Angkor, the era of the great temple states was at an end. Shrivijaya, too, declined from the thirteenth century onward: Mongol depredations stifled trade with China in the thirteenth century, and in the fourteenth century, Shrivijaya's main trading partner in India, the Chola empire, fell to another Indian power. With the loss of its trading contacts, Shrivijaya was left high and dry.

Of the four great states of twelfth-century Southeast Asia, only East Java, with an expanding trade in pepper, cloves, and nutmeg from its outlying islands, was to grow stronger in the centuries that followed. When European navigators found their way to Southeast Asia in the fifteenth century, it was the spices of the Moluccas that beckoned. By then, the glory of Pagan and Angkor was no more than a memory.

A RENAISSANCE OF LEARNING

As western Europe struggled to emerge from the Dark Ages, a new interest in learning began to stir in its monasteries, cathedrals, and courts. Though most intense in France, the thirst for knowledge seized thinkers as far afield as Scotland and Italy.

A crippling gulf separated twelfth-century scholars from the cultural and intellectual heritage of the ancient world. The instability that resulted from the dissolution of the Roman Empire had scattered the knowledge of centuries, leaving—at least in western Europe—only a few treasured remnants salvaged from the wreck of classical culture.

The ancient knowledge had not been eradicated everywhere, however. In the Greek-speaking eastern half of the Roman Empire, scholarly traditions had remained unbroken, and the Arabs as well, after their explosive expansion during the seventh and eighth centuries, had developed a cultured civilization that adopted and advanced the classical Greek tradition of academic inquiry.

With the gradual return of stability to western Europe, people of intellect established contacts with Byzantium and the Muslim world. Much progress followed the fall of Moorish Toledo to Christian forces in 1085. Christian translators collaborated with Jewish and Arabic scholars to unlock the wealth of classical and Arabian ideas stored in the Spanish libraries in the fields of medicine, philosophy, astronomy, natural history, music, and mathematics.

Another transmission point for knowledge was the cosmopolitan kingdom of Sicily, where Norman, Greek, and Muslim thinkers had long cooperated. Scholars who traveled to Palermo in pursuit of knowledge found clerks employed at the royal court *(above)* working in all three scholarly languages—Greek, "Saracen" (Arabic), and Latin.

The result of these activities was an intellectual renaissance that swept the Christian west, reaching its peak in the second half of the twelfth century: No side of life remained untouched by the new spirit of critical inquiry.

The theologian Hugh of Saint Victor, as seen above, lectures in the city of Paris.

Drawn by the fame of a succession of brilliant teachers, students traveled from all over Europe to the cathedral schools of Rheims, Chartres, Laon, and Paris. At these centers of learning—precursors of the universities—Latin, the universal language of educated Christendom, made knowledge accessible to all nationalities.

The primary subject of study—as well as the justification for all forms of intellectual inquiry—continued to be the word of God as handed down in holy writ; but a new spirit of inquiry and scrutiny was replacing the previous attitude of unquestioning acceptance. The first steps were taken in the long task of reconciling mystical interpretations of the faith with the demands of reason and logic as expressed by such thinkers as Aristotle and the sixth-century Roman Boethius.

As an aid to systematic study of the scriptures, the marginal comments, or glosses, of generations of scholars were collected and standardized in fresh editions that gained wide circulation.

Text and parallel comment are skillfully compressed into a harmonious and legible form by a scribe in this copy of the first five books of the Old Testament that once belonged to Thomas Becket.

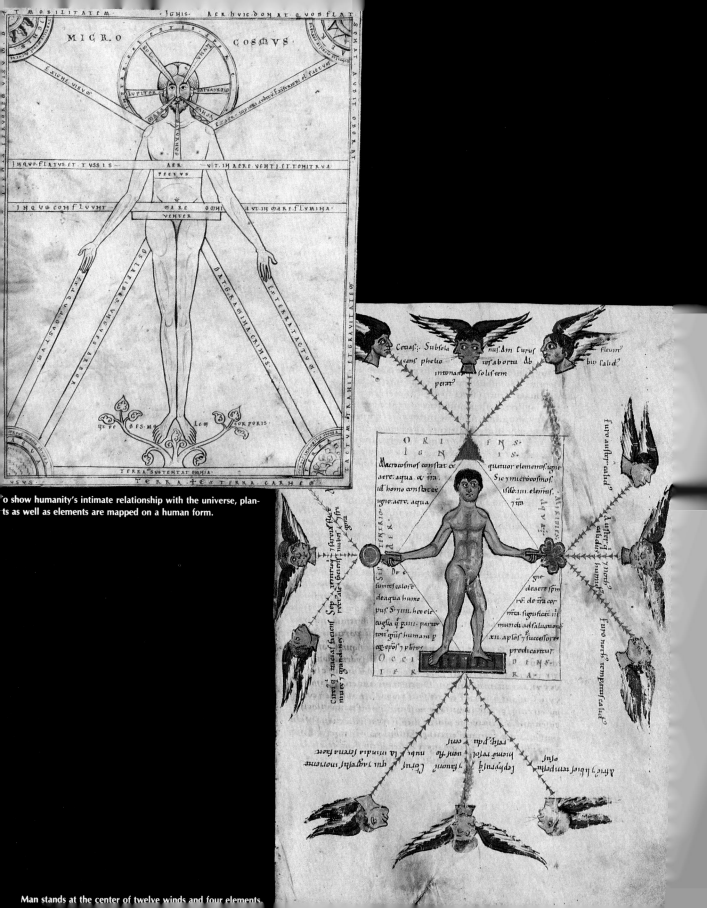

To show humanity's intimate relationship with the universe, plants as well as elements are mapped on a human form.

Man stands at the center of twelve winds and four elements.

THE PHILOSOPHICAL DEBATE

In the changing intellectual climate, thinkers began to progress from the theological study of God's word to a consideration of the nature of the world and of humankind itself. Because they regarded the natural world as an expression of God's intentions, such scholars sought to find an underlying divine pattern rather than to make an empirical study of concrete phenomena.

A human being was seen as both a part of the world and also a microcosm containing within himself all the principles and elements—earth, air, fire, and water—of which the macrocosmic world was composed. Many attempts were made *(far left and left)* to give diagrammatic expression to this relationship.

The new mathematical insights that the Christian world owed to Arabian thought were particularly exciting to medieval scholars. Calculation had already been made simpler than in Roman times by the introduction at the beginning of the eleventh century of the abacus, which put ones, tens, and hundreds in different columns; now the translation of a treatise on Arabic numerals, which unlike the Roman system included zero, allowed calculations in the decimal system to be written down. To contemporary minds it seemed that numerical ratios underlay all creation, especially the relations of the musical scale *(right)*.

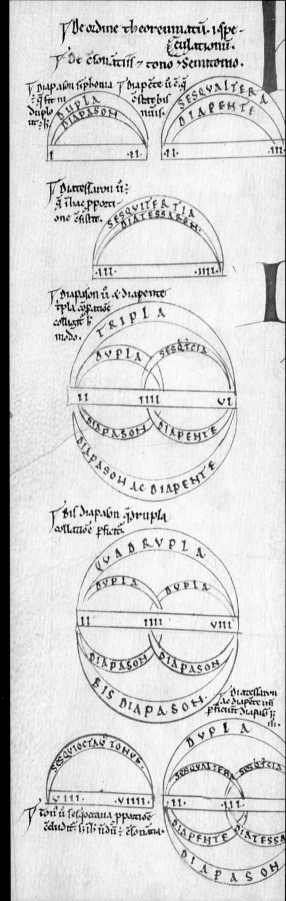

A series of proportional arc diagrams express the mathematical ratios, first formulated in classical Greece, that govern the intervals of the musical scale.

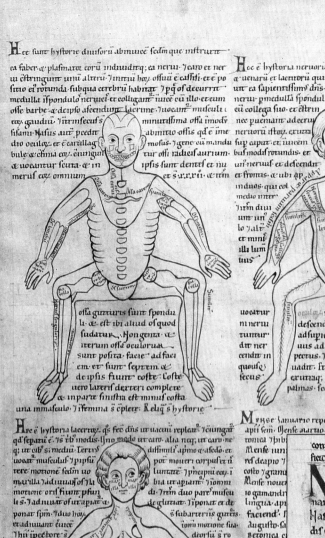

These anatomical diagrams were derived from the Greek doctor Galen.

Known to the Romans, crowfoot was a medieval remedy for dog bites.

in herbal medicines used by the Romans, and anatomy taught according to principles laid down by the Greek physician Galen. In the twelfth century, the school revived surgery and made important advances in anatomical knowledge, but emphasis remained firmly on the practical aspects of medicine, with little attention being paid to the underlying theory. The real revolution occurred after 1130, when scholars in Toledo began translating the works of the eleventh-century Arab philosopher and scientist Avicenna. In a canon more than a million words long covering every aspect of health, Avicenna took pains to show that medicine was a science, not an empirical art, thus helping raise the discipline to a new level of theoretical dignity.

1 A doctor directs the pounding of herbs.

2 An epileptic is treated by surgery.

3 Dots map the correct points for cautery.

4 A surgeon operates to

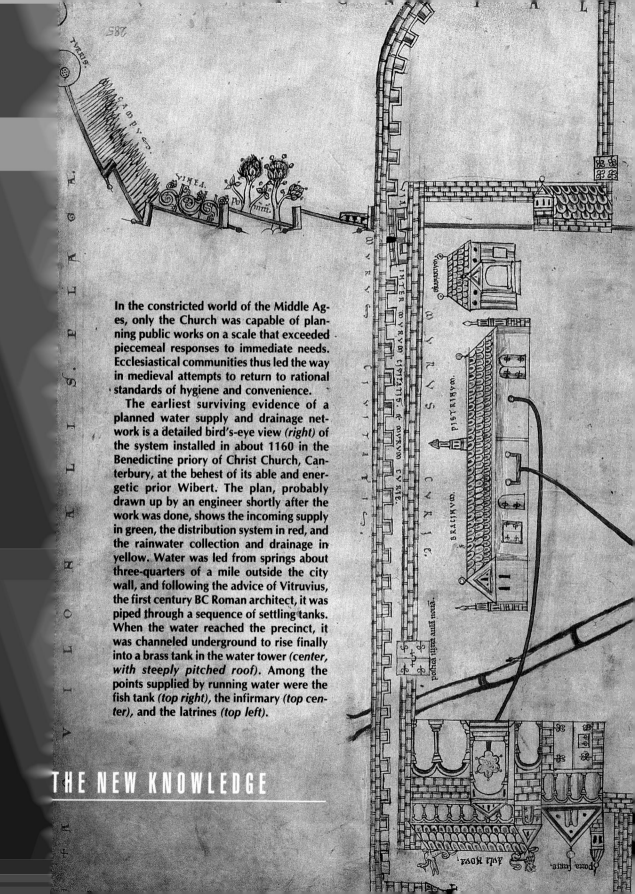

In the constricted world of the Middle Ages, only the Church was capable of planning public works on a scale that exceeded piecemeal responses to immediate needs. Ecclesiastical communities thus led the way in medieval attempts to return to rational standards of hygiene and convenience.

The earliest surviving evidence of a planned water supply and drainage network is a detailed bird's-eye view *(right)* of the system installed in about 1160 in the Benedictine priory of Christ Church, Canterbury, at the behest of its able and energetic prior Wibert. The plan, probably drawn up by an engineer shortly after the work was done, shows the incoming supply in green, the distribution system in red, and the rainwater collection and drainage in yellow. Water was led from springs about three-quarters of a mile outside the city wall, and following the advice of Vitruvius, the first century BC Roman architect, it was piped through a sequence of settling tanks. When the water reached the precinct, it was channeled underground to rise finally into a brass tank in the water tower *(center, with steeply pitched roof)*. Among the points supplied by running water were the fish tank *(top right)*, the infirmary *(top center)*, and the latrines *(top left)*.

THE NEW KNOWLEDGE

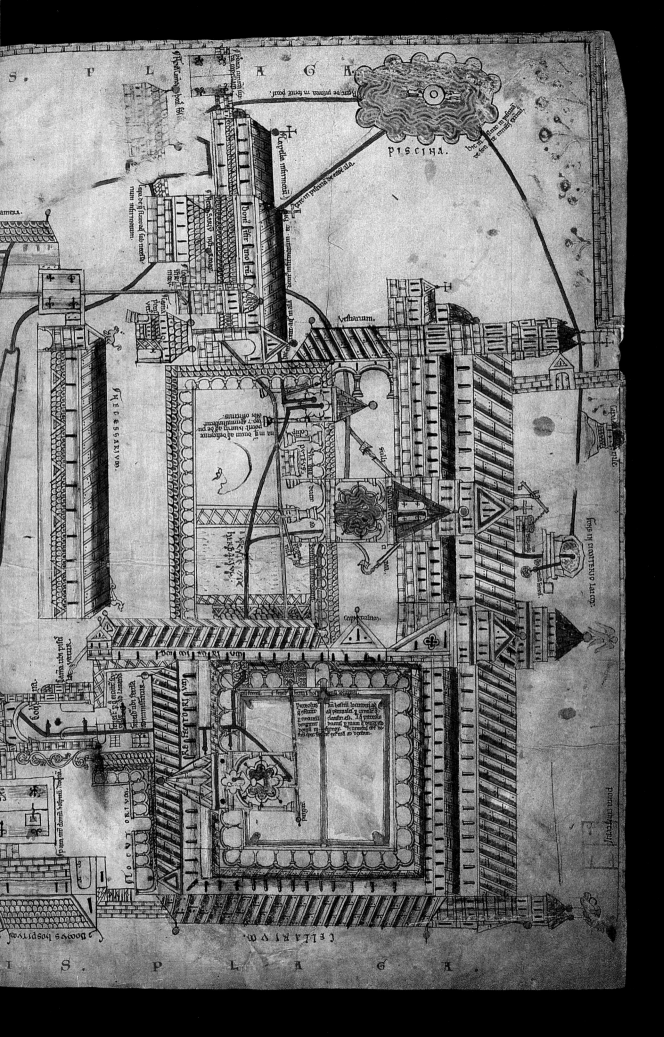

1100-1110	1110-1120	1120-1130	1130-1140	1140-1150
Henry I accedes to the English throne while his elder brother Robert, duke of Normandy, is on crusade (1100).	The city-state of Florence becomes a commune, ruled by an association of nobles in the name of the people (1115).	The philosopher Peter Abelard's *Theologia*, an attempt to apply logical analysis to metaphysics, is declared heretical (1121).	Abbot Suger, councilor to the French kings Louis VI and Louis VII, begins rebuilding the royal abbey of Saint Denis in the new Gothic style (1132).	The Benedictine monk Grati produces an immense compition of ecclesiastical laws an tries to resolve the contradictions he has exposed (1140).
The French poem *Chanson de Roland*—the first of many epics of knightly exploits—is written (c. 1100)	The founding by Saint Bernard of the Cistercian abbey of Clairvaux in central France marks the start of this monastic order's huge expansion (1115).	The Concordat of Worms divides the investiture of bishops between the ecclesiastical and lay powers, creating a truce in the struggle for dominance between the papacy and the German emperors (1122).	On the death of Henry I of England, his nephew Stephen of Blois seizes the throne (1135). Henry's daughter Matilda contests Stephen's action and civil war breaks out.	Venice and Rome become c munes governed by councils elders (1143).
Henry I of England defeats his brother Robert at the Battle of Tinchebrai and thus gains Normandy (1106).	Alfonso of Aragon wins Saragossa from the Muslims (1118).			With the help of a crusading force from northern Europe, fonso I of Portugal captures bon from the Almoravid Mus lims (1147).
With the ascent of Louis VI, the Capetian dynasty of France begins to prosper (1108).	The religious military Order of the Knights Templars is founded in Jerusalem (1118).	Matilda, the daughter of Henry I of England, marries Geoffrey Plantagenet of Anjou (1129).	The ruler of Portugal, a vassal of the king of Leon, declares his land an independent kingdom and becomes Alfonso I (1139).	

EUROPE

After the success of the First Crusade, Raymond of Toulouse takes Tripoli and sets up the county of Tripoli (1109).		Christian knights gain the city of Tyre from the Muslims (1124). Zengi, the Turkish ruler of Mosul in Mesopotamia, conquers the key northern Syrian city of Aleppo (1128).		Zengi overruns the Crusader state of Edessa, triggering the Second Crusade (1144). During the Second Crusade, Crusaders attack but fail to t Damascus (1148).

THE MIDDLE EAST

INDIA AND AFGHANISTAN

	Kyanzittha, king of Burma, who built the Ananda Temple at Pagan, dies (1113). Suryavarman II claims the throne of Angkor, Cambodia (1113); his reign sees the erection of the Angkor Wat temple complex.			

SOUTHEAST ASIA

TimeFrame AD 1100-1200

50-1160	1160-1170	1170-1180	1180-1190	1190-1200
s and Oxford universities are ded (c. 1150). ry Plantagenet, grandson of ry I of England, marries nor of Aquitaine and thus omes one of the greatest ces in France (1152). lerick I of Germany is elected lerick I of Germany (1152). the death of Stephen of s, Henry Plantagenet becomes ry II of England (1154). ry the Lion, duke of Saxony, ranted the duchy of Bavaria rederick Barbarossa (1156).	Frederick Barbarossa, seeking to impose his rule over northern Italy, destroys Milan (1162). The Constitutions of Clarendon, a document produced for Henry II of England, attempts to bring the clergy under the criminal law of the land. Thomas Becket, archbishop of Canterbury, defies the Constitutions of Clarendon and flees to France (1164). The Lombard League of sixteen Italian cities vows mutual support against Barbarossa (1167).	Thomas Becket returns to England, only to be murdered in Canterbury Cathedral by four of Henry II's knights (1170). Chrétien de Troyes writes the romances *Lancelot* and *Perceval*, whose narratives are based on events at the court of the mythical king Arthur (c. 1170). Frederick Barbarossa is defeated by the Lombard League at the Battle of Legnano (1176). The Third Lateran Council regulates papal elections (1179).	The able king Philip II of France, nicknamed Augustus, succeeds to the throne (1180). Henry the Lion, duke of Saxony, is exiled from Germany after making many enemies through ruthless expansion (1182). Frederick Barbarossa concludes the Treaty of Constance with the cities of Lombardy (1183). Richard I of England, known as the Lion-Hearted for his prowess in battle, succeeds Henry II (1189).	Richard I of England captures Cyprus (1191). The complete reconstruction of Chartres Cathedral in the Gothic style begins (1194). Pope Innocent III takes office and preaches the Fourth Crusade (1198).
e late Zengi's son Nur al-Din es the important Syrian city Damascus (1154).	After the kingdom of Jerusalem invades Egypt, the caliph in Cairo invites Nur al-Din to send a Syrian force to protect Egypt; the Christian knights withdraw without a fight. Nur al-Din's general Shirkuh is appointed vizier of Egypt by its caliph; on his death a few weeks later, Shirkuh's second-in-command, Saladin, becomes ruler of Egypt in his turn (1169).	On the instruction of the Syrian ruler Nur al-Din—an adherent of Sunni Islam—Saladin converts Egypt from Shiite to Sunni practice (1171). Saladin's forces conquer the rich country of Yemen (1174). On the death of Nur al-Din, Saladin invades and conquers all of Syria except Aleppo (1174). Seljuk Turks defeat the armies of Byzantium resoundingly at Myriokephalon (1176).	Saladin captures Aleppo, virtually completing the encirclement of the Christian states in the Levant (1183). Saladin defeats the Christian forces at the Battle of Hattin and captures Jerusalem, together with most of the other cities of Palestine and southern Lebanon (1187). Guy, ousted king of Jerusalem, besieges the Muslims at Acre (1189).	Frederick Barbarossa, taking part in the Third Crusade, drowns in Turkey (1190). After a two-year siege, the Muslims are driven out of Acre by Crusaders under Richard I of England; Richard wins the Battle of Arsuf (1191). Saladin and Richard sign a treaty that leaves the Syrian coast in Christian hands and allows Christians access to Jerusalem (1192). Saladin dies and is succeeded by his three sons (1193).
askaracharya, the celebrated lian astronomer and mathetician, composes *Lilavati*, his ssic opus in verse on arithtic and algebra (c. 1150). e magnificent city of Ghazni Afghanistan, headquarters of e Ghaznavid dynasty, is deoyed by the ascendant rulers Ghur (1150).		The Ghurid ruler Ghiyas al-Din establishes a sultanate in Afghanistan (1173). Lakshmana Sena, the third member of the Sena dynasty ruling Bengal, ascends the throne and proceeds to extend his rule as far as Benares and Assam (c. 1179).	Muizz al-Din Muhammad, the brother of the Sultan of Ghur in Afghanistan, wrests the Punjab from the last of the Ghaznavid dynasty (1186).	Muizz al-Din Muhammad is defeated by Rajputs at Tarai, near Delhi (1191). Muizz al-Din Muhammad returns to Tarai and vanquishes the Rajputs (1192). Muizz al-Din Muhammad's slave and general Qutb al-Din takes Delhi (1192); he begins the construction of the Qutb Minar victory tower. General Ikhtiyar takes Bihar and Bengal on behalf of Muizz al-Din Muhammad (1193).
ryavarman II dies (c. 1150). s death begins a period of inability and rebellion among e Khmer people of Cambodia.		Taking advantage of the Khmer's neglected frontier defenses, the Chams, rivals from South Vietnam, invade Cambodia, overrunning Angkor and ransacking temples and sanctuaries. The Chams kill the Khmer king, leaving Angkor in a state of anarchy (1177).	Jayavarman VII ascends the throne of Angkor (1181) after routing the Chams in a naval battle. His reign marks a new upsurge of Cambodia's power.	Jayavarman VII's army overwhelms the kingdom of Champa (1190). Cham slaves are employed as laborers on Angkor Thom, the Khmer's stupendous new capital.

BIBLIOGRAPHY

BOOKS

Ahmad, Aziz, *Studies in Islamic Culture in the Indian Environment.* Oxford: Clarendon Press, 1964.

Alberuni's India. Ed. and transl. by E. C. Sachau. London: Trübner & Co., 1910.

Auboyer, Jeannine, and Roger Goepper, *The Oriental World.* London: Paul Hamlyn, 1976.

Aung-Thwin, Michael, *Pagan: The Origins of Modern Burma.* Honolulu: University of Hawaii Press, 1985.

Baker, Derek, ed., *Medieval Women.* Oxford: Blackwell, 1978.

Barber, Richard, *The Devil's Crown: Henry II, Richard I, John.* London: British Broadcasting Corp., 1978.

Barraclough, Geoffrey, *The Medieval Papacy.* London: Thames & Hudson, 1968.

Bautier, R. H., *The Economic Development of Medieval Europe.* London: Thames & Hudson, 1971.

Bechert, Heinz, and Richard Gombrich, eds., *The World of Buddhism.* London: Thames & Hudson, 1984.

Bhattacharya, Sachchidananda, *A Dictionary of Indian History.* Calcutta: Calcutta University Press, 1967.

Billings, Malcolm, *The Cross and the Crescent.* London: British Broadcasting Corp., 1987.

Bishop, Morris, and the Editors of Horizon Magazine, *The Horizon Book of the Middle Ages.* London: Cassell, 1969.

Bloch, Marc, *Feudal Society.* Vols. 1 and 2. London: Routledge & Kegan Paul, 1965.

Boase, T. S. R.:
Death in the Middle Ages. London: Thames & Hudson, 1972.
Kingdoms and Strongholds of the Crusaders. London: Thames & Hudson, 1971.

Bony, Jean, *French Gothic Architecture of the Twelfth and Thirteenth Centuries.* Berkeley: University of California Press, 1983.

Bosworth, C. E., *The Ghaznavids 994-1040.* Edinburgh: Edinburgh University Press, 1963.

Bradford, Ernle, *The Sword and the Scimitar.* London: Victor Gollancz Ltd., 1974.

Briggs, L. P., *The Ancient Khmer Empire.* Philadelphia: The American Philosophical Society, 1951.

Brooke, C. N. L., *The Twelfth Century Renaissance.* London: Thames & Hudson, 1969.

Brooke, Christopher, *The Structure of Medieval Society.* London: Thames & Hudson, 1971.

Brooke, Rosalind, and Christopher Brooke, *Popular Religion in the Middle Ages: Western Europe 1000-1300.* London: Thames & Hudson, 1984.

Brown, Roxanna M., *The Ceramics of South-East Asia: Their Dating and Identification.* Kuala Lumpur: Oxford University Press, 1977.

Campbell, Marian, *An Introduction to Medieval Enamels.* London: Her Majesty's Stationery Office, 1983.

Chandler, D. P., *A History of Cambodia.* Boulder, Colo.: Westview Press, 1983.

Chenu, M. D., *Nature, Man and Society in the Twelfth Century.* Chicago: University of Chicago Press, 1968.

Chibnall, Marjorie, *Anglo-Norman England 1066-1166.* Oxford: Blackwell, 1986.

Cipolla, Carlo, ed., *The Middle Ages.* Vol. 1 of *The Fontana Economic History of Europe.* London: Fontana, 1976.

Clanchy, M. T., *England and Its Rulers 1066-1272.* Oxford: Blackwell, 1983.

Coedes, G., *The Indianized States of South-East Asia.* Honolulu: East West Center, 1968.

Collon-Gevaert, Suzanne, et al., *A Treasury of Romanesque Art.* Transl. by Susan Waterston. New York: Phaidon, 1973.

Cottrell, Leonard, *Lost Worlds.* London: Elek Books, 1964.

Doshi, Saryu, *Pageant of Indian Art: Festival of India in Great Britain.* Bombay: Marg Publications, 1983.

Dronke, Peter, ed., *A History of Twelfth-Century Western Philosophy.* Cambridge: Cambridge University Press, 1988.

Duby, George:
The Chivalrous Society. London: Edward Arnold, 1977.
The Early Growth of the European Economy: Warriors and Peasants from the Seventh to the Twelfth Century. London: Weidenfeld & Nicolson, 1974.
History of Medieval Art 980-1440. London: Weidenfeld & Nicolson, 1986.
The Rural Economy and Country Life in the Medieval West. London: Edward Arnold, 1968.

Duggan, Charles, *Twelfth Century Decretal Collections and Their Importance in English History.* London: Athlone, 1963.

Durliat, Marcel, *L'Art Roman.* Paris: Éditions d'Art Lucien Mazenod, 1982.

Elliot, H. M., *History of India as Told by Its Own Historians.* 10 vols. Ed. by John Dowson. London: Trübner & Co., 1867-69.

Enlart, Camille, *Les Monuments des Croisés dans le Royaume de Jérusalem: Architecture Religieuse et Civile.* Paris: P. Geuthner, 1925.

Evans, Joan, ed., *The Flowering of the Middle Ages.* London: Thames & Hudson, 1966.

Fawtier, Robert, *Capetian Kings of France 987-1328.* London: Macmillan, 1960.

Finucane, Ronald C., *Soldiers of the Faith: Crusaders and Moslems at War.* London: J. M. Dent & Sons Ltd., 1983.

Foss, Michael, *Chivalry.* London: Michael Joseph, 1975.

Fourquin, Guy, *Lordship and Feudalism in the Middle Ages.* London: Allen & Unwin, 1976.

Fuhrmann, Horst, *Germany in the High Middle Ages c. 1050-1200.* Cambridge: Cambridge University Press, 1987.

Gabrieli, Francisco, *Arab Historians of the Crusades.* London: Routledge & Kegan Paul, 1969.

Galbert de Bruges, *The Murder of Charles the Good, Count of Flanders.* Transl. by J. B. Ross. Oxford: Oxford University Press, 1960.

Ganshof, François, *Feudalism.* London: Longman, 1964.

Gauthier, Marie-Madeleine, *Émaux du Moyen Âge Occidental.* Fribourg: Office du Livre, 1972.

Giteau, Madeleine, *The Civilization of Angkor.* New York: Rizzoli, 1976.

Groslier, Bernard, and Jacques Arthaud, *Angkor: Art and Civilization.* Transl. by Eric E. Smith. London: Thames & Hudson, 1957.

Groslier, George, *Recherches sur les Cambodgiens.* Paris: Augustin Challamel Éditeur, 1921.

Grover, Satish, *The Architecture of India: Islamic.* Delhi: Vikas, 1981.

Grunebaum, G. E. von, *Classical Islam.* London: Allen & Unwin, 1970.

Gupte, R. S., *Iconography of the Hindus, Buddhists and Jains.* Bombay: D. B. Taraporevala Sons & Co., 1972.

Habib, M., *Politics and Society during the Early Medieval Period.* Vol. 1. New Delhi: People's Publishing House, 1974.

Haig, Wolseley, *Turks and Afghans.* Vol. 3 of *The Cambridge History of India.* Cambridge: Cambridge University Press, 1928.

Hall, D. G. E., *A History of South-East Asia.* London: Macmillan, 1968.

Hall, Kenneth, and John Whitmore, eds., *Explorations of Early Southeast Asian History.* Ann Arbor: University of Michigan, 1976.

Hallam, E. M., *Capetian France.* London: Longman, 1980.

Hallam, Elizabeth, ed., *The Plantagenet Chronicles.* London: Weidenfeld & Nicolson, 1986.

de Hamel, Christopher, *A History of Illuminated Manuscripts.* Oxford: Phaidon, 1986.

Hardy, Peter, *The Muslims of British India.* Cambridge: Cambridge University Press, 1972.

Hell, Vera, and Hellmut Hell, *The Great Pilgrimage of the Middle Ages.* London: Barrie and Rockliff, 1966.

Henderson, G., *Gothic.* London: Penguin Books, 1967.

Holt, P. M., *The Age of the Crusades.* London: Longman, 1986.

Hyde, J. K., *Society and Politics in Medieval Italy 1050-1350.* London: Macmillan, 1973.

Ishizawa, Masao, et al., *The Heritage of Japanese Art.* Tokyo: Kodansha International, 1982.

Jones, Peter Murray, *Medieval Medical*

Miniatures. London: The British Library, 1984.

Kalman, B., and J. L. Cohen, *Angkor: The Monuments of the God-Kings.* London: Thames & Hudson, 1975.

Kedar, B. Z., *Crusade and Mission.* Guildford: Princeton University Press, 1984.

Keen, Maurice, *Chivalry.* London: Yale University Press, 1984.

Kempers, A. J. B., *Ancient Indonesian Art.* Oxford: Oxford University Press, 1959.

Kidson, Peter, *The Medieval World.* London: Paul Hamlyn, 1967.

Kirsch, A. T., *Southeast Asian History and Historiography.* Ithaca: Cornell University Press, 1976.

Knowles, David, *The Monastic Order in England.* Cambridge: Cambridge University Press, 1963.

Kulke, Herman, and Dietmar Rothermund, *A History of India.* London: Croom Helm, 1986.

Lawrence, C. H., *Medieval Monasticism.* London: Longman, 1984.

Leff, Gordon, *Medieval Thought.* London: Merlin Press, 1980.

Lewis, Bernard:
Islam: From the Prophet Muhammad to the Capture of Constantinople. New York: Walker & Co., 1976.
The Jews of Islam. London: Routledge & Kegan Paul, 1984.
The Muslim Discovery of Europe. London: Norton, 1982.
The World of Islam. London: Thames & Hudson, 1976.

Lewis, Suzanne, *The Art of Matthew Paris in the Chronica Majora.* Aldershot: Scolar Press, 1987.

Lindberg, David C., ed., *Science in the Middle Ages.* Chicago: University of Chicago Press, 1978.

Lindsay, J., *The Troubadours and Their World of the Twelfth and Thirteenth Centuries.* London: Muller, 1976.

Lomax, D. W., *The Reconquest of Spain.* London: Longman, 1978.

Lopez, R. S., *The Commercial Revolution of the Middle Ages.* Cambridge: Cambridge University Press, 1976.

Losty, Jeremiah P., *The Art of the Book in India.* London: The British Library, 1982.

Luce, G. H., *Old Burma-Early Pagan.* 3 vols. Locust Valley, N. Y.: J. J. Augustin, 1969-70.

Lyons, M. C., and D. E. P. Jackson, *Saladin.* Cambridge: Cambridge University Press, 1982.

Mango, Cyril, *Byzantium.* London: Weidenfeld & Nicolson, 1980.

Matthew, Donald, *Atlas of Medieval Europe.* Oxford: Phaidon, 1983.

Mayer, Hans Eberhard, *The Crusades.* Oxford: Oxford University Press, 1972.

Mazzeo, Donatella, and C. S. Antonini, *Monuments of Civilization: Ancient Cambodia.* London: Cassell, 1978.

Moore, R. I., *The Origins of European Dissent.* Oxford: Blackwell, 1985.

Morgan, Nigel, *Early Gothic Manuscripts 1190-1250.* Vol. 4 of *A Survey of Manuscripts Illuminated in the British Isles.* Oxford: Oxford University Press, 1982.

Morris, Colin, *The Discovery of the Individual 1050-1200.* London: S.P.C.K., 1972.

Mujeeb, M., *The Indian Muslims.* London: Allen & Unwin, 1967.

Mullins, Edwin, *The Pilgrimage to Santiago.* London: Secker & Warburg, 1974.

Munz, P., *Frederick Barbarossa.* London: Eyre & Spottiswoode, 1969.

Nath, R., *History of Sultanate Architecture.* Delhi: Abhinav, 1978.

Nazim, M., *Sultan Mahmud of Ghazna.* New Delhi: Munshiram Manoharlal, 1971.

Needham, Joseph, ed., *Science and Civilisation in China.* Vol. 5. Cambridge: Cambridge University Press, 1985.

Nizami, K. A., *Some Aspects of Religion and Politics in India during the Thirteenth Century.* London: Asia Publishing House, 1967.

Pacaut, Marcel, *Frederick Barbarossa.* Transl. by A. J. Pomerans. London: Collins, 1970.

Panofsky, Erwin, ed.:
Abbot Suger on the Abbey Church of St. Denis and Its Art Treasures. Princeton: Princeton University Press, 1979.
Renaissance and Renascences in Western Art. London: Paladin, 1970.

Pe Maung Tin, *The Glass Palace Chronicle.* Transl. by G. H. Luce. Oxford: Oxford University Press, 1926.

Platt, Colin:
The Atlas of Medieval Man. London: Book Club Associates, 1979.
The English Medieval Town. London: Secker & Warburg, 1976.

Queller, D. E., *The Fourth Crusade.* Leicester: Leicester University Press, 1978.

Richard, Jean, *The Latin Kingdom of Jerusalem.* 2 vols. Oxford: North-Holland Publishing Co., 1979.

Riley-Smith, J. S. C.:
The Crusades: A Short History. London: Athlone Press, 1987.
The First Crusade and the Idea of Crusading. London: Athlone Press, 1986.

Riley-Smith, Louise, and Jonathan Riley-Smith, *The Crusades: Idea and Reality.* London: Edward Arnold, 1981.

Robinson, Francis, *An Atlas of the Islamic World.* Oxford: Phaidon, 1980.

Rogers, Michael, *The Spread of Islam.* Oxford: Elsevier-Phaidon, 1976.

Rowland, Benjamin:
Art in Afghanistan. London: Allen Lane, 1971.
The Art and Architecture of India. Harmondsworth, England: Penguin Books Ltd., 1953.

Runciman, S., *A History of the Crusades.* 3 vols. Cambridge: Cambridge University Press, 1951-54.

Russell, F. H., *The Just War in the Middle Ages.* Cambridge: Cambridge University Press, 1975.

Schnitger, F. M., *The Archaeology of Hindoo Sumatra.* Leiden: E. J. Brill, 1937.

Sharma, R. S., *Indian Feudalism.* London: Macmillan, 1965.

Siberny, E., *Criticism of Crusading 1095-1274.* Oxford: Clarendon Press, 1985.

Sitwell, Osbert, *Escape with Me!* Oxford: Oxford University Press, 1984.

Sivaramamurti, C.:
The Art of India. New York: Harry Abrams Inc., 1977.
South Indian Bronzes. Delhi: Lalit Kala Akademi, 1963.

Smail, R. C., *Crusading Warfare 1097-1193.* Vol. 3 of *Cambridge Studies in Medieval Life and Thought.* Cambridge: Cambridge University Press, 1956.

Southeast Asia, by the Editors of Time-Life Books (Library of Nations series). Alexandria, Virginia: Time-Life Books, 1987.

Southern, R. W., *The Making of the Middle Ages.* London: Arrow, 1959.

Stierlin, Henri, *The Cultural History of Angkor.* London: Aurum Press Ltd., 1984.

Subhadradis Diskul, M. C., ed., *The Art of Srivijaya.* Oxford: Oxford University Press, 1980.

Ta-Kuan, Chou, *Notes on the Customs of Cambodia.* Bangkok: Social Science Association Press, 1967.

Thapar, Romila, *A History of India.* Vol. 1. London: Penguin Books, 1968.

Ullmann, Walter, *A Short History of the Papacy in the Middle Ages.* London: Methuen, 1974.

Waley, D. P., *The Italian City Republics.* London: Longman, 1978.

Walker, Benjamin, *Hindu World.* 2 vols. London: Allen & Unwin, 1968.

Watson, Francis, *A Concise History of India.* London: Thames & Hudson, 1974.

Watt, William M., *The Majesty That Was Islam.* London: Sidgwick & Jackson, 1974.

White, Lynn, Jr., *Mediaeval Technology and Social Change.* Oxford: Clarendon, 1962.

Wolters, O. W., *The Fall of Srivijaya in Malay History.* Ithaca: Cornell University Press, 1970.

Yadava, B. N. S., *Society and Culture in Northern India in the 12th Century.* Allahabad: Central Book Depot, 1973.

OTHER SOURCES

Age of Chivalry: Art in Plantagenet England 1200-1400. (Royal Academy of Arts catalog) London: Royal Academy of Arts, 1987.

Aung-Thwin, M.:
"A Reply to Lieberman." *Journal of Asian Studies* 40 (1). Ann Arbor: University of Michigan Association for Asian Studies, 1980.
"The Role of Sasana Reform in Burmese History." *Journal of Asian Studies* 38 (4). Ann Arbor: University of Michigan Association for Asian Studies, 1979.

Constable, G., "The Second Crusade as Seen by Contemporaries." *Tradition* (New York), Vol. 9, 1953.

Daw, Thin Kyi, *Artibus Asiae Supplementum* (Switzerland), Vol. 2, no. 23, 1966.

English Romanesque Art 1066-1200. (Hayward Gallery catalog) London: Arts Council of Great Britain, 1984.

Gesick, Lorraine, ed., *Centers, Symbols, and Hierarchies.* Yale University Southeast Asian Studies Monograph No. 26. New Haven: Yale University Press, 1983.

Hollister, C. W., and J. W. Baldwin, "The Rise of Administrative Kingship: Henry I and Philip Augustus." *American Historical Review* (Washington, D.C.), Vol. 88, 1978.

Jacques, C., *Southeast Asia in the 9th to 14th Centuries.* Ed. by D. G. Maar and A. C. Milner. Singapore: Institute of Southeast Asian Studies, 1986.

Kulke, Hermann, *The Devaraja Cult.* Data Paper No. 108. Ithaca, N.Y.: Cornell University, Southeast Asia Program, 1978.

Lieberman, V. B.:
"A Note on Burmese Religious Landholdings." *Journal of Asian Studies* 40 (4). Ann Arbor: University of Michigan Association for Asian Studies, 1981.
"The Political Significance of Religious Wealth in Burmese History." *Journal of Asian Studies* 39 (4). Ann Arbor: University of Michigan Association for Asian Studies, 1980.

Mabbett, I. W., "Kingship in Angkor." *Journal of the Siam Society* 66 (2). Bangkok: Siam Society, 1978.

Miksic, John, *Bulletin de l'École Française d'Extrême-Orient,* Vol. 74, 1985.

Page, J. A., *An Historical Memoir on the Qutb: Delhi.* Calcutta: Government of India Central Publication, 1926.

Riley-Smith, J. S. C., "Crusading as an Act of Love." *History,* Vol. 65. London: Historical Association, 1980.
"Santiago de Compostela." *Europalia 85 Espaa.* Belgium: Crédit Communal, 1986.

Smail, R. C., "Latin Syria and the West, 1149-1187." *Transactions of the Royal Historical Society* Ser. 5, 19. London: Offices of the Royal Historical Society, 1969.

van Liere, W. J., "Traditional Water Management in the Lower Mekong Basin." *World Archaeology* 11 (3). London: Routledge & Kegan Paul.

Wolters, O. W., "Restudying Some Chinese Writings on Srivijaya." *Indonesia* 42. Ithaca: Cornell University Press, 1986.

Zwalf, Wladimir, *Buddhism: Art and Faith.* London: British Museum Publications Ltd., 1985.

ACKNOWLEDGMENTS

The following materials have been reprinted with the kind permission of the publishers: Page 27: "Lords, look at the best knight you have ever seen . . .," quoted in *Chivalry*, by M. Keen, London: Yale University Press, 1984. Page 62: "have destroyed the altars . . .," quoted in *The Crusades: Idea and Reality*, by L. Riley-Smith and J. Riley-Smith, London: Edward Arnold, 1981. Page 87: "The plain was covered . . .," and: "Women and children . . .," both quoted in *Arab Historians of the Crusades*, by Francisco Gabrielli, Berkeley: University of California Press, 1978. Page 98: "The whole country of India . . .," quoted in *A Concise History of India*, by Francis Watson, London: Thames & Hudson, copyright © 1974 and 1979 Francis Watson.

The editors also wish to thank the following individuals and institutions for their valuable assistance in the preparation of this volume:
England: Bristol—M. D. Lambert, Reader in History, Department of Theology and Religious Studies, University of Bristol; P. L. Reynolds, Department of Theology and Religious Studies, University of Bristol; Paul Williams, Department of Theology and Religious Studies, University of Bristol. Cambridge—C. N. L. Brooke, Dixie Professor of Ecclesiastical History, University of Cambridge. Canterbury—Canon Derek Ingram-Hill, Canterbury Cathedral. Colchester—Neil Fairbairn. Leeds—Graham A. Loud, Lecturer in Medieval History, University of Leeds. London—Janet Backhouse, Curator of Illuminated Manuscripts, British Library; Iris Barry; Yu-Ying Brown, Japanese Curator of Oriental Collections, British Library; Charles Burnett, Warburg Institute, University of London; John Cayley, Oriental Collections, British Library; Anthony Christie, Lately Chairman of the Centre of Art and Archaeology, School of Oriental and African Studies, University of London; David Crouch, Institute of Historical Research, University of London; Brian Durrans, Deputy Keeper of the Ethnography Department, British Museum; John Guy, Assistant Keeper of the Indian Department, Victoria and Albert Museum; Ralph Hancock; J. P. Losty, Curator of Prints and Drawings, India Office Library and Records; Mehrdad Shokoohy, School of Architecture and Landscape, Thames Polytechnic; Deborah Thompson; Brian A. Tremain, Photographic Service, British Museum. Nottingham—Bernard Hamilton, School of History, University of Nottingham. Oxford—Nicholas Vincent. Southampton—Colin Morris, Professor of Medieval History, University of Southampton.
France: Paris—François Avril, Curateur, Département des Manuscrits, Bibliothèque Nationale; Béatrice Coti, Directrice du Service Iconographique, Éditions Mazenod; Antoinette Decaudin, Documentaliste, Département des Antiquités Orientales, Musée du Louvre; Nick Growse; Marie-Odile Roy, Service Photographique, Bibliothèque Nationale.
Scotland: Edinburgh—Paul Strachan.
U.S.A.: Los Angeles—Paul E. Cheveddon.

PICTURE CREDITS

INDEX